DISRAELI, DEMOCRACY
AND THE TORY PARTY

DISRAELI, DEMOCRACY AND THE TORY PARTY

———◆———

CONSERVATIVE LEADERSHIP AND ORGANIZATION AFTER THE SECOND REFORM BILL

BY

E. J. FEUCHTWANGER

DEPUTY DIRECTOR OF EXTRA-MURAL STUDIES
AND SENIOR LECTURER, UNIVERSITY OF SOUTHAMPTON

CLARENDON PRESS · OXFORD
1968

Oxford University Press, Ely House, London W. 1

GLASGOW NEW YORK TORONTO MELBOURNE WELLINGTON
CAPE TOWN SALISBURY IBADAN NAIROBI LUSAKA ADDIS ABABA
BOMBAY CALCUTTA MADRAS KARACHI LAHORE DACCA
KUALA LUMPUR HONG KONG TOKYO

PRINTED IN GREAT BRITAIN
BY HAZELL WATSON AND VINEY LTD
AYLESBURY, BUCKS

ACKNOWLEDGEMENTS

I AM grateful to all those who gave me access to papers and documents, and would like to thank Lord Cairns, Lord Harrowby, the Duke of Richmond and Gordon, and Lord Salisbury for permission to quote from private papers in their possession. I am similarly indebted to the Department of Manuscripts at the British Museum, the National Trust, the Public Record Office and National Register of Archives, and the National Union of Conservative and Unionist Associations. Special thanks are due to Dr. J. F. A. Mason of Christ Church for helping me with the Salisbury Papers, and to Miss W. D. Coates for her advice on private papers generally.

Many people have helped me in writing this book. I received valuable advice at various stages from Professor H. J. Hanham, Mr. C. H. D. Howard, and the late Sir Lewis Namier. I would like to thank my colleagues in the University of Southampton, particularly Professors Bromley, Patterson, and Rothwell, and Mr. F. C. Mather of the Department of History, and Professor Frankel of the Department of Politics. I am grateful to the University and to my Department for having given me a sabbatical term. My secretaries, Mrs. A. Wharmby, Mrs. C. Glover and Mrs. M. Cook, laboured hard in preparing the manuscript. Last but not least my wife gave me invaluable help in matters of style and in proof-reading.

CONTENTS

INTRODUCTION

THE history of England in the Victorian era is a well-charted sea. Each generation, however, must rewrite its past, and we are now sufficiently far removed from the nineteenth century and its circumstances to be able to see many things more clearly than our predecessors, or at any rate differently. In the narrower field relevant to the present study there has been much important reassessment. Professors Gash and Hanham have added new dimensions to our view of the political system, and Professor Briggs has thrown fresh light on the complex social transformations of the age. Major modern biographies of leading figures, for example Robert Blake's *Disraeli*, have deepened our understanding of the interplay of personalities and social forces. Specific aspects have been newly investigated: for instance, John Vincent's book on *The Formation of the Liberal Party* has drawn our attention to political and social movements, whose impact on the parliamentary scene had not hitherto been fully apparent. To all these writers and many others I owe a debt.

This book tries to make a contribution to the process of reassessment. It deals with the Conservative party between the second and the third Reform Bills, a crucial period in the evolution of the modern party system. It claims to be no more, no less than a study of history, but it has implications for the work of the political scientist who is concerned with the morphology of political parties.

I have looked at the Tory party in this period from the centre, and from the angle of the parliamentary party. This procedure seemed to me well suited to the subject: a parliamentary grouping, with a long pedigree, compelled by the widening of the franchise to develop and organize new sources of electoral support. On this score the Conservative party differs substantially from the Liberal party of the same period: the Whigs and Radicals were also parliamentary groups, but the impact of extra-parliamentary movements and pressures on them, and on the process of their consolidation into Gladstonian Liberals was much greater. The Liberals were more often responding to spontaneous demands from outside; the Conservatives were from their parliamentary base reaching out to potential new voters. Modern Toryism can be defined as a continuing belief in the need for authority and a governing class in politics, combined with an acceptance of the democratic *imprimatur* conferred by a mass electorate on the elite. The manner in which the Tory party reacted to the tides of popular democracy, produced by the Reform Bill of 1867, accords well with this view. It seems to make sense, therefore, to look at the Tory party from its established parliamentary base, and in this study I have mainly relied on the traditional sources, the private papers of the parliamentary leaders and the large body of political biography, to tell my story.

It can now be clearly seen that the part played by the Tories and by Disraeli in the passage of the Reform Bill of 1867 was not the result of deliberate long-range calculation. Nevertheless, Disraeli and those Conservatives who fully supported him in his complex manoeuvres in 1867 were at any rate prepared to 'shoot Niagara' and were quick to adjust to the consequences once the deed had been done. The new situation faced the party with problems both of leadership and organization; the old sources of Tory support had to be reinstated, while new electoral bases had to be won. Leadership involved the management of the parliamentary party, as well as an effective appeal to the wider voting public. The personalities of the leaders, their political problems, the composition and nature of the parliamentary Conservative party, and the Tory electoral appeal form the subject of the first part of this book.

The country gentlemen were still the predominant element in the parliamentary Conservative party of the 1870s. They had been 'educated' to accept the great change of 1867, but the process of education had been reluctantly undergone and had been only partially successful. It continued to be difficult to persuade the rank and file of the Tory squirearchy that the Conservative party could no longer be entirely theirs, but had to gain the allegiance of new social groups. Outside Parliament, the English counties and rural areas in general still formed the bulwark of Tory electoral strength; the unity of the landed interest, landowners and tenant farmers, was still taken for granted. The Tory strength in the countryside was, however, not sufficient to give the party a majority in the House of Commons. Moreover the unity of the landed interest was a tradition surviving from the age of the Corn Laws, and the agricultural depression of the 1870s was beginning to crack it. Household suffrage in the counties, looming over the horizon, was soon to alter the situation fundamentally, to the probable disadvantage of the Conservative party.

The leaders had therefore to look to the larger boroughs for reinforcement, even if the rank and file did not see the need for this. The building up of organization was one way of strengthening the Conservative party in the boroughs, but there also had to be a positive appeal through policies and programmes to new classes of voters. It was not only a matter of attaching a growing number of working-class voters to the Conservative cause, but also of making progress among the commercial and professional middle classes in the towns. There was no Marxist incompatibility between these two requirements. The middle-class Radicals in Parliament, who had been the main driving force in reopening the question of parliamentary reform in the 1860s, had acted in the belief that strengthening the respectable working-class vote would help them in reducing the power of the aristocracy. On the Conservative side, too, it was realized that the Tory working man would not materialize without middle-class leadership. The fact that the employers of labour were still on the whole in the Liberal camp did, however, make it easier for the Conservatives to satisfy some of the more articulate demands of labour. Nor must we regard the working class vote as monolithic: the gulf between the skilled artisan and the lumpen proletariat of large towns could be very large. Some contemporary voters regarded Tory successes among the urban voters as no more than a 'revolt of the residuum', a passing mood of the fickle and ignorant mob at the bottom of the social order, on which no permanent reliance could be placed. Regional factors were still of the greatest importance, as could be seen from the Tory victories in Lancashire in 1868.

As a result of the growth of a Tory interest in the towns, there appeared in the House of Commons a contingent of Con-

servative borough members. They naturally tended to find a
common viewpoint on many topics. Few of them attained
office; their social background put most of them slightly apart
from the mass of Tory members belonging to the landed
gentry. They were, however, not rebellious as a group, for they
were still too anxious to gain full acceptance. The party leaders
recognized the borough members as a significant group representing important interests and were prepared to entertain
their opinions, though rarely their claims to office.

The task of leading the Conservative party in the 1870s thus
involved the containment of considerable tensions. Among the
Tory leaders of the time only Disraeli was a statesman of the
first calibre, an originator of new policies and directions. His
position as leader was, however, weak, at least until 1874. The
main reason for this was that he was held responsible for the
Reform Bill of 1867 and was thus identified with a policy which
was detested by many Tories, which had not proved successful
in 1868, and was itself the main focus of the tensions in the
party. Before his return to power in 1874, Disraeli's energies
were devoted to ensuring his political survival, putting the party
organization into trim to take advantage of Gladstone's growing
unpopularity, and sketching a Tory programme for the future
in general terms. Once back in power he had to play safe with
party unity and the policy of giving the Conservative party a
broader electoral base had to be pursued with caution. In forming his second ministry in 1874 Disraeli paid due regard to
the predominance of the landed gentry in the party and to the
claims of the great Tory families. He took only a distant interest
in the measures of social reform promoted by his Government,
and left the details to the ministers immediately concerned.

Among Disraeli's colleagues, only two, the fifteenth Earl of
Derby and Lord Salisbury, possessed major political status in
their own right. Many Conservatives preferred Derby to Disraeli as party leader; his name and personality had a wide
electoral appeal, yet Tories of the old school felt safe with him.
Only his own reluctance to take first place prevented his
accession to the leadership. Salisbury was the chosen leader of
all those Conservatives who conceived resistance to democratic
change to be the chief purpose of their party, and to whom an
appeal to new classes of voters by outflanking their political

opponents appeared to be an unethical proceeding. Salisbury was politically estranged from Disraeli at least until 1872, but he never allowed himself to be used to split the party. Some of Disraeli's senior colleagues had achieved their eminence without the aid of a great aristocratic position or family connection, for example Lord Cairns and Gathorne Hardy, and the Tories were on this score often less restrictive than their opposite numbers among the Whigs. On the whole, however, the Conservative party, if sometimes bold in measures, was still orthodox in men.

In spite of the tensions with the party caused by the new electoral conditions, the Tories were a remarkably coherent parliamentary force after 1867. This unity was not, however, dependent on extra-parliamentary party organizations. We were as yet far removed from the modern position where the meaning of party resides largely in the formidable structures which exist outside Parliament. Nevertheless, the efforts made by the Tory leaders, and Disraeli in particular, to create a better party organization, more in tune with the new circumstances, became perhaps the most important permanent legacy of the period. The Tories were the pioneers here, and their refurbished central organization, eventually consisting of the Conservative Central Office and the National Union, antedates the reform of the Liberal headquarters. Again it is evident that with the Tories the initiative came from the leaders, not from the grass roots. The leaders were, as in the case of the Reform Bill, responding to circumstances and had little notion of the permanent significance of what they were doing. Only in the 1880s did the party organization move out of the shadows, to become for a moment the battleground of a fierce internal conflict. The tension between the Old Toryism and the New Conservatism had in fact beset the party organization from its inception, just as it had posed the main problem for effective party leadership.

The second part of this book deals with the story of the Conservative party organization from 1867 until the eve of the General Election of 1885. It is a story well known in its broad outline, but this account adds fresh detail and seeks to present a rounded picture. The angle from which I have looked at the organization is again from the centre, for it is here that the most striking innovations were made, the foundation of the National Union, and the Conservative Central Office. Limited in significance as these moves were in their immediate context, in the long run they have changed the nature of the British party system.

Note. Two important books appeared too late to be referred to in the present work: Maurice Cowling, *1867 Disraeli, Gladstone and Revolution. The Passing of the Second Reform Bill* (Cambridge, 1967); and Paul Smith, *Disraelian Conservatism and Social Reform* (London and Toronto, 1967). They cast much additional light on the events and personalities discussed here.

PART ONE

The Parliamentary Party

I

DISRAELI'S POSITION AS LEADER

THE personalities and the aims of the leaders have generally counted for much in the history of English political parties. This was true of the aristocratic parliamentary groupings, hardly deserving the name of party, of the eighteenth century. It remained true of the more broadly based parties of the nineteenth century. The Whigs of the 1850s were not ashamed to answer to the name of Palmerstonians. Their successors, the Liberals of the sixties, seventies, and eighties, were often accused of being not a cohesive party, but only the heterogeneous and ill-assorted following of Gladstone. The Tories were perhaps so natural and indestructible a grouping that they were able to survive periods when leadership was not only absent, but when the very conception of it was compromised by a profound crisis of confidence, as in the years after Sir Robert Peel's defection over the Corn Laws. Nevertheless the Tory party, too, had to have leadership in order to become capable of wielding power again. Disraeli emerged as the only man of sufficient stature to supply it.

This is not the place for adding to the extensive biographical literature on Disraeli.[1] This chapter has the much narrower concern of discussing his role as party leader during the last fifteen years of his life. By then he had already borne the brunt of leadership for nearly two decades. Disraeli's biographers, popular and academic, have emphasized his early political struggles and the precariousness of the eminence he achieved in the protectionist rump of the Tory party after 1846. Even from the massive documentation of Monypenny and Buckle, there emerges little sense of the continuing precariousness of Disraeli's position as party leader right up to the electoral

[1] W. F. Monypenny and G. E. Buckle, *Life of Benjamin Disraeli*, remains useful for the student because of its full documentation. All references here are to the new and revised edition in two volumes published in 1929, abbreviated Buckle. Robert Blake, *Disraeli* (London, 1966), is the standard modern biography.

triumph of 1874. Yet this is the most striking conclusion to be drawn from the record of the years between 1868 and 1874. Disraeli's succession to the nominal leadership and to the premiership in 1868 by no means confirmed beyond doubt his place at the head of the party. In fact, the situation on the morrow of electoral defeat in 1868 was exactly the opposite, and Disraeli's position was again completely insecure. His future was once more deeply involved in the general process of adjustment which his party had to undergo.

The weakness of Disraeli's position after 1868 was due to a variety of factors. The particular brand of Toryism, for which he stood, had suffered spectacular defeat in 1868 and he appeared to have shot his bolt. Those hostile to the policy of reform, whether prominent or obscure, were on the whole opposed to Disraeli's leadership. The overwhelming nature of the Liberal victory made coherent opposition and strong leadership, for the time being, very difficult. Over Irish Church disestablishment and other parts of the Liberal programme Disraeli judged it prudent to offer only qualified opposition, but this was not calculated to unite the Conservative party enthusiastically behind him. Disraeli's own grip on the reins slackened after his resignation in 1868: the prospect of another long spell in opposition after more than 20 years of it was discouraging; his age and indifferent health made it doubtful if he could ever take office again; literary preoccupations supervened.[2] Moreover the Conservative party, like the Liberal party, was made up of different sectional interests, though the friction between these was less spectacular than the disagreements in the opposite camp. The task of leadership was thus inherently difficult, especially for Disraeli who was not intimately associated with any particular group in the party.

The insecurity of Disraeli's hold on the leadership between 1868 and at least 1872 is perhaps best illustrated by the story of the Conservative leadership in the House of Lords during those years. In the nineteenth century the leader of a party in the Lords was on a level with the leader in the Commons, and the Prime Minister often sat in the Upper House. The lead in the Lords might therefore decide the leadership of a party as a whole. When Derby retired from the premiership in February

[2] Buckle, ii. 511–17.

1868 Lord Malmesbury led the Conservative Peers, but he in his turn wished to lay down the burden after the election of December 1868.

In the discussions which now arose concerning his successor the name of Lord Salisbury was almost never absent.[3] This is surely astonishing when it is remembered that Salisbury was Disraeli's most prominent opponent in the party. As Lord Cranborne, he had, with Lord Carnarvon and General Peel, resigned from the Conservative Cabinet over the Reform Bill in May 1867. Ever since, he had left no doubt about the bitterness he felt towards the author of that bill and all that he stood for. Prominent Tory Peers, such as the Dukes of Marlborough and Richmond, who now considered Salisbury as a possible leader in the Lords, must have known that co-operation between him and Disraeli would be out of the question, and that therefore the latter's position as leader of the party as a whole would be seriously compromised.[4] On this occasion the problem was fairly easily resolved. Lord Cairns, former Lord Chancellor, and a close political associate of Disraeli, was another widely supported candidate for the lead amongst the Conservative Peers. Disraeli, having made it clear that Salisbury was unacceptable to him prevailed upon Cairns to undertake the task, and for the moment the threat of a major leadership crisis in the party was removed.

The respite was short-lived. Cairns found his position during the session of 1869 unsatisfactory and had been unable to lead effectively over the Irish Church Disestablishment Bill, the major measure of the session.[5] He considered that Salisbury and Stanley, who had just entered the House of Lords as the fifteenth Earl of Derby, were the two most important personalities on the Tory side, but he had little hope that these two could act in harmony on many issues, and he feared that both of them would draw considerable numbers of Conservative Peers in opposite directions. This situation confirmed Cairns in his intention of laying down the leadership.[6] From Disraeli's point of view it was now essential that Derby, the Liberal

[3] Richmond Papers, Cairns to Richmond, 11 Dec. 1868; also Earl of Malmesbury, *Memoirs of an Ex-Minister* (1884), ii. 388.
[4] Richmond Papers, Marlborough to Richmond, 15 Dec. 1868.
[5] Buckle, ii. 452.
[6] Hughenden Papers, B/XX/Ca, Cairns to Disraeli, 19 Nov. 1869.

Conservative, and not Salisbury, the High Tory, should succeed Cairns. At that very moment Salisbury had again stressed his bitter opposition to Disraeli in an article in the *Quarterly Review* on 'The Past and the Future of Conservative Policy'.[7] Support for Salisbury was strong, but widespread awareness that the problem of communication between him and the existing leader in the Commons would be insurmountable finally swung opinion to support Derby.[8] To Disraeli's consternation, Derby declined the proffered honour. Perhaps he knew his limitations, which were later to become obvious to the world in general. But to Disraeli this refusal was little short of a disaster, and he sent his faithful secretary, Montagu Corry, to plead with Derby and to stop him from sending the news to *The Times* and the *Standard*. The best that Derby could offer was to ease matters between Disraeli and Salisbury.[9] Panic reigned in the Disraeli camp:

I found Colville at the Carlton, after dinner, already copying the letter for the newspapers, and strongly confirmed in his determination to send it at once by the advice of Lord Redesdale and Lord Chelmsford, and by other circumstances which I will tell you of to-morrow. You may imagine, therefore, that my task was neither easy nor short. So far, however, I have succeeded that for the moment and reluctantly he holds his hand and has written to Lord Derby to say that he feels himself unable alone to take the responsibility of publishing what must be fatal to the hopes of the whole Conservative party—and he must decline to do so until he has had an opportunity of consulting his friends to-morrow. . . . I hope therefore that no confident report of what has occurred will appear in print, though I have my doubts, as no secret has been made of the matter at the Carlton—strange to say.[10]

Carnarvon now proposed a scheme by which Salisbury would become leader, without confidentially communicating with Disraeli. The position at this juncture is fully set out by Gathorne Hardy, later Secretary of State for War, in a letter to Cairns:

[7] *Quarterly Review*, Oct. 1869.
[8] Cairns Papers, Carnarvon to Cairns, 16 Feb. 1870.
[9] Richmond Papers, Colville to Richmond, no date, bundle 1870.
[10] Hughenden Papers, B/XX/Co, Corry to Disraeli, 20 Feb. 1870. For Colville and other lesser Figures in the Conservative Party, see Glossary of Names, pp. 227–44.

I write to tell you of a long interview I have had with Carnarvon at his request. He has been strongly urging Salisbury the last two days to accept the position on the understanding that it is a leadership *in and for the Lords* and that he need not and will not hold any confidential communication with our leaders here. He thinks that he has made much impression but as Salisbury has gone down to Hatfield this evening I dread the influences there. Failing him he has tried hard with the Duke of Richmond and does not despair in case of real difficulty of persuading him to accept. Carnarvon is really hearty and most anxious to prevent anything of secession or disruption and has promised Richmond that he in any event would sit by him and would do his best to bring Salisbury with him. He asked me if I thought that Disraeli would take any step to make Salisbury's accession easy. I replied as I strongly feel that D.'s position in this House must be in the lead or nowhere. While here he must lead and his own view as you know was and probably is that by his lead the best hope of securing the future of the party exists. I thought you would like to know something of my talk with Carnarvon. I suppose his leading would not do. Indeed I do not think health or nerve would allow of his taking it. Disraeli looks ill and the Speaker pleasantly told him last night on his reappearance that he had never seen such a change in a man in a fortnight.[11]

Salisbury, seeing the insuperable obstacles to his assumption of the leadership, now put himself out of the running. The Duke of Richmond, a relatively minor political figure, emerged to save the unity of the party and was elected.[12] Here is his own account of these events:

You will no doubt have been as much surprised as I was to learn that after taking twenty-four hours to consider, Derby declined to accept the post of leader. We therefore had a small meeting on Tuesday last and deputed Carnarvon to try Salisbury. He, however, declined also; we were therefore left without a leader. Malmesbury urged me very much to take it, as did Carnarvon. Colville told me that my doing so would be very generally acceptable to the party and I therefore very reluctantly assented. You know how much such a position (though very flattering) is contrary to all my taste habits etc.[13]

---

[11] Cairns Papers, 22 Feb. 1870.
[12] The invitation was conveyed by Colville. See Richmond Papers, Colville to Richmond, no date, bundle 1870.
[13] Cairns Papers, Richmond to Cairns, 27 Feb. 1870.

Little of the tension of these events and of the threat they posed to Tory unity penetrated to the general public. The press, whatever its political complexion, generally welcomed the prospect of Derby assuming the lead, and was disappointed when he refused. Salisbury was widely mentioned as the most acceptable alternative. Even the *Standard*, the Conservative newspaper with the largest circulation, saw in him the only possibility once Derby had refused.[14] It was generally realized that Salisbury might not find co-operation with Disraeli easy, but *The Times* did not consider this obstacle at all insuperable.

Disraeli thus narrowly succeeded in averting a course of events which would in all probability have ended his leadership of the Conservative party. Many leading Tories had made it clear that they were able to contemplate such a prospect with equanimity, and some had even welcomed it. Froude wrote in 1870: 'I have been among some of the Tory magnates lately. They distrust Disraeli still, and will never again be led by him. So they are as sheep that have no shepherd. Lord Salisbury's time may come. But not yet.'[15]

If this was the position at the top of the party, the situation was no different at the grass roots. Striking evidence for the weakness of Disraeli's support among provincial Tories comes from the story of the great Conservative political demonstration, which eventually took place in Manchester in April 1872.[16] Lancashire was one of the few bright spots for the Tories in the General Election of 1868. In this area, the Tory working man was, for various reasons, a reality and Disraeli's hope that an enlarged electorate might be to the advantage of the Conservatives was here borne out by events. At the time of the 1868 election, the possibility of a ceremonial visit by Disraeli to the County Palatine had been mooted, and the idea was revived from time to time afterwards. By 1870 John Gorst, whom Disraeli had put in charge of the new Central Conservative Office, was anxious to promote the visit as a means of signalling a revival of Tory fortunes in the country generally. According to Gorst, Algernon Egerton, the member for South-east Lancashire, had put himself at the head of the movement to invite

---

[14] *Standard*, 23 Feb. 1870.
[15] Froude distrusted Disraeli and disliked both political parties.
[16] See also below, pp. 115 ff.

Disraeli. Yet after the lapse of a few weeks Egerton himself had to write to Disraeli far more soberly:

Without entering at any length into the present state of our local politics, the case, in my belief, stands thus—the Conservatives of the middle and lower classes are, generally speaking, warmly in favour of asking you to come here, and this is also the feeling of the gentry in N.E., and S.E. Lancashire, on the other hand in N. and S.W. Lancashire the gentry are not in favour of holding any political demonstration at present; they consider that the Conservative cause needs no strengthening in their districts, and there is a section of them who have not forgiven your Reform Bill (though they cannot complain of its results, as far as they are concerned.) I am also informed that Lord Derby would decline any large political meeting under present circumstances, and I am convinced that his presence would be indispensable at any meeting purporting to represent the Conservatives of the county. I therefore am of the opinion that we cannot invite you to a 'county' meeting. [Christmas Day 1870].[17]

In these circumstances Disraeli could not possibly have contemplated accepting the invitation and exposing himself to the risk of failure. It is interesting to note that Lord Derby, whom Disraeli had been obliged to back in order to keep Salisbury from the leadership in the Lords, was yet himself so little inclined to share a platform with the former associate of his father. All the prominent men of Lancashire Conservatism, R. A. Cross, Lord Sandon, both later members of Disraeli's government, and Samuel Graves, the great Liverpool shipowner and M.P. for the City, judged the time for a demonstration inopportune in 1870, especially if the support of Lord Derby could not be obtained.

In August 1871, Graves began a renewed move for a Conservative demonstration, but this time he was thinking not so much of an invitation to Disraeli personally as of one to several prominent Conservative party leaders jointly. Graves felt that the moment was very favourable so far as opinion at large was concerned, and he therefore considered it worthwhile to make a fresh approach to the Master of Knowsley.[18] This was Sandon's reaction to the proposal:

I do not myself like the idea of a public appearance of the members of the late Cabinet in Lancashire—as you know, I do not hold a

[17] Hughenden Papers, B/XIII/109a. Material relating to the Lancashire visit is in bundle A/IV/N/58–96.
[18] Harrowby Papers, L/132, Graves to Sandon, 23 Aug. [1871].

very high opinion of their capacity and I feel sure that such an appearance would tell against us in the country in two ways—firstly: it would be said—it is after all a struggle for place between two Cabinets and though the present one is bad enough we are not prepared to accept the feeble Conservative Cabinet robbed of some of its strongest men by the defection of General Peel, Salisbury and Carnarvon—and secondly such a demonstration would warn off the Liberals who are gradually inclining to our side, as they would be told that the movement in the country is a purely Conservative party one, that they must pass beneath the yoke of our old party leaders if they give up their own side.[19]

Cross felt that there was little point in asking the Conservative leaders to come down if they had no definite policy to put before the country. Again Lord Derby's co-operation seemed to him essential, and he doubted if it would be forthcoming. Thus the proposal for a demonstration hung fire for several months longer. The opposition to Disraeli's leadership was therefore not confined to the country gentlemen and the squirearchy; even men like Cross and Sandon, who could be regarded as belonging to the progressive wing of the party, are here seen to have adopted a decidedly sceptical and detached attitude.

In the meantime the anti-Disraeli movement at the top of the party reached its climax at a gathering of prominent Tories at Burghley House at the end of January 1872.[20] For several days there were inconclusive discussions about the leadership problem. There was a good deal of feeling that the party would be better off under Derby than under Disraeli. The opposition to Disraeli throughout the party was thus both personal and political. To many Tories a Jewish literary man at the head of the party was only tolerable if he achieved results, and in electoral terms Disraeli's successes had certainly not been spectacular. His flexible policies over twenty years, culminating in the second Reform Bill had inspired deep distrust.

At the beginning of the parliamentary session of 1872 Disraeli began to reassert himself. He reprimanded his colleague in the Lords, the Duke of Richmond, for being insufficiently co-operative. The alarmed Duke was driven to seek comfort and reassurance from Lord Cairns, who was always at his elbow

---

[19] Harrowby Papers, L/306, Sandon to Graves, 1 Sept. 1871.
[20] Buckle, ii. 513.

as political guide and mentor. Cairns wrote back, '. . . you know that last year, and in 1870, he was down in the mouth and rather repelling meetings to concert plans etc: now he thinks things are looking up, and awakening himself, he turns round and insists that every one else is asleep . . .'[21]

Cross, who had taken a prominent part in putting the Conservative case on the Ballot Bill in the session of 1871, asked Disraeli for his opinion about the tactics to be followed on this bill in the coming session. The leader's words had about them the ring of a marching order given by a general to his troops, 'The government would like the bill to linger in the Commons and distract attention from other subjects. Our policy is the reverse.' and 'Let the Whig peers throw it out if they like. I should not attempt to influence their course one way or the other.'[22] Disraeli was firmly back in the saddle.

The signal was now given, probably from Hughenden, to start preparations in earnest for a big political demonstration in Lancashire. Disraeli's triumphant reception in Manchester in April 1872 and his famous Free Trade Hall speech did much to quell doubts about his leadership. The Lancashire visit was remarkable as the first occasion on which Disraeli attempted to address himself directly to a mass audience. Gladstone had long established himself as a great popular platform orator and the Conservative leader was never to the end of his career able to equal him in this respect. Yet Disraeli's visit to Manchester showed that he, too, could spark off popular enthusiasm and that his personality had mass appeal. *The Times*, in a leading article on 3 April 1872, said, 'If he were the most potent of ministers instead of the chief of the weakest Opposition which Parliament has known for many years, he could not have met with a more hearty welcome.' London had already acclaimed Disraeli when he drove from the thanksgiving service at St. Paul's after the Prince of Wales' recovery from typhoid fever in February 1872, and he received further proof of his popularity when he addressed the National Union of Conservative and Constitutional Associations at the Crystal Palace in June of

[21] Richmond Papers, 23 Jan. 1872. See also Robert Blake, *Disraeli*, p. 521.
[22] Cross Papers, Add. MS.51265, 23 Dec. 1871. For the passage of the Ballot Bill through Parliament, see Cornelius O'Leary, *The Elimination of Corrupt Practices in British Elections 1868–1911* (1962), pp. 74 ff.

that year.[23] The worst dangers to Disraeli's position as leader appeared to have been surmounted, provided the momentum of the Conservative revival could be maintained.

Disraeli was aware, however, that, in order to qualify his party for office and to strengthen his personal position, it was necessary not merely to arouse popular enthusiasm and to profit from the mistakes of his opponents, but also to meet the taunts that the Conservatives had no policy. He therefore used his big speeches at Manchester and at the Crystal Palace to outline a programme. The policy which emerged was an amalgam of the personal political views he had always held, of views common to Conservatives in general and of responses to immediate problems. He emphasized support for the Monarchy, a point not only appropriate to Conservatism, but given special significance by the Republicanism prevalent in some quarters in the previous few years. In proclaiming the Conservative Party as the pillar of the Established Church, Disraeli was restating a traditional tenet of Toryism, which had remained as topical and relevant as ever. Social reform on the other hand was a new plank in Disraeli's programme; it arose out of the current political situation and out of the demands of the moment, and was also an example of Disraeli's personal political philosophy of making Toryism into a bond between different social classes in the nation. Support for the Empire and for its further development was a new and unconventional policy with great potentialities for the future. In this matter Disraeli proved far seeing and possessed of that feeling for the spirit of the age, of which he made so much in his speech at Glasgow in the following year. In proclaiming the Conservatives as the party of the Empire, Disraeli was not only responding to the widespread criticism of Gladstone's weak external policy but was also establishing a clear contrast between himself and his opponents.

The speeches of 1872 are hardly by modern standards a political manifesto.[24] There is little reference to specific measures, and general lines of policy are only broadly sketched.

[23] Sir William Fraser, *Disraeli and His Day* (1891), pp. 374–6; Buckle, ii. 533.
[24] *Selected Speeches of the late Rt. Hon. The Earl of Beaconsfield*, ed. by T. E. Kebbel (1882), ii. 490 (Manchester speech), ii. 523 (Crystal Palace speech).

The machinery, by which political parties work out their programmes nowadays, did not then exist and it would not have been expedient for Disraeli to be too specific. Detail was never his strong point. He continued to emphasize that a fully fledged policy could only emerge once the party had taken office and from the information that would then become available to the leaders.

Even after these successful public initiatives, confidence in Disraeli was neither firmly based nor universally shared in the Conservative party. Any break in the rising tide of electoral approval could bring renewed attacks on his leadership. The *Spectator*, commenting on Disraeli's standing after the parliamentary session of 1872, thought that in spite of the reconciliation of Salisbury and Carnarvon he still suffered from the deep-seated distrust of the country Conservatives, who blamed him for 1867 and all that flowed from it. Many sections of the party were beginning to feel, so the the paper declared, that most of what they wanted to conserve had been given away, either by Disraeli, or by Gladstone with little opposition from Disraeli.[25] Lady Knightley, the wife of Sir Rainald Knightley, one of the most intrepid and irreconcilable Tory opponents of Disraeli, wrote in her diary at this time: 'Mr. Lowe and R fell to talking politics, recalling the time when they worked so hard together in 1866 and had so nearly created a strong Constitutional party to see it all destroyed the following year, and *selon eux* the country ruined by Mr. D.'[26]

Disraeli's refusal to take office in March 1873 presented fresh opportunities for criticism. He and his colleagues appear to have had no difficulty in making up their minds that neither the circumstances in Parliament nor in the country were at that juncture favourable enough for them to take office. The only close colleague of Disraeli's whose attitude was in doubt was Cairns. Disraeli had consulted him some weeks earlier about this possible contingency, and his view then was that the party should not take office. *Ex post facto* he was apparently less certain, as the following letter to him from Gathorne Hardy indicates:

[25] *Spectator*, 20 July 1872, p. 904.
[26] *The Journals of Lady Knightley of Fawsley*, ed. by Julia Cartwright (1915), p. 230, 3 May 1872.

The explanations are over but not quite to my mind. I think Disraeli was wrong in dwelling so much on the necessity of our making up our policy on many questions after we are in office. That assures almost perpetual exclusion. With regard to the course which he has pursued there is a thorough and general agreement among the best of our men. I admit your view has force but the present House would be so hostile and the election so uncertain that I think three months office might be followed by great discomfiture. I felt so strongly that I could not have taken office and Hunt at least was of the same mind, but it was needless to consider this matter as Disraeli adopted the view more strongly than he generally does.[27]

The arguments which determined Disraeli and his associates in their refusal to accept the Queen's commission are ably set out by Northcote:

I am afraid I cannot give you any dates; but I think it pretty clear that you could not meet Parliament, with an administration formed, until Easter week, and that you could not dissolve until the beginning of May. It would be a most inconvenient time for interrupting public and private business; and you would moreover go to the country at a great disadvantage, from having been obliged on the one hand to huddle up a good deal of important work which ought to be done deliberately, and on the other hand not having had time to mature with your colleagues a scheme of policy. My own belief is, that if you took office now you would find it necessary to carry on the session to its natural termination, say perhaps early in July, and to dissolve in the summer with the possibility of having to call us together in the autumn. I cannot say how strongly I feel against the idea of your taking office just now. Gladstone may endeavour to drive you to do so, and may say that having taken the responsibility of defeating his ministry on a vital question you are bound to replace them. If our action upon the University bill had been in any way concerted with the Roman Irish there would be force in this argument; but it would be monstrous to hold that we were stopped from voting against a bill which on independent grounds we thought a bad one by the fact that a body of men with whom we had no relations whatever, and of whose intentions we really had no reliable information up to the last moment, determined also to vote against it on grounds of their own. If we were to accept Gladstone's doctrine we should give colour to the assumption from which he draws his inference, and he would take care to make the most of our alliance with Rome when he went to the hustings.

[27] Buckle, ii. 547; Cairns Papers, Hardy to Cairns, 20 Mar. 1873.

But looking at the matter broadly, and in the interest of the Conservative cause as distinct from that of the present representatives of the Conservative party, I am strongly convinced that time is required to mature the fast ripening Conservatism of the country, and to dispel the hallucinations which have attached a great mass of moderate men to the Liberal cause. I believe that the disintegration of Gladstone's party has begun and that nothing but precipitancy on our part can arrest it. He has expended the impetuous force which brought him into office, and now is brought face to face with new, or rather old, difficulties which he can hardly surmount without alienating one or the other wing of his party. If he goes on with the Extreme section, a large body of his moderate supporters will rank themselves with the Conservatives, if he quarrels with the Extreme section they will become the Opposition, while the conduct of affairs will fall to the acknowledged Conservatives, who will obtain the support of the moderate Liberals. But if we appeal to the country before the breach in the Liberal ranks is fully made, and before the policy of the Extreme men is fully developed, we shall consolidate them; the Extreme men will hold back a little and the moderate advance a little and there will be more confusion and confiscation.[28]

Similar arguments were used by Disraeli in public to justify his action to his party. There was undoubtedly a section of Tories who were dissatisfied with the decision not to take office—the 'ravenous' members of the party, as someone called them.[29] The *Standard*, a newspaper which rarely deviated from the official Conservative party line and which was always reluctant to wash dirty linen in public, was puzzled and bewildered.[30] On the other hand some inveterate enemies, like the Knightleys, now considered Disraeli's refusal to take office statesmanlike.[31] There was a widespread feeling that if the party took office it would be better off under Derby. Colonel Taylor, the Conservative Whip, told Disraeli quite frankly that, while on a dissolution they might get a majority of a hundred seats in England, the nominal leadership of Derby would be an advantage.[32]

[28] Iddesleigh Papers, Add. MS.50016, Northcote to Disraeli, 14 Mar. 1873.
[29] Richmond Papers, Charles Peel to Richmond, 15 Mar. 1873.
[30] *Standard*, 18 Mar. 1873.
[31] *Journals of Lady Knightley*, 15 Mar. 1873.
[32] Hughenden Papers, B/XX/T, Taylor to Disraeli, 14 Mar. 1873. See also below, p. 55.

It may be imagined how gravely Disraeli's position with his party would have been shaken if the gamble of refusing office in March 1873 had not eventually paid off. For many Tories, Disraeli's leadership continued to be merely the lesser of two evils: better an irksome leader than a dangerous friend, as *The Economist* put it.[33] Even at the moment of triumph in 1874, when Disraeli's lifelong struggle to make the Conservatives into the majority party was at last crowned with success, there were still voices calling for a different Premier. Lord Russell, who could claim to be the Whig elder statesman in the Lords and who had made common cause with the Tories on numerous occasions, wrote to Richmond, 'As a change of Government seems imminent, I wish to communicate my solitary impression. If you or Derby is to be the head, I wish to keep my seat in the House of Lords and to support the new Government. If Mr. Disraeli is to be the head, I shall cross over at once and sit on the Opposition side of the House.'[34] Cairns suggested to Richmond that he reply to Russell that 'should the result of the elections which are now taking place through the country lead to the formation of a Conservative Government I hope at a crisis like the present its policy will meet with your approval under whomsoever it may be formed', but privately he commented to Richmond, 'Poor old Lord Russell can't hear of any political movement without trying to have a finger in the pie. I was under the impression that he sat in Opposition to us at the present time: but it is little matter where a man who comes to the House once in the session, and then can't hear anyone, and can't be heard himself, sits'.[35]

Once invested with the patronage of office, Disraeli was never again in danger, in spite of ill health and the relatively meagre results of his first two years of power. The usual explanation for the barrenness of his ministry in domestic legislation is that the Prime Minister, lacking in physical vigour, was unable to contemplate heavy parliamentary battles. Another reason for

[33] *The Economist*, 29 Nov. 1873, p. 1436 in a comment on Disraeli's speeches at Glasgow. See also Buckle, ii. 603–8.
[34] Richmond Papers, Russell to Richmond, 8 Feb. 1874.
[35] Richmond Papers, Cairns to Richmond, 10 Feb. 1874. According to Lady Derby there was a scheme to offer Lord Russell a place in the Cabinet as a compliment (Lady G. Cecil, *Life of Robert, Marquis of Salisbury* [1921–32], ii. 47).

Disraeli's comparative inertia may have been his reluctance to take any further risks with party unity and with his personal position, now that there was at last the prospect of a secure spell in office after fighting off so many challenges.

The composition of Disraeli's government points in the same direction. The prominent place allotted to the representatives of the great Tory families has often been noticed. Of these, the two most politically important accessions were those of Salisbury and Carnarvon, whose presence in the Government made a renewed challenge from the right wing of the party unlikely. The controversy about Ritualism in the Church of England, which was likely to engage the Government's attention in its first few weeks of office, might well have caused both these staunch High Churchmen to stay out. For the rest, requests to Disraeli by, or on behalf of, the scions of the great Tory houses often achieved their object. On the other hand, men without aristocratic connections, but with considerable claims on grounds of merit, political weight, or services to the party in many cases received no preferment.[36] The same impression is created by the inordinate amount of time and energy that was spent in the autumn of 1875 with the grievances, alleged or real, of Lord Henry Lennox, the Duke of Richmond's brother, against the Treasury. Disraeli, Northcote, Cairns, and Richmond all made valiant efforts to spare Lord Henry the necessity of leaving the Government.[37]

Disraeli's choice of men was thus distinctly conservative, while the eventual legislative achievements of his administration were modest. The Premier's political instincts, however, remained radical: he was always at pains to avoid associating his party or the Government with anything smacking of reaction, and was anxious to preserve their broad mass appeal. This can be clearly seen from two interventions by the Premier in the field of educational policy, where retrograde pressures

[36] Hughenden Papers, B/XII/A. This bundle contains much material on the formation of the 1874 Administration. See *The Times*, 3 Mar. 1874, on the predominance of county members in the new Government. See also below, Chapter III, for the composition of Disraeli's Government in 1874. Requests for office from some of the middle class members sitting for large boroughs, such as Wheelhouse, the member for Leeds, fell on deaf ears.

[37] See Hughenden, Iddesleigh, Cairns, and Richmond Papers throughout 1875. Also Buckle, ii. 631, 823; R. Blake, op. cit., p. 684.

in the Conservative Party were strong. In the 1874 session the
Endowed Schools Bill in its original form provided for the return
to Church management of schools which had been brought
under the Endowed Schools Commission. The bill was to some
extent a sop to Salisbury and others, who had been brought to
the brink of resignation by the Government's course on the
Public Worship Regulation Bill.[38] Eventually, however,
Disraeli himself dropped those clauses of the Endowed Schools
Bill most offensive to people concerned about educational
progress, and only the abolition of the Endowed Schools Commission and the transfer of its functions to the Charity Com-
missioners remained.[39]

An even more striking illustration of Disraeli's reluctance to
sponsor what he considered a reactionary course, especially if,
as he seems to have suspected in this case, it had the support of
the High Church party, is provided by one of his interventions
on the Education Bill of 1876. The school boards, provided for
in the Education Act of 1870, had become a thorn in the side of
many a Tory squire and parson. Their abolition, in areas where
the existing voluntary schools were considered to fulfil educational needs adequately, was strongly demanded by many Tory
county members of the old school. The Cabinet consequently
decided that, if a clause providing for the abolition of unnecessary school boards should be moved from their own back
benches, it should be accepted. As expected, such a clause was
moved by Albert Pell, a prominent Tory county member.[40]
Without warning, however, Lord Sandon, who as Vice-President of the Committee of Council on Education was in charge
of the bill, found himself confronted with the Prime Minister's
refusal to accept Pell's clause. Other members of the Cabinet

---

[38] This was the bill to counteract the spread of Ritualism within the
Church of England. It was a private member's bill introduced by the Archbishop of Canterbury and the Government supported it.
[39] See Cecil, op. cit., ii. 62–4; Buckle, ii. 673. Viscount Sandon, the Vice-
President of the Committee of Council on Education, expressed uneasiness
about the retrograde character of the bill at an early stage (Hughenden
Papers, B/XXI/Sandon, 18 July 1874). Dr. J. H. Rigg, the prominent
Methodist, wrote to Sandon that for Methodists the bill (in its original
form) 'will go far to rehabilitate the Liberal ministry in favour and even
to procure condonation for Mr. Gladstone.' (Harrowby Papers, LIII/358,
16 July 1874).
[40] See below, Chapter III, p. 64.

remained strongly in favour of accepting a proposal likely to give so much satisfaction to Conservative grass root sentiment. Sandon appealed to Salisbury:

I must tell you confidentially of the great peril which hangs over Pell's clause for abolishing unnecessary school boards—which I consider one of our most important moves, which is immensely popular with all our party in the House of Commons, and will be most acceptable to all the country except the big towns. As you will remember it was early decided in the Cabinet to accept such a proposal if made by our friends and I have been repeatedly assured by the Committee of Cabinet that they wish me to press it and consider it of primary importance. Before I committed the Government to it in the House of Commons on Thursday, I asked Cross, Northcote and Hardy, whether after hearing the wild opposition of Forster and Co., they still wished the Government to commit itself, and they all agreed I should do so and should interpose in the debate at the moment I did. I confess I have been disappointed that no member of the Cabinet came forward during yesterday's hot debate to support me, when I was violently attacked for reaction etc.

The danger to the clause lies in this—Mr. Disraeli told me yesterday that he should settle the question of adhering to Pell's proposal at Monday's Cabinet, and spoke most strongly against the proposal —he said the Government had made a fatal mistake in supporting it, that the move against school boards was held by the Opposition to be 'made by the Sacerdotal party', and gave me to understand that he would throw us over. I really believe no greater blunder could be committed at this moment than to abandon the clause. We have all our party and most of the country with us—and Forster has made a great mistake, and he will find when his friends meet their constituents in the autumn, in supporting unnecessary school boards and opposing the popular option. Of course we all knew he would fight hard to save his children, and that we must have a struggle for such a gain.[41]

Disraeli's treatment of the merchant shipping question in 1875 shows a similar anxiety to avoid the charge of 'reaction'. Plimsoll had aroused public opinion with the cry of 'coffin ships'. The Government was already short of parliamentary time and Disraeli was personally strongly committed to the

[41] Salisbury Papers, Sandon to Salisbury, 22 July 1876. For the debates on Pell's clause, see *Hansard*, vol. ccxxx, 20 July 1876 and following days. Also Harrowby Papers, vols. LIII and LV. Disraeli relented under pressure from his colleagues and Pell's clause was accepted.

Agricultural Holdings Bill, designed to enable the tenant to secure the benefit of unexhausted improvements. The Prime Minister was anxious to show that the Ministry's devotion to the welfare of the agricultural interest extended to tenants, as well as to landlords. If the Agricultural Holdings Bill was to be completed, there would be no time left to deal comprehensively with the merchant shipping question. Rather than face the charge that the Tories were not as earnest in the pursuit of social welfare and as alive to humanitarian considerations as their opponents, Disraeli introduced a temporary Unseaworthy Ships Bill and thus appeased the Plimsoll agitation.[42]

If Disraeli was thus anxious to rebut any notion of retrogression, he was not prepared to exert himself greatly to accomplish a striking record of domestic legislation. He left this task to his lieutenants, Cross, Northcote, Sclater-Booth and others and, if anything, exercised a restraining influence. He backed up Cross against the rest of the Cabinet over trade union legislation, but otherwise took little active interest in what the Home Secretary and other ministers were doing in the field of social reform.[43] When Cross put forward a proposal for dealing with the government of London, Disraeli's reaction was characteristically negative:

I am quite decided never to embark on a scheme for the Government of London.

I would rather at present, under any circumstances, leave the matter alone. We came in on the principle of not harrassing the country and I shrink from prematurely embarking on such questions as Railway Reform, University Reform and the one respecting which you have written to me today.[44]

Disraeli was only too well aware that the Tory tradition of social reform was opposed to the imposition of any blueprints and intensely suspicious of Whitehall interference with local interests.[45]

[42] For the Merchant Shipping question in 1875, see Andrew Lang, *Life, Letters and Diaries of Sir Stafford Northcote, First Earl of Iddesleigh* (1889), ii. 78–82; W. S. Child-Pemberton, *Life of Lord Norton* (1909), Chapter XXXVII; David Masters, *The Plimsoll Mark* (1955); *Hansard*, 18 Feb.–2 Aug. 1875 (vols. ccxxii–ccxxvi).

[43] R. Blake, op. cit., pp. 553–6.

[44] Cross Papers, Add. MS. 51265, 22 Oct. 1874.

[45] See D. Roberts, 'Tory Paternalism and Social Reform in Early Victorian England', *American Historical Review*, vol. LXIII, No. 2 (Jan. 1958), p. 323.

Assessing the position of the Government early in 1875, *The Economist* saw three sections in the Conservative Party: the country party, believers in old watchwords, uneducated to new ideas, finding the Government a little too liberal for their liking; the second section, the men of business in the Cabinet—simply moderate Liberals on the wrong side; the third section, the over-educated part of the Cabinet, consisted notably of the Prime Minister himself. 'He is the inventor of "Democratic Conservatism"; that a low suffrage in England is safe only if you go low enough. He appeals to the outsiders, the non-voting element, to the "people" in the least agreeable sense. He advocates a Plimsoll policy, secures the road to India, will throw away the "dry bones" of parliamentary economy.' This was the voice of a shrewd, though unsympathetic, contemporary.[46]

In fact Disraeli was, in his personal predilections, a mixture of aristocratic and democratic impulses. His background was by no means as humble as popular opinion generally conceived it. He had declared it one of the objectives of his party to maintain the recognition of the aristocratic principle in the constitution.[47] He had persuaded himself that his own origins were highly patrician and had therefore no difficulty in identifying himself with the aristocracy. In his youth he conquered, and became part of London Society.[48] In his later political and private life he surrounded himself with aristocratic personages. Gladstone's popular performances in the country were thoroughly uncongenial to him and he was never really convinced of his popularity with the masses.[49] He was in a sense so un-English that the masses probably never understood him though they may not have disliked him.[50] Yet the very prejudices of many of his followers, the very stuff of Toryism, against which he had to battle so much in the long process of education, often brought out the radical element in Disraeli's personal

---

[46] 'The State of Parties', *The Economist*, 15 Jan. 1875, p. 62.
[47] For a long and explicit public declaration of his faith in the Monarchy and the House of Lords, see the Manchester speech, *Select Speeches*, ed. Kebbel, p. 490. See also *Leaves from the Note-Books of Lady Dorothy Nevill*, ed. by R. Nevill (1907), p. 75, for Beaconsfield's attachment to aristocratic government.
[48] R. Blake, op. cit., pp. 504 ff.
[49] *The Reminiscences of Lady Dorothy Nevill*, ed. R. Nevill (1906), p. 204.
[50] 'The Causes of Mr. Disraeli's Popularity', *Spectator*, 6 Apr. 1872, p. 426.

make-up, an element as real as his aristocratic leanings.[51] Moreover he realized, with his highly developed political instinct, that in the circumstances of the age the Tory party must be a mass party, even though he no longer had the vigour after 1874 to carry out a popular policy on a large scale, and make it prevail against the powerful obstacles it was bound to encounter.

Disraeli's performance in the premiership was usually much admired by friend and foe alike, but at times it aroused a storm of criticism in the most diverse quarters. Reginald Brett, later Viscount Esher, despite his youth a shrewd and independent observer of the political scene, with personal access to many of its leading figures, noted in his *Journals* on the occasion of Disraeli's retirement to the Lords:

> His great merit is that he is a perfect captain of a side; that he has a true judgement about men's abilities, claims and propensities. He not only can choose his eleven correctly but keep them charging and backing each other up. No other minister in recent times has had his knowledge of character and skill in dealing with various capabilities. His Ministry is the result of admirable skill and arranging. And on the whole they behave better than any set of Ministers ever known.[52]

On the other hand Disraeli's lack of vigour and what was sometimes called 'want of business aptitude' were frequently noticed, especially during the first three sessions of his Government. While it was generally conceded that he was a man of imagination, it was widely said that he lacked attention to detail, that he was unable to give careful supervision to his ministers, and that he was imperfectly acquainted with all the legislative proposals which his Government had laid before Parliament.[53] Even Disraeli's famed parliamentary skill was

[51] Cf. Shaftesbury's pungent comment on Disraeli becoming Premier: 'Disraeli Prime Minister! He is a Hebrew; this is a good thing. He is a man sprung from an inferior station, another good thing in these days, as showing the liberality of our institutions. But he is a leper, without principle, without feeling, without regard to anything, human or Divine, beyond his personal ambition.' (reported by G. W. E. Russell, *Prime Ministers and Some Others* [1918], Chapter IV).
[52] *Journals and Letters of Reginald, Viscount Esher*, ed. by Maurice V. Brett (1934), i. 37, 30 Aug. 1876.
[53] 'The Situation of the Government', *The Economist*, 22 May 1875, p. 606.

variously assessed. Sir Henry Lucy, that seasoned parliamentary reporter, speaks of the great hold that Disraeli had on the House of Commons during the first session of his second premiership and of his ability to fill the House as soon as he rose to his feet. Others found grave fault with his handling of the Public Worship Regulation and Endowed Schools Bills, the two most controversial measures of that session;[54] the sudden changes, of course, some of which have been referred to earlier, were ascribed to his lack of foresight and fundamental absence of principle.

Disraeli's translation to the Upper House, his emergence into the European limelight, and his Near Eastern policy turned him into a figure larger than life. At the height of his triumphs Beaconsfield had gained a position stronger than the majority of Prime Ministers ever achieve. His opponents began to talk of 'personal government', and the favour he enjoyed at Court aroused deep suspicion.[55] On the other hand the policy of imperialism never had the enthusiastic support of all sections of Conservatism. The increasingly important section of Conservatives with commercial and industrial connections, some of whom sat in the Commons as the representatives of the great cities, voiced their anxiety as the tension grew.[56] Nonetheless, it was widely held that, if Beaconsfield had chosen to go to the country after his return from Berlin, he would have been certain of another term in office. Advice to dissolve Parliament reached him and other members of the Government from many quarters. The question was discussed in Cabinet, but feeling against ending a parliamentary term prematurely was strong. The state of Beaconsfield's health may also have made him

---

[54] 'The Government and the Session', *Spectator*, 8 Aug. 1874, p. 996; H. W. Lucy, *A Diary of Two Parliaments* (1885), vol. i; *The Disraeli Parliament 1874–1880*, p. 39, 7 Aug. 1874; 'The Session and the Ministry', *Edinburgh Review*, vol. 286, p. 549, Oct. 1874.

[55] 'Lord Beaconsfield and Personal Government', *The Economist*, 23 Nov. 1878, p. 1370.

[56] Cf. R. Tennant's speech to the Leeds Chamber of Commerce, reported in *The Times*, 16 Jan. 1878; also, indicating the anxiety of borough members, a telegram from J. Torr, M.P. for Liverpool, to his fellow member for the city, Sandon, on 19 Dec. 1877, asking about the reasons for the early summons of Parliament. This was sent on to Corry by Sandon, with the note: 'What reply can I give?' (Harrowby Papers LV/25). See also below, Chapters III and VIII.

reluctant to risk an electoral battle at that moment.[57] Even if he had won then, or in 1880, his time was inexorably drawing to a close.

The most interesting points to emerge during the last year of Beaconsfield's life, after his defeat in 1880, were his attitude to the developing tension between Northcote and the Tory free lances, soon to be known as the Fourth Party, and his outlook and expectations for the future. Instinctively Beaconsfield's sympathies must have lain with the young rebels, who were making life difficult for the orthodox leaders. Equally, he must have been disappointed in the performance of Northcote and the rest of his successors in the Commons; their parliamentary qualities were put to a sterner test in opposition than in office. There is evidence from at least three of the four principals of the Fourth Party that Beaconsfield gave them encouragement.[58] The exact degree of this encouragement is difficult to estimate; there is equally strong evidence that Beaconsfield never wavered in his loyal co-operation with Northcote as leader of the party in the Commons, and that at one point the veteran leader assured him that he would help in 'looking after the Fourth Party'.[59] Beaconsfield was by this time so near the end of his career, and at so Olympian a height, that he could hardly have been expected to intervene decisively in a dispute which had yet to reach its most acute phase. T. H. S. Escott, a well-informed political writer and editor, expressed the view that Beaconsfield ought to have come to Northcote's rescue by other means than 'semi-serious remonstrances sent through Mr. Spofforth';[60] while Balfour, recording a conversation

[57] See also below p. 140; R. Blake, op. cit., pp. 656–7; H. J. Hanham, *Elections and Party Management* (1959), pp. 227–9. A. B. Forwood, the prominent champion of Tory Democracy at Liverpool wrote to Sandon at this time: 'The question of the hour is "Will there be, and should there be, a dissolution". The general response of our supporters is that it would be wise for the Government to go to the country, if you can only find a strong enough challenge from Gladstone and Hartington. . . . Use the flood tide and do not let taxes and the short memory of the populace efface, as it may next year, the recollections of what was done this.' (Harrowby Papers, vol. L, no date).

[58] See Sir H. D. Wolff, *Rambling Recollections* (1908), ii, 263; also W. S. Churchill, *Life of Lord Randolph Churchill* (1906), i. 154; A. J. Balfour, *Chapters of Autobiography* (1930) p. 148.   [59] Buckle, ii. 1461.

[60] T. H. S. Escott, *Randolph Spencer-Churchill, as a Portrait of His Age* (1895), p. 128. For Spofforth, the Conservative party agent, see below, Chapter V.

with Beaconsfield in January 1881, emphasized the latter's isolation from his late Cabinet colleagues and his contempt for
them.[61]

It is perhaps more profitable to try to assess Beaconsfield's
views on the position of the Conservative party after the great
defeat of April 1880 and on the outlook for the future. All
observers reported that the débâcle did not leave the old
statesman dispirited.[62] His life's work, the creation of the
modern Conservative party, capable of attracting a mass
electorate and obtaining a parliamentary majority, was not in
ruins but had only suffered a temporary setback. He obviously
felt that the Tory party remained capable of attracting substantial support from all sections and classes in the community.
But, as the year wore on, this general confidence was often
overshadowed by gloom. In his talk with Balfour soon after
the election, in which he had refused to be downcast, Beaconsfield also foresaw that the equalization of the county and
borough franchise would be the most far-reaching change likely
to come from the Liberal Government. To meet this challenge
he planned to use the House of Lords, where the Conservatives
retained the majority, to enforce a simultaneous treatment of
franchise extension and redistribution of seats. Beaconsfield
calculated that redistribution would cause almost insuperable
difficulties and thus the whole project might be made to
founder. Tactically this prescription was no doubt far seeing,
and in 1884 events very nearly bore him out. In spite of all
wooing of the boroughs the strong Conservative position in the
counties was still the backbone of the party, and Beaconsfield's
vision of the future seems to have been chiefly inspired by fear
of losing this bulwark. It is difficult to imagine that, if he had
still been in charge when the crisis came, he would have confined himself to a purely negative blocking action. In 1880 he
could not, of course, have foreseen the events which decisively
rescued the Conservative party from the danger of becoming
once again a permanent minority party.

At the first rally of Conservative M.P.s and Peers after the
election of 1880, held at Bridgwater House in May 1880,

---

[61] Salisbury Papers, Balfour to Salisbury, 24 Jan. 1881.
[62] A. J. Balfour, *Chapters of Autobiography*, pp. 124–7. Andrew Lang,
Northcote, ii. 176–8.

Beaconsfield warned his followers against 'the party of revolution, perhaps 100 in number'.[63] As the year advanced he saw emerging grave threats to the whole system of land tenure on which the proud position of the aristocracy still rested. The Gladstone Government's legislation to deal with the ills of Ireland, the Compensation for Disturbance Bill, later the Land Bill, all seemed to him part of a grand assault on this central citadel. To Lady Chesterfield he wrote gloomily, 'It is a revolutionary age, and the chances are that even you and I may live to see the final extinction of the great London season, which was the wonder and admiration of our youth. . . .'[64] He was particularly concerned about divisions appearing in the camp of the landed interest. A clash of this kind was brought into the open by a relatively minor piece of Government legislation known as the Ground Game, or Hares and Rabbits Bill. Its purpose was to make it obligatory to include in all land leases a clause leaving it to the tenant to deal with ground game damage to crops. Many representatives of landlords and tenants from the Tory benches took opposite sides on this Bill, a considerable sense of discomfort was produced in the party and even Beaconsfield felt troubled.[65]

The Liberal and Radical attack on the landed interest created opportunities for the recruitment of some of the Whigs to the Tory side, and Northcote was constantly writing to Beaconsfield about expected and possible combinations. The aged leader attached little importance to these efforts; 'The Whigs may be indignant, but they are pusillanimous' he wrote to Lady Bradford.[66] Beaconsfield's fears for the landed interest, the bulwark of the Tory party, are understandable; the greatest danger to Britain's farmers and landowners, however, did not arise from events in Ireland, but from economic depression and foreign competition.[67] Beaconsfield had been unable to find any remedies against these evils when he was in power, and he found none now. His final abdication from the life-long pursuit

[63] Buckle, ii. 1448.
[64] *The Letters of Disraeli to Lady Bradford and Lady Chesterfield*, ed. by The Marquis of Zetland (1929), ii. 279, 27 June 1880, to Lady Chesterfield.
[65] Ibid., ii. 278, 14 June 1880, to Lady Bradford. See also below, Chapter III, and D. Southgate, *The Passing of the Whigs* (1962), p. 368.
[66] Ibid. II. 280, 4 July 1880, to Lady Bradford.
[67] See below, Chapter IV.

of political power may have blunted his subtle political sensitivity. Between his radical instincts and his aristocratic leaning he now came down heavily on the side of the latter and, at the end of his life, fear at times predominated over constructive plans for the future.

II

THE CONSERVATIVE FRONT BENCH

ISRAELI reached and kept the leadership of the Conservative party through his exceptional qualities as a man and a politician. He towered over his colleagues. Nevertheless, the Tories were Disraeli's party far less than the Liberals were Gladstone's. Among the Conservative parliamentary leaders there were many who had established their own political position and could not be disregarded. The wider circle of office holders mirrored the variety of groups and interests to be found in the party. In this chapter the front bench is taken to consist of those who held office in the Government of 1874. Sixteen men sat in the Cabinet at various times between 1874 and 1880. Of these, five were major political figures who carried enough weight to contribute significantly to shaping the course of the Government: Derby, Northcote, Hardy, Cairns and Salisbury. Their personalities, policies, and relations with each other are of the greatest importance.

Derby,[1] who was for a long time Disraeli's reluctant rival for the premiership, owed his position less to his personal ambition or perhaps even ability than to the fact that he was the head of the House of Stanley and the son of his father. In fact there was long-standing distrust between father and son: the fourteenth Earl doubted his son's capacity for leadership and disliked his liberal Church views.[2] Yet the fifteenth Earl enjoyed a personal reputation which many more ambitious men might have envied: to the public mind his image suggested high-minded and disinterested moderation. He was never an instinctive Tory, and always something of a Liberal even before he changed his party. His father had also crossed the floor of the House, having started life as a Whig, and the Whigs disliked him as a

---

[1] There is no standard biography of Derby. See *Speeches of the Fifteenth Earl of Derby*, ed. by T. H. Sanderson and E. S. Roscoe (1894), 2 vols.
[2] R. Blake, *Disraeli*, p. 446.

renegade.[3] The fifteenth Earl had spent most of his political career in close alliance with Disraeli as a progressive Conservative, but his personal popularity, with the middle classes in particular, transcended the confines of the party. In 1866 he might have become the head of a coalition government of Whigs and Tories, a combination which would probably have involved the exclusion of his father and of Disraeli.[4] His high political standing, especially between 1870 and 1874, owed much to this detachment from narrow party allegiance and during those years he was, as we have seen, strongly favoured for the Conservative leadership. The party, then still struggling for a majority, might have reaped the benefit if, at its head, there had been a Liberal aristocrat with a Cross-bench mentality. Derby claimed after he had joined the Liberals that he had never been a high Tory or even a Tory at all: he had never sympathized with Jingoism, and had always seen the uselessness of resisting the march of popular ideas.[5] This was Derby's definition of Conservatism:

A Conservative policy, as it seems to me, tells its own story—to distrust loud professions and large promises; to place no confidence in theories for the regeneration of mankind, however brilliant and ingenious, to believe only in that improvement which is steady and gradual and accomplished step by step; to compare our actual condition, not with the ideal world which thinkers have sketched out, but with the condition of other countries at the present day, and with our country at other times; to hold fast what we have till we are quite sure that we have got hold of something better instead.[6]

We have discussed earlier the important part played by Derby in Lancashire, one of the key marginal areas, and the relative detachment from Disraeli and other Tory leaders which he showed, at least until 1872. It is remarkable how Derby was, despite his own reluctance, persistently mentioned as a possible

---

[3] For the fourteenth Earl, see W. D. Jones, *Lord Derby & Victorian Conservatism* (1956).

[4] M. Cowling, 'Disraeli, Derby and Fusion, October 1865 to July 1866', *Historical Journal*, VIII, 1 (1965), p. 67.

[5] *Speeches of the Fifteenth Earl of Derby*, ii. 95, (Liverpool, 4 Jan. 1882). See also 'Lord Derby's Position', *The Economist*, 25 Oct. 1879, p. 1223. In 1866 there was the hope in some quarters that Stanley would form a Third Party (See A. P. Martin, *Life of Robert Lowe* [1893] ii. 308).

[6] *Speeches of the Fifteenth Earl of Derby*, i. 267 (Edinburgh, 18 Dec. 1875).

Tory Prime Minister even after the fortunes of the Conservative Party, and of Disraeli personally, had taken a turn for the better. During the ministerial crisis of March 1873 there were widespread rumours that a Conservative ministry would be headed by Derby, even though by this time Disraeli had firmly re-established his position.[7] Only Derby, so it was said, could have expressed the lower-middle-class mood of apprehension, which had been the main cause of the revulsion against Gladstone's Government.[8] Even by 1874 rumours of a Derby administration were not dead, and both Lord and Lady Derby seemed to have reckoned with the possibility that he might be asked to fill the first place.[9]

After the formation of Disraeli's Cabinet Derby remained the most obvious successor to the leadership if ill health should at any time force the Prime Minister to retire. In August 1876, before agreeing to the Queen's proposal that he should continue to lead the Government from the Lords, Disraeli made an apparently genuine effort to get Derby to accept the premiership. The Foreign Secretary declined to consider the offer or to serve under anyone else. Ostensibly this was the reason for Disraeli's decision to continue in office with a peerage. Derby had thus deliberately refused the highest office for the second time. He did not feel he possessed the qualifications or the temperament for the first post. His tenure of the Foreign Office after 1874 opened the eyes of many to the flaws in his character: irresolution and lack of initiative.[10]

From 1876 onwards, as the Near Eastern crisis deepened, Derby's political role began to change. His presence at the Foreign Office was, to those who above all else cherished the preservation of peace, a guarantee that sober counsel would prevail. On the other hand his resignation, long threatened before being finally carried out, was, to many, a signal of ultimate danger. When it became clear in 1879 that Lord Derby had thrown in his lot with the Liberals, the event was of considerable importance. None knew then what the future would hold for the political parties, and a man like Derby, with

---

[7] *The Economist*, 15 Mar. 1873, p. 305. *Spectator*, 15 Mar. 1873, p. 328. *Standard*, 14 Mar. 1873.

[8] 'The loss of the Tory Opportunity', *Spectator*, 22 Mar. 1873, p. 365.

[9] Lady G. Cecil, *Life of Salisbury*, ii. 44.

[10] *Journals of Reginald, Viscount Esher*, vol. i, 23 Aug. 1875.

his broad appeal to all moderates, might come to hold the key to the formation of a government. *The Economist* saw in his secession a sign that 'Tory Democracy, the kind of Toryism now in the ascendant' was not to the taste of all men in the party. As it turned out, the fifteenth Earl of Derby's apostasy did not become an event of great significance, and was soon lost in the general Liberal advance and sweep back to power.

Sir Stafford Northcote was for many years one of Disraeli's most faithful lieutenants and closest political friends, and eventually succeeded him as leader of the House of Commons. Northcote's biography was written soon after his death and is inadequate;[11] his reputation for posterity was moreover mainly determined by the part he played in the dual leadership phase between 1880 and 1885. He came to be regarded as weak, pusillanimous and lacking in powers of decision. This judgement was not far from the truth. He was an ineffective leader of the House after 1876, and when events compelled him to play a political role of the first order after 1880 he proved an utter failure. Nevertheless, the large number of letters and memoranda from Northcote's hand that have come down to us show him to have been a politician who, if not of the first rank, was yet a man of great experience, shrewdness and integrity. Reginald Brett, later Lord Esher, wrote this apt characterization of him when he became leader of the house in 1876:

. . . Northcote, the sort of politician peculiar to Great Britain. A country gentleman with a fair education and all domestic virtues, simple and honourable, and continually rising to the occasion as demands are made upon him. There is no genius in him but much capacity for sheer hard work, and some talent in arranging what he has to say. Added to this he has the necessary sense of humour.[12]

Northcote brought indefatigable industry almost amounting to pedantry to the host of administrative and parliamentary problems clamouring for his attention. A strong and sound instinct for political pitfalls and lurking dangers preserved him and those who took his advice from many mistakes. Even on larger issues Northcote's opinion was worth hearing. His mental processes had been formed entirely within the framework of

[11] Andrew Lang, *Life, Letters and Diaries of Sir Stafford Northcote, First Earl of Iddesleigh* (1889), 2 vols.
[12] *Journals of Reginald, Viscount Esher*, i. 37.

parliamentary and constitutional government, and like many men of this kind he was liable to overestimate the risk of radical decision and new departure. This tendency often sapped his ability to act.[13] Politically Northcote was completely a man of the centre: he might just as well have been a moderate Liberal and had as much in common with Whigs as with Tories. In 1866 he would have been happy to join a Whig-Tory coalition.[14] He was not associated with any particular wing of the party and his relations with his colleagues were uniformly good. He was in almost constant communication with Disraeli—there are over four hundred letters preserved, dating from 1866 to 1881.[15] Many are long epistles of the thinking aloud kind, carefully weighing up the pros and cons of problems.

Northcote had a consistent and clearly defined political attitude in two fields, economic and foreign affairs. In economics and finance he was a stronger more convinced adherent of the orthodox Manchester School than many Conservatives at this period. He had, after all, spent many years at the start of his career sitting at the feet of Gladstone, and to the disgust of many Tories the personality of the Liberal leader never quite lost its hold over him. On the other hand, Northcote could never be extremist or doctrinaire and in many instances he was willing to accept some dilution of the pure milk of Political Economy. In the 1870s collectivism was just beginning its advance and the problem of exceptions to or breaches of the rules of *laissez faire* arose with increasing frequency. Northcote was personally responsible for the drafting of the Friendly Societies Bill, part of the Conservative social reform programme of 1874–5. The aim of this bill was to subject the Friendly Societies to just enough control to enable the general public to judge their soundness, without involving the Government directly in their operations.

Legislation on merchant shipping was another problem

---

[13] See Lord George Hamilton, *Parliamentary Reminiscences and Reflections, 1868–1885* (1917), p. 141.

[14] M. Cowling, 'Disraeli, Derby and Fusion', *Historical Journal*, VIII, 1 (1965), pp. 65 ff.

[15] These letters are now in the Iddesleigh Papers, but were formerly in the Hughenden Papers.

which engaged Northcote's attention in 1875. Action was being forced on the Government by the pressure of public opinion, roused by Plimsoll's agitation. On the other hand, the Government could not afford to damage the competitive position of the British Merchant Marine nor offend the powerful shipping interests considerably represented on the Tory benches. Northcote's attitude to the problem, characteristic of his whole outlook on economic matters, was expressed in a letter to Farrer, the Permanent Secretary at the Board of Trade:

The principle on which, as I conceive, we must legislate is that of bringing both classes of force, Government interposition and shipowners' responsibility, fairly into play. I am not disposed to rely exclusively on either. Even if there were no excitement, I should favour a certain amount of Government interposition; and under existing circumstances I have no doubt that it is inevitable, and that the true policy even of the laissez-faire school would now be, to endeavour to guide the Plimsoll movement, not to try to stem it; and at the same time endeavour to enforce the shipowners' responsibility, concurrently with the strengthening of official control. I want to say to the shipowners, in the face of the nation, we mean to do our part, and at the same time to insist on your doing your part, to prevent preventible evils: we recognize your general merits, and won't indorse all that is said against you: we recognise the immense importance of your industry, and desire, not only in justice to you but on behalf of national interests and those of all classes (including sailors themselves) which are connected with you, to get you fair play and secure you from needless restrictions; we desire too to help you to improve the character of your seamen, and to meet the difficulties of carrying on your business with imperfect means of enforcing discipline; but on the other hand we must insist that you shall not evade your responsibilities under the specious plea of freedom of contract, which is (or may be) a good enough plea as between the contracting parties, but is one to be very jealously scrutinised when it affects the lives of other persons.[16]

Northcote's basic approach in foreign affairs was liberal. In November 1875, when the Government was in the throes of purchasing the Suez Canal shares, he wrote to Disraeli:

The end and object which we have in view is to secure for ourselves an uninterrupted passage to the East. We don't want exclusive

[16] Iddesleigh Papers, Add. MS. 50052, 20 Nov. 1875. See also above, p. 19.

privileges, and we don't want territory. Neither, as I take it, do we want to mix ourselves up more than is inevitable with the maintenance of Egypt or of Turkey, or to make ourselves responsible for their proceedings. What would suit us best would be an international arrangement, by which the Canal could be placed under the guardianship of all the powers interested in maintaining the communication, and which would also provide for the execution of the works necessary for its maintenance. . . .[17]

Over the Eastern Question, Northcote sided with the pacific wing of the Cabinet, but his inability to be firm and clear-cut led him into all sorts of obscurities and prevarications. Thus Disraeli was led to describe the views of the Chancellor of the Exchequer, to the Queen, as 'utterly futile' and 'approaching silliness'.[18]

Why did Disraeli choose Northcote to succeed him as Leader of the House in 1876, thus giving him a reversionary claim to the party leadership? As early as January 1876 Sandon and Carnarvon considered Northcote the most suitable candidate for the leadership.[19] The Queen seems also to have regarded him as Disraeli's most likely successor in the Leadership of the House of Commons.[20] As a man of the centre he was clearly well placed and his experience and industry were additional qualifications. Hardy, the other possible candidate, was too closely identified with a particular section of Toryism, the High Church party. Northcote's faithful devotion to Disraeli, his high integrity and, on the other hand, lack of original ideas were probably just what the Prime Minister wanted at this point, when it was necessary for him to retain a tight grip on affairs from the Upper House. According to Sir Henry Drummond Wolff, Disraeli told him, shortly before his death, that when appointing Northcote Leader of the House, he did not anticipate the return of Gladstone to active politics nor the magnitude of the Liberal victory of 1880.[21] Wemyss Reid takes the view that Northcote's decline started from the moment he became Leader of the House. Before that everybody thought well of him; thereafter he

[17] Iddesleigh Papers, Add. MS. 50017, 22 Nov. 1875. See also Andrew Lang, op. cit., ii. 82–7.
[18] Buckle, ii. 1066.
[19] See below, p. 44.
[20] Buckle, ii. 831.
[21] Churchill, *Life of Lord Randolph Churchill* (1906), i. 157.

proved himself unable to deal with obstruction either by conciliation or by the terror of the law; finally he lost his temper.[22]

Nevertheless Northcote succeeded in maintaining his position as a principal member of the Government and as one of those in line for the succession to the party leadership. His appeal as a potential leader was to those who wanted businesslike government and disliked expensive adventures. On the morrow of the Conservative defeat in 1880, *The Economist* mused on what might have happened in case of a narrow Conservative victory: Lord Beaconsfield would soon have retired and there might have been government by Northcote, 'sound business government with no thought of adventure'. Instead, Northcote became leader of the Opposition in the House of Commons. His ambitions were high. Like many others he looked forward to a split in the Liberal ranks which might bring the Conservatives back to office before a full parliamentary term had elapsed. Northcote felt that his own leadership on the Tory side offered the best chance of a Whig secession from Gladstone and he was already beginning to see in Salisbury his most serious rival. On 28 April 1880 he wrote in his diary:

. . . I think it is likely enough that a Conservative Cave may be formed on the Liberal side, with perhaps Goschen as its centre and that if we manage our Opposition discreetly we may often join hands with them, and perhaps ultimately bring some of them to take part in a Conservative Cabinet. That could not, however, be under Lord Beaconsfield nor probably under Salisbury or any other Peer of our party. It might possibly take place under myself . . . F. Stanley spoke anxiously to me, on his own behalf, and also, as he said, for Smith and Sandon, against any step being taken which would seem to imply that Salisbury was to inherit the lead of the party. Lord B. is now much under the Hatfield influence; and Arlington Street [Lord Salisbury's town house] is a most convenient place for our headquarters. If our party councils were always to be held there, it would give the owner a position which might lead to embarrassment if the Chief were to retire.[23]

Northcote soon encountered rough water on his own side. His studied moderation irked many Tories and when that

[22] Sir T. Wemyss Reid, *Politicians of To-day* (1880), 2 vols. 'Sir Stafford Northcote'.
[23] Iddesleigh Papers, Add. MS. 50063A.

famous ginger group, the Fourth Party, began to emerge it was not only at loggerheads with him over tactics, but rightly suspected him of giving high priority to the advancement of a coalition with the Whigs. On 14 May 1880, when the new session of Parliament had only just opened, and the first rumble of the Bradlaugh case was heard, Balfour wrote to Lord Salisbury:

Northcote will find some difficulty in driving his team. The division on Tuesday was as much directed against him, as it was against Bradlaugh. Harry Thynne (when I told him that it was a great pity to divide, seeing that for once our leaders and sound agreement were on the same side) said he would not agree: for it would teach North-cote *not to be always jumping up and agreeing with the other side* without first consulting his friends! Fortunately strict discipline is not much required in opposition; still it would be a pity, if our people below the gangway get into the habit of thinking that Northcote's having voted one way is sufficient reason for their voting the other![24]

Soon the chorus of criticism swelled and Northcote's position could not have been strengthened by Beaconsfield's discreet encouragement of the Fourth Party. Northcote was openly attacked at a party meeting on 20 August 1880 at the Carlton, but at the same meeting he also found his defenders. The attack came, however, from all sections of the party. Balfour, who had spoken at the meeting on behalf of the Fourth Party, explained the situation at length to Salisbury; he ended thus:

. . . Dizzy, with whom I have had some conversation tells me that Northcote complains that the independent members never consult him. In so far as this is true it arises from the fact that nobody has any confidence as to the motives which may prompt his advice. He appears to have a real dislike to doing anything which may annoy the opposition—or which may modify the very excellent opinion which they now entertain about him: and it is the suspicion that this rather than a far-seeing caution is the real reason why he counsels inaction, which prevents him from obtaining the confidence of those who do not happen to share his peculiar views on the subjects. I have now grumbled enough about poor Northcote:—who after all is a man of many virtues . . .[25]

[24] Salisbury Papers. Balfour to Salisbury, 14 May 1880. For Harry Thynne, see below, pp. 57f.
[25] Salisbury Papers, Balfour to Salisbury, 25 Aug. 1880. See also Kenneth Young, *Arthur James Balfour* (1963), p. 68.

In face of all these difficulties Northcote maintained his position solidly; the correspondence between him and the former Prime Minister went on as before, and he continued to consult his leader faithfully on many of the minutiae of House of Commons affairs. When Disraeli died in April 1881, Northcote was still indispensable in the Commons. All his possible rivals for the leadership were Peers: Salisbury, Cairns, Richmond. Attempts were made to invest Salisbury with the sole leadership and Northcote was greatly annoyed by rumours in the press that his claims were to be set aside. He was, however, much reassured by the fact that the Queen seemed to regard him as Disraeli's true successor.[26] Northcote was too important to be passed over and Salisbury was too loyal a colleague to allow this to happen. Thus began the dual leadership.

Gathorne Hardy was, apart from Disraeli himself and Northcote, the most prominent Conservative front bencher in the Commons. He had attained this position through his own ability and without the help of influential aristocratic family connections.[27] Hardy's chief political characteristic was a tough kind of Toryism, which stood in marked contrast to Northcote's liberal Conservatism. Hardy was also a strong High Churchman and in the Conservative Cabinet he was therefore on many issues thrown into the company of Salisbury and Carnarvon. The particular colour of his political beliefs was, however, not quite the same as that of Salisbury's intellectual high Toryism, and he was perhaps less detached from the flow of public opinion at large.

In the early 1870s, when Disraeli's position was weak and Derby was reluctant to come forward, Hardy was seen by some as a potential contender for the party leadership.[28] His published diary is too self-deceptive to give clear evidence whether he nursed such ambitions at that stage. It shows, however, that Hardy was very unsympathetic towards Disraeli in the early stages of his career and remained frequently critical even after

[26] Iddesleigh Papers, Add. MS. 50063A, Northcote's Diary, 5 May 1881.
[27] For Hardy, see *Gathorne Hardy, First Earl of Cranbrook. A Memoir with Extracts from his Diary and Correspondence*, ed. by the Hon. Alfred E. Gathorne Hardy (1910), 2 vols.
[28] 'The Conservative Leadership', *The Economist*, 18 May 1871, p. 608. 'The Boisterous Conservatives', *Spectator*, 12 Mar. 1870, p. 320.

he had entered the Cabinet in 1866.[29] He seems to have taken pride in the fact that Disraeli regarded him in the early 1870s, and after 1874, as his right-hand man in the Commons and by this time collaboration between the two men was cordial. There are many testimonies to Hardy's qualities as a hard-hitting debater: as a parliamentary fighter he had no rival amongst Disraeli's frontbench colleagues.[30]

The offer of the War Office came as a surprise to Hardy in 1874. It was one of the chief spending departments and had assumed particular importance at this time owing to Cardwell's Army Reforms, but it was hardly the ideal stepping stone to the leadership. During the first two sessions of the 1874 Parliament, Cross and Northcote were much more in the limelight than Hardy, who was engrossed in the work of his department. This was one of the arguments put forward by Disraeli when in August 1876 he first began to hint to Hardy that he would prefer Northcote to succeed him. It was also pointed out to Hardy that it would be difficult to combine his heavy administrative duties at the War Office with the party leadership. Such were the excuses offered to reconcile Hardy to Northcote's preferment. Between these two men there had been rivalry dating back to the period before they both entered the Cabinet on the same day, though the rivalry was usually friendly enough.[31] Hardy's sense of disappointment at this check to his career is evident from his diary, but he accepted the decision loyally.

In the protracted crisis on the Eastern Question which now followed, Hardy was in fact of more use to Beaconsfield than Northcote. He was the firmest and most consistent advocate of a strong policy in a Cabinet in which the supporters of conciliation and compromise were well represented. In this way he helped the Premier to steer his precariously balanced course. When allowing his claims to the leadership to be set aside in 1876, Hardy had made it a condition that he should

---

[29] For example, entry in his Diary, 7 Mar. 1867: 'I had more talk with Disraeli, whose fault is that he is always looking for what will suit others, rather than what is sound in itself.' (*Gathorne Hardy, A Memoir*, i. 203)

[30] Lord George Hamilton, *Parliamentary Reminiscences and Reflections 1868–1885*, p. 141. According to Hamilton, Hardy went to the House of Lords in 1878 because Northcote had thrown him over in debate.

[31] *Gathorne Hardy*, i. 189.

have a peerage when he wanted it. He availed himself of the opportunity of Derby's resignation in March 1878 to enter the Upper House, and was transferred to the India Office. In the following year there fell to him the immediate responsibility of dealing with the situation in Afghanistan, which, in some people's opinion, was the main cause of the Conservative defeat in 1880. Once he had left the Commons, Hardy, or Cranbrook as he now became, was a lesser figure, for as a new-comer to the Lords he could not rival the established Tory leaders in that chamber.

Lord Cairns was throughout the 1870s an important figure in the inner circle of Conservative leaders. Of all Disraeli's closest associates he was most genuinely a self-made man, having come up the traditional ladder of the law. Another characteristic which distinguished him from his colleagues was his strong and lifelong adherence to low-church, ultra-Protestant views. This religious outlook coloured many of his activities: he was connected with the Church Missionary Society, the Bible Society, and Exeter Hall, and was a Moody and Sankey supporter. This must have been a bar to understanding and sympathy with many of his political friends in the Conservative party. His intellectual grasp, however, was sufficiently powerful to enable him to maintain a high level of political realism. Thus the defence of the Irish Established Church was of particular concern to Cairns as an Ulsterman. Yet when he saw that disestablishment had become inevitable he set himself to secure the best obtainable terms by compromise.[32] He appears to have disliked the 1867 Reform Bill, but once it had passed the Commons emerged as a strong defender of it in the Lords. In 1884, in similar circumstances, he worked on the whole for compromise, although fundamentally opposed to and afraid of a further extension of the franchise.[33] In spite of his legal training and intellect, and his fierce Evangelicalism, Cairns cannot therefore be accused of want of flexibility and narrowness of political outlook, a view of him held by some of his colleagues. Nevertheless it seems unlikely that he was ever a strong candidate for the party leadership, although on some occasions there

[32] See J. B. Atlay, *The Victorian Chancellors* (1908), vol. ii, Chap. XIV.
[33] There is much unpublished material on Cairns' attitude in this crisis in the Salisbury Papers.

was talk of it.[34] His short tenure of the leadership in the House of Lords has been referred to earlier: the chief obstacle to his resuming this more limited position on later occasions was that he lacked the great aristocratic background to sustain it.

Even if Cairns was not a strong contender for the leadership, he was immensely useful to the party and the Government of which he was a member and to Disraeli personally. None of his colleagues, except Salisbury, could rival him in sheer intellectual power. He made up, by grasp of detail and capacity for work, for what he lacked in imagination and intuitive understanding. He collaborated closely with Disraeli in building up the party organization between 1870 and 1874 and was the first man to be consulted by the leader when the news of a dissolution of Parliament burst unexpectedly in January 1874.[35] Cairns is said to have kept minutes and records of Cabinet meetings for his colleagues.[36] Disraeli and others frequently praised his great capacity and judgement and acknowledged the help they had received from him. One incident remains puzzling: Hardy records in his Diary that at the Burghley House meeting in January 1872 Cairns took the lead in raising the question of Disraeli's continuance in the leadership. It is certainly true that Cairns appears to have been anxious at this time about Disraeli's political apathy.[37] Apart from this the two men seem to have collaborated closely then and at other times. Cairns was, like Disraeli himself, a professional man in politics and detached from all vested interests.

Lord Salisbury proved himself in time the most successful and powerful personality among the inner circle of Tory leaders. The great question mark which hung over his political career after his resignation from the Cabinet in 1867 was when and how

---

[34] 'The Elections', *The Economist*, 3 Apr. 1880, p. 378, commented that, if the Conservatives had won, Lord Beaconsfield would have retired and there might have been a Cairns Government, in which case experience of the past two years, open triumphs, secret surrenders, would have been repeated. Cairns was often in bad health and there was a general feeling that he would be unable to bear the physical burden of leadership. See Atlay, op. cit.

[35] H. E. Gorst, *The Fourth Party* (1906) where it is repeatedly emphasized that Cairns was the only Conservative front bencher, apart from Disraeli, who took an interest in party organization before 1874.

[36] Viscount Cross, *A Political History, Privately Printed for my Children* (1903), p. 23.

[37] Richmond Papers, Cairns to Richmond, 23 Jan. 1872; see above, p. 11.

his reconciliation with Disraeli could be brought about. To some extent this was a problem of policy. Salisbury, it is true, was far too intelligent to waste his energies in hankering after the past and accepted the great change of 1867 once it had become a fact. He remained, nevertheless, a stern advocate of resistance to the advance of democracy and to attacks on property and traditional privilege. That certain changes were inevitable and that resistance to them was not only fruitless but liable to produce explosive situations was an argument that made little appeal to Salisbury. The tactical manoeuvres, the outflankings and about-turns dear to Disraeli seemed to Salisbury only to hasten disastrously the onward march of Radicalism. This attitude emerged again and again from Salisbury's writings and speeches, at least up to 1872.[38] Thereafter events produced a *rapprochement* between the attitudes of Salisbury and Disraeli. In an article in the *Quarterly Review* of October 1872 Salisbury used practically the same arguments against another Conservative minority government which led Disraeli to refuse office the following March[39] When a Tory majority was returned in 1874, circumstances had removed virtually all political obstacles to Salisbury's assumption of office in the new Government. The only concrete issue which had to be resolved between him and Disraeli was how far the Government would refrain from bringing in or supporting legislation against Ritualism.[40]

The disappearance of political differences between Salisbury and the party leader still left a residue of dislike and distrust on the part of the former. Many biographies and autobiographies of the period give evidence of Salisbury's great personal bitterness against Disraeli for what he considered treachery and surrender in 1867. By 1869 their wives were still not on speaking terms.[41] In 1874 Salisbury still found it very hard to bring himself to make personal contact with Disraeli. Only the fact that there was no political issue which could have served as a valid

---

[38] For example on the Army Regulation Bill, *Hansard*, vol. CCVII, col. 1849, 17 July 1871, and on the Ballot Bill, *Hansard*, vol. CCXI, col. 1491, 10 June 1871.
[39] 'The Position of the Parties', *Quarterly Review*, October 1872. See also reference to this article in 'Lord Salisbury on Tory Prospects', *Spectator*, 19 Oct. 1872, p. 1320.
[40] See Lady G. Cecil, *Life of Salisbury*, ii. 43–51; Buckle, ii. 633.
[41] *Journals of Lady Knightley*, p. 162, 13 Mar. 1869.

excuse for declining to enter the Government, and the complete isolation which would have ensued made Salisbury conquer his great inner reluctance to resume relations. These personal difficulties disappeared quickly and completely once Salisbury had entered the Cabinet. After a few months not even the considerable strains and stresses of the Public Worship Regulation Bill and the Endowed Schools Bill could bring about a break. Thereafter, and particularly during the Near Eastern Crisis, Disraeli and Salisbury became close and harmonious collaborators.

The evolution of Salisbury's attitude is mirrored in the transformation of Lord Carnarvon's feelings towards Disraeli. Lord Carnarvon was Salisbury's closest political associate, another strong High Churchman who had also resigned in 1867. At that time Carnarvon's antipathy to Disraeli was as profound as that of Salisbury; in writing to the Duke of Richmond, who was on the point of entering the Cabinet, he shows strikingly how much Disraeli was held personally responsible for what was conceived to be a catastrophe and how much he was distrusted:

Perhaps I ought not to have spoken as freely as I did this evening of one of your present colleagues. I did not do so with the wish to prejudice you against him but rather because he was uppermost in my thoughts and because I conscientiously believe him to be the author of the present difficulty. What I said therefore to you was said to you alone—not that I should shrink if there was any necessity from saying what I think: but that I do not desire to seem to make mischief or even to give way to the bitterness which I can hardly help feeling when I see the ruin to which he has brought a great party. But having said so much I must say one word more—you enter the Cabinet comparatively unfettered by what has up to this time passed: and I would urge strongly on you that you trust in this most delicate question of reform to no-one's facts, figures or judgment but your own. I am convinced that we are in a very critical position. Household suffrage will produce a state of things in many boroughs the results of which I defy anyone to predict. In Leeds for example the present number of electors are about 8,500. With household suffrage they will become about 35,000. Is there anyone who dares to say what will be the character and tendency of that constituency? It may be good or bad: but it is a revolution. The Conservative party is in imminent danger of going to pieces now if indeed it does not disappear in the deluge that the Government are bringing on.

The compensation and securities which were proposed when I knew anything of what was passing in the Cabinet were I believe illusory. The Whigs, who have not scrupled on former occasions to go far, are now dismayed. The very meetings in London, with Potter & Co. at their head, are prepared to accept your scheme—Bright is afraid that you are going too fast—the step that you take will be irrevocable—these are all considerations which at least show that the situation is an unparalleled one and full of anxiety. There are I suspect many to whom it will be extremely painful to oppose the Government but who will do so rather than assist in what they believe to be a revolution and I think that they will be right. But even if they throw you out the mischief will be done.[42]

Time assuaged Carnarvon's political differences with Disraeli and his personal feelings seem to have softened more quickly than Salisbury's:

I had a short cruise with Carnarvon . . . and found him very friendly in tone. Very much alarmed at the possibility of a great attack on the land, suspicious of Gladstone and of an attempt to set tenant against landlord etc. Speaking of the Reform bill he said he must admit on looking back that he had been overmuch frightened about it, and that it had worked out better than he expected. He said nothing about yourself, but told me he had felt Lord Derby's conduct to him at the time of the rupture very keenly, though they had made it up personally before Lord Derby's death. He praised your Manchester speech warmly, and said he could not recall an expression with which he did not agree. Lowe seems quite to have lost the influence he at one time had over him.[43]

The Duke of Richmond was the only man, apart from the five major Tory leaders discussed here, who in the 1870s and early 1880s had a fleeting chance of obtaining the over-all leadership of the party. The story of his almost accidental elevation to the leadership in the House of Lords has been told. In spite of his eminent position Richmond never proved much of a political personality in his own right. He relied greatly on Lord Cairns for advice on all major and minor difficulties, and

---

[42] Richmond Papers, Carnarvon to Richmond, 11 Mar. 1867.
[43] Iddesleigh Papers, Add. MS. 50016, Northcote to Disraeli, 23 Sept. 1872. Later Lady Chesterfield helped to bring Carnarvon, her son-in-law, and Disraeli closer. See also Sir Arthur Hardinge, *Life of the Fourth Earl of Carnarvon* (1925), ii. 54 and 58–63. Disraeli, however, did not always have a high opinion of Carnarvon. See Buckle, ii. 815.

the Lord Chancellor was Richmond's constant comforter and counsellor.[44] There was a possibility, mainly technical, of Richmond becoming Prime Minister in 1874. Two years later, when Disraeli's health seemed to be failing, the possibility was more real, as a memorandum by Lord Sandon shows:

Carnarvon dined with me alone this evening. When we discussed the question of the Duke of Richmond becoming Prime Minister in the event of Disraeli resigning (from ill health), we both agreed, notwithstanding personal regard for the person in question, that such an appointment would be fatal to the Conservative Party, as he has no knowledge of the feeling of the country, or anything approaching to intellectual grasp—but we both agreed the danger of his having the position was a real one, as H.M. may be favourable and Lord Derby in the Lords is likely to be afraid of the responsibility of the leadership, the Lord Chancellor is a sworn friend of the Duke of Richmond, being of the same narrow political intellect or rather want of it in *political* matters (not legal or oratorical in which the latter is no mean master)—and it may be difficult in the House of Commons to decide between the pretensions of Cross and Northcote. The latter we both agree was clearly pointed out for the lead.[45]

Sandon had at this time much reason to dislike Richmond. As Vice-President of the Committee of Council on Education he was Richmond's subordinate and the preparation of the Education Bill of 1876 was causing friction between the two men.[46] Sandon was keen on educational progress, while Richmond had little knowledge of the subject and less enthusiasm for it. When Lord George Hamilton succeeded Sandon in 1878, he complained to Beaconsfield about having to serve under someone so inferior in ability and standing to his late chief Salisbury. The Premier replied: 'The Lord President, though punctilious, is a high-minded and upright gentleman, and you must get on with him as best you can.'[47] The formal importance of Richmond's position declined after Beaconsfield entered the Upper House in 1876. In 1881 he took a prominent part in arranging for the election of Salisbury as leader of the Conser-

[44] Disraeli was well aware that Richmond was much under the influence of Cairns, see Hardinge, op. cit., ii. 52.

[45] Harrowby Papers, LV/181, 18 Jan. 1876.

[46] There are frequent references to this friction in the Harrowby and Richmond Papers.

[47] Lord George Hamilton, *Parliamentary Reminiscences and Reflections 1868–1885*, p. 151.

vative Peers and thus the possibility of his assuming the lead finally disappeared.[48] Three new men entered the 1874 Government, R. A. Cross, Lord Sandon, and W. H. Smith, of whom the first achieved Cabinet rank immediately and the other two before the life of that Parliament had run its course. The three had often made common cause while the party was in opposition. They figure in a list of 'troublesome men in the party' sent by Taylor, the Chief Whip, to Disraeli. The list also included Raikes, F. S. Powell, and Birley of Manchester, all of them on the left of the party.[49] When Disraeli was about to form his Government in 1874, Noel, another of the Whips, recommended Cross, Sandon, and Smith for inclusion in the administration as useful new blood.[50] Cross also had the recommendation of Derby and his appointment was a tribute to Lancashire, the stronghold of urban Conservatism.[51] Thus he achieved the rare distinction of reaching an important Cabinet post without previous experience of office. He cannot, however, be regarded as a representative of Tory Democracy; he belonged to an old Lancashire family and in the preparations for the 1872 Manchester demonstration he had been by no means an enthusiastic advocate of the Disraeli visit.[52] The connection with Lancashire could cause uncomplimentary comment, 'A perky and self-satisfied representative of that strange compound of Orange bigotry and political stupidity of which Lancashire Toryism is composed.'[53] Disraeli himself wrote of Cross at a moment of irritation, after only two months in office; 'This comes of giving high office to a middle class man.'[54] In a letter to Lord Sandon, written when the visit

[48] See Richmond Papers, Bundle 1881.
[49] Hughenden Papers, B/XX/T, Taylor to Disraeli, undated, probably 1873. For Hugh Birley, a highly respected borough member, see below, p. 77. Raikes played a prominent role in the foundation of the National Union of Conservative and Constitutional Associations; see below, Chapter V.
[50] Hughenden Papers, B/XII/A, Noel to Disraeli, 12 Feb. 1874.
[51] Buckle, ii. 629. Cross was often regarded as a spokesman for Derby, particularly during the Near Eastern Crisis. See F. J. Dwyer, 'R. A. Cross and the Eastern Crisis of 1875–8', *Slavonic & East European Review*, vol. 39 (1961), pp. 440–58.
[52] See above, p. 10.
[53] Sir T. Wemyss Reid, *Politicians of To-day*, 'Mr. Cross'.
[54] *Letters of Disraeli to Lady Bradford and Lady Chesterfield*, i. 72, 18 Apr. 1874 to Lady Bradford.

to Lancashire was under discussion in August 1871, Cross gives
a characteristic picture of his political outlook—middle of the
road, aware of political realities, cautious, concerned with
concrete matters:

I have not the very slightest doubt in my own mind that the
country would most heartily welcome the Conservative Party if
they could see that they did not merely seek office but had some
thoroughly sound views of their own which they really were determined for the sake of the Country to carry out. The country is I
believe thoroughly disgusted with party fights because they have
begun to look upon party government here as the same thing as
party government in Australia, as wholly consisting in the possession of office. This Government has certainly laid itself open to
severe criticism but it is of little use holding meetings in Lancashire
for mere criticism however severe and however just unless you will
go further and put forward views of your own by which you are
prepared to stand or fall. But this is exactly just the *one thing of all
others* which I feel so strongly we ought to do—and it can be done as
it seems to me in one of two ways. The first and best is undoubtedly
that the members of the late Government should after serious counsel among themselves and with their friends come down with some
statesmanlike well defined policy not of dram drinking but of sober
earnest work which has been left alone and laid aside only too long.
I will take your own words willingly 'Social, administrative and
economical reform.' I would add colonial policy so as to unite our
empire.[55]

As Home Secretary, Cross became the chief executant of
Conservative social reform; he was not an originator of new
lines of policy, but an accomplished and business-like super-
visor of affairs which circumstances and the activities of others
had brought to the fore. Once in office there was never any
doubt about his party orthodoxy.

Lord Sandon entered the Government in 1874 as Vice-
President of the Committee of Council on Education, an important position at a time when educational questions were so often
in the forefront of political controversy. Sandon's father, the
second Earl of Harrowby, had at one stage been a Peelite and
was a member of Palmerston's government from 1855 to 1857.
In his later life the second Earl was active in ecclesiastical
matters; he was a Liberal Churchman. On the threshold of his

[55] Harrowby Papers, LII/246, 28 Aug. 1871.

own political career Sandon had an offer of a Secretaryship to Henry Labouchere, Colonial Secretary in the same Palmerston government of which his father was a member; it was a step which might determine the whole future of his political life, and he turned for advice to Carnarvon, an old friend from his undergraduate days at Christ Church. Carnarvon replied:

If you feel that you are a thorough Tory in principles—I use the word Tory in its old and better sense—and that your mission will be rather to repress innovation than to liberalise, then I think your acceptance of office though now advancing will ultimately retard you—if you do not feel so strongly on these points I think you will gain much in training.[56]

Sandon accepted the offer and entered Parliament unopposed as a Liberal Conservative, representing Lichfield until 1859. In 1861 he married into the high Tory aristocracy, and his father-in-law, the Marquis of Exeter, offered him, in 1866, his pocket borough of Stamford in succession to Sir Stafford Northcote.[57] He eventually re-entered Parliament for Liverpool in 1868, a borough with which his family had long-standing connections, and his link with the political life of the city became close.[58]

In background and situation Sandon was thus well qualified to straddle the gap between the high Tories and the new Conservatism of the boroughs. Together with Smith, and to a lesser extent Cross, Sandon had interested himself in educational questions while the Conservatives were in opposition and this may have led to his appointment in 1874. Sandon and Smith sat on the London School Board. On education many Tories, in particular the squirearchy, were frankly retrograde in outlook: they did not believe in education for the lower orders and especially disliked school boards.[59] In promoting educational progress Sandon had to fight against this dead weight within his own party. In ensuring progress he had also to protect and advance the cause of denominational teaching, for which the

[56] Harrowby Papers, XXXIX/25, 30 Nov. 1855.
[57] Ibid., LII/370.   [58] See below, Chapter VIII.
[59] See above, p. 18. The Harrowby Papers contain much material on Sandon's educational policy, and on the preparations for the Education Act of 1876, particularly in volume LV. See also F. Adams, *History of the Elementary School Contest* (1880), written from the Radical point of view.

Conservative Party held a special brief. The Education Act of 1876, which owed its passage mainly to his energy, was a notable achievement and put its author in line for promotion. In February 1877 the Prime Minister toyed with the idea of making Sandon Lord Privy Seal. Lord John Manners, who was also a candidate for the post, mentioned, as a particular advantage of Sandon's promotion, that it would satisfy feeling in the boroughs.[60] When Ward Hunt died in July 1877 Sandon was considered both for the Admiralty and as the Chief Secretary for Ireland;[61] and in April 1878 he at last achieved Cabinet rank when he succeeded Adderley at the Board of Trade, which only now attained the status of a first class department.

W. H. Smith was a man destined to rise high in the party. It was a sign of the times that he was a Conservative at all. A son of middle-class tradespeople, a Wesleyan by origin, though later received into the Church of England, he had built up a great business and immense wealth. This was the typical career of a great many who sat on the Liberal benches. Smith had several chances to stand as the Liberal candidate. His biographer suggests that one of the reasons that turned him away from the Liberal side was that, perhaps owing to Whig prejudice against a tradesman, he failed to secure election to the Reform Club.[62] In 1865 he stood as Liberal-Conservative candidate for Westminster, in a three-cornered contest against John Stuart Mill, standing as a Radical, and Captain Grosvenor, Whig. An exchange of letters with Colonel Taylor, the Conservative Whip, made it clear that he did not consider himself a member of the Conservative party, but was looking to an ultimate fusion of the followers of Palmerston and Derby into one great Liberal-Conservative party. Although Westminster was a forlorn hope for the Conservatives, W. H. Smith came close to winning, and received a letter of sympathy from Disraeli. His acquaintance with the Conservative party organization, particularly in London, dates from this contest and he never thereafter ceased to take a close interest in party organization. His

---

[60] Charles Whibley, *Lord John Manners and his Friends* (1925), ii. 175.
[61] R. Blake, op. cit., p. 630.
[62] Sir H. E. Maxwell, *Life and Times of W. H. Smith* (1893), i. 116. For a modern account, see Viscount Chilston, *W. H. Smith* (1965).

victory at Westminster in 1868 was, apart from those in Lancashire, one of the few striking Conservative successes of that election.

During the next few years he, Sandon and Cross formed a ginger group on the left of the Conservative Party. On the Irish Church Bill these three members tried to infuse spirit into a disheartened opposition. In the Education Bill debates they pressed for a single London School Board and helped the Government to obtain it; they were less insistent than the rest of the Conservative party on the rights of the Church of England. On the Ballot Bill Smith was again prominent in persuading his party to allow the Bill to pass the Commons without damaging amendments. He was disgusted with Disraeli's Bath Election Letter on which his comment was; 'Disraeli has ruined himself and rendered reconstruction of parties—new choice of leaders—almost inevitable.' When Disraeli included Smith in the 1874 Government he was therefore placing a possible 'caver' and giving recognition to the new Conservatism in the Metropolis. This was well worth the murmurs of 'the bookstall man' which, according to Smith's biographer, the appointment occasioned amongst the squirearchy. Smith filled a junior but important post in the Treasury, and as was to be expected found it easy to co-operate with a man of Northcote's liberal views. Smith quickly became a pillar of respectability, whose views were completely orthodox and who was widely trusted. The way was open for him to become a member of the Cabinet in 1877, and Beaconsfield commended him to the Queen in these words: '... of a character similar to Mr. Cross—in mind, manner, energy, but more weighty and with much repose.'[63] He was soon to be one of the leading lights of the party.

Of Disraeli's six remaining Cabinet colleagues in the Government of 1874 two were veterans, Lord John Manners and Lord Malmesbury, and a third, Ward Hunt, had received his

[63] Chilston, op. cit., p. 94. On 14 June 1879 the *Spectator* wrote, '... if the country likes a little political sleep—and at times clearly it does like a little political sleep, for we have always agreed with Mr. W. H. Smith that the Conservative working man is by no means a fiction of Conservative brains, but as genuine a fact as the Conservative shopkeeper or the Conservative landowner—why should it not take its rest under a great Administration such as Mr. Smith would give us . . .' (quoted by Maxwell, op. cit., ii. 6).

promotion to Cabinet rank in 1868.[64] Hicks Beach was a young and relatively new man, having first entered official life as an Under Secretary at the Home Office in 1868. In some ways he was a typical representative of the Tory squirearchy, but his high intelligence and political competence soon put him on the ladder of promotion. In the 1880s he was to be the Conservative front bencher most sympathetic to Lord Randolph Churchill and his friends.[65] The Duke of Northumberland, who entered the Cabinet when Derby resigned in 1878, seems to have owed his position to Beaconsfield's desire to make up for the loss of a Stanley by the adhesion of a Percy, and similar considerations must have contributed to the inclusion of the Hon. F. A. Stanley, later sixteenth Earl of Derby, as Secretary of State for War.

The junior posts in Disraeli's Government were shrewdly distributed to satisfy various sections and groups in the party, to offer opportunity to rising talent, to place possible rebels and 'cavers' and to meet the claims of different parts of the country. As in the major appointments, the claims of the great Tory families formed an important consideration. The Stanleys, Hamiltons, Lennoxes, Herberts, Cecils and many others were all represented.[66] On the other hand, as has been noted, none of the representatives of the great industrial boroughs, except Sandon, received an appointment, though it is fair to point out that informed political comment did not mention any of them for possible promotion.[67]

It was most important to give the fullest possible representation to the agricultural interest, to whose needs and desires the county members, who still formed the bulk of the Parlia-

---

[64] 'Mr. Ward Hunt's Conservatism', *Spectator*, 8 Nov. 1873, p. 1396. In this article Ward Hunt's views are praised as an excellent example of modern Conservatism, as opposed to Toryism; he is said to be cautious, distrustful of innovations, yet not believing too much in paternal government.

[65] See Lady V. A. Hicks Beach, *Life of Sir Michael Hicks Beach* (1932), vol. i. chap. IX.

[66] Buckle, ii. 635. *The Times*, commenting on Lord Pembroke's appointment as Under Secretary at the War Office, wrote on 3 Mar. 1874, 'Mr. Disraeli has always shown himself singularly conscious of the charm the early command of a great inheritance backed by a long descent conveys.'

[67] See *The Times*, leading article on prospects for junior Government appointments, 24 Feb. 1874.

mentary Conservative Party, were very sensitive. Within the agricultural interest it was necessary to give confidence both to landlords and tenant farmers, both bulwarks of Conservative strength in the counties. Sir Massey Lopes, a county member from Devonshire, who had made rating his special subject, became Civil Lord of the Admiralty, an appointment pleasing to landlords and farmers. In accepting, Lopes expressed the hope that the interests of the ratepayer would receive consideration from the Government.[68] Sir Henry Selwin-Ibbetson, a well-known parliamentary figure, who took a special interest in the problem of rural intemperance, became an Under Secretary at the Home Office and in the reshuffle of March 1878 took Smith's place at the Treasury. The appointment of Clare Sewell Read, member for South Norfolk, as Parliamentary Secretary to the local Government Board under Sclater-Booth was even more clearly aimed at the farmers, rather than the owners of land. In his letter of acceptance Read called himself 'a through and through countryman' and mentioned that he held more advanced views on ground game and tenant compensation than some of the Government.[69] Issues of this kind were of passionate concern to tenant farmers and tended to bring them into opposition to the land owners. Read's views soon got him into trouble: in May 1875 he declared at a meeting of the Central Chamber of Agriculture that he was in favour of the Agricultural Holdings Bill, then before Parliament, being made compulsory, though he feared that the House of Lords would not pass a compulsory bill. This bill was intended to secure to the tenant the benefit of unexhausted improvements, but it was on a permissive basis only. Read's speech brought complaints from the Duke of Richmond to the Prime Minister and requests that he be restrained. Breaking point came in November 1875, when Read resigned in protest against regulations on the import of diseased cattle not being made uniform in England and Ireland. The farmers of England made Read a presentation in recognition of his stand. His resignation was much regretted by the Whips and other members interested in the farming vote. Read's job was offered to John Gorst, and

[68] Hughenden Papers, B/XII/A, Lopes to Disraeli, Feb. 1874.
[69] Ibid., B/XII/A, Read to Disraeli, 24 Feb. 1874. See also T. E. Kebbel, *Lord Beaconsfield and Other Tory Memories* (1907), p. 118.

after his refusal[70] was accepted by Thomas Salt, the member for Stafford, who had banking and commercial connections.

The appointment of Rowland Winn as an assistant Whip was recommended to Disraeli by Taylor on the ground that it would please Henry Chaplin, who could be regarded as the most widely respected and influential representative of the Tory squirearchy.[71] Taylor also suggested that Winn's appointment would be pleasing to Lincolnshire and Yorkshire. Lancashire, which had so greatly contributed to the Conservative victory, not only had Derby and Cross in the Cabinet, but also Algernon Egerton as Secretary to the Admiralty. The appointment of Smith was, as we have seen, a tribute to the Conservative revival in the Metropolis. The High Church party received satisfaction through the offer of the post of Lord Chamberlain to Lord Bath, the appointment of his brother, Lord Henry Thynne, as Whip and Treasurer to the Household, and Lord Beauchamp as Lord Steward,[72] and in 1878 through the appointment of J. G. Talbot as Parliamentary Secretary to the Board of Trade.

If family interest was still the most important single principle in Disraeli's political appointments, he must nevertheless be given credit for having cast his net wide in the formation of the 1874 administration. The Tories were never as exclusive as the Whigs, so that men like Cairns, Northcote and Hardy could be the political equals of great magnates like Richmond, Salisbury, Lord John Manners and others. New blood was introduced; obvious failures, like Sir John Pakington and Sir Charles Adderley, were sooner or later removed;[73] young men like Edward Stanhope, who became Parliamentary Secretary to the Board of Trade in 1875 to support the incompetent Adderley, were given their chance. The Conservative front bench, in its great men as well as in its lesser occupants, was thus representative of nearly the whole gamut of Conservatism as it was in the 1870s. This was one of the factors which kept the party so solidly together for six years, prevented any important movement of dissidence and maintained the Conservative majority intact until the end of the 1874 Parliament.

---

[70] Hughenden Papers, B/XXI/Gorst, to Disraeli, 20 Nov. 1875.
[71] Ibid., B/XII/A, Taylor to Disraeli, no date.
[72] Buckle, ii. 633.
[73] For Adderley's point of view, see W. S. Childe-Pemberton, *Life of Lord Norton* (1909), Chapters XXXVII and XL.

III

WHIPS AND BACKBENCHERS

I T is hardly surprising that amongst the leaders of the
Conservative Party in the 1870s there existed a variety of
factions and shades of opinion. If we look now at the more
outstanding figures and groups amongst the backbenchers an
even greater diversity meets the eye. Nevertheless, the party's
performance in Parliament, especially when in office, reveals
few breaches of unity. The party of the Right, pledged to
consolidation and conservation, always finds it easier to preserve harmony in its ranks than the party of the Left which has
to agree on a positive course of action. In the Conservative
party, after the Second Reform Bill, united action in Parliament
was much helped by the social homogeneity of members which
transcended their differences of opinion and attitude. In the
main, Tory M.P.s still came from one closely inter-connected
social class, the landed gentry, and even those from outside
this narrow circle tended to conform to its code of behaviour.
Divisions in the Tory party were not the stuff from which
dramatic party splits are made: they were discernible only to
the experienced political observer.

The personalities of the Whips, the way in which they were
appointed and discharged their functions, afford much insight
into the nature of the Conservative party at this period. Virtually all those connected with the Whips' office were county
members and had close ties with the landed aristocracy. This
social background was evidently considered necessary for the
task of persuading and managing men of a similar stamp. Four
men held the office of Conservative Chief Whip from 1866 to
1885, the devolution from one to the other being gradual:
Colonel T. E. Taylor, the Hon. Gerard Noel, Sir William Hart
Dyke and Rowland Winn, all of them county members with
aristocratic connections. Colonel Taylor had sat in the House
as member for County Dublin continuously since 1841. He first
began to act as a Whip in 1855 under Sir William Jolliffe (later

Lord Hylton) and became Patronage Secretary in 1866. Taylor was, therefore, Chief Whip throughout the difficult period of Conservative minority government. In his communications with the party leaders, particularly with Disraeli, there was nothing of the master-servant relationship; he enjoyed an independent political position and was on terms of close acquaintance with many important figures. His influence on policy was slight, but his advice on appointments carried some weight with Disraeli, who also gave him credit for his part in the passage of the Reform Bill of 1867.[1] Serious friction developed in the summer of 1868 between Taylor and Ward Hunt, the Chancellor of the Exchequer, about the management of the forthcoming elections.[2] This did not prevent Disraeli from appointing Taylor Chancellor of the Duchy of Lancaster a few weeks before the 1868 Government went out of office. The Chief Whip was thus rewarded for his services, but this preferment did not preclude his return to the Whips' duties after the General Election.

Gerard Noel, second son of the first Earl of Gainsborough, succeeded Taylor for the last weeks of Disraeli's administration; he had been a Lord of the Treasury since 1866 and Taylor's chief assistant. Noel was not strikingly successful as a Whip and there are some indications that he could not maintain harmony amongst his assistants in the Whips' office.[3] On the other hand, with the party out of office after 1868, the nature of his task was very different from that which Taylor had discharged so successfully earlier on. Noel was more sympathetic than Taylor to members who stood apart from the orthodox representatives of the landed interest: he recommended that Sandon be asked to move the rejection of the Third Reading of the Irish Church Bill in 1869 and he suggested the inclusion of Smith, Cross, Sandon and Sewell Read in the 1874 Government.[4] It was on his recommendation that John Gorst succeeded Spofforth as

---

[1] See article on Taylor in the *Dictionary of National Biography*. For Taylor's influence on Disraeli during the Reform Bill debates, see also William White, *The Inner Life of the House of Commons*, ii. 71–72.

[2] Hughenden Papers, B/XX/Hu.

[3] Ibid., B/XXI/Whitmore. Complaints by Henry Whitmore, an assistant Whip, against Noel, 1868–9.

[4] Ibid., B/XXI/Noel, to Disraeli, 11 May 1868; B/XII/A, Noel to Disraeli, 12 Feb. 1874.

party agent in 1870; a new chapter in party organization was thereby initiated.[5] Noel continued to be Chief Whip until 1873, when ill health forced him to retire temporarily. In the meantime William Hart Dyke, who had first appeared as a Whip in 1868, took a larger share of the work and was helped by Taylor, who had never ceased to interest himself in Whipping and party management. Rowland Winn was another Assistant Whip who now came increasingly into the picture. In December 1873 it was seen that Noel was still not well enough to return to duty for the 1874 session; it was therefore arranged that Taylor should once more take charge, in collaboration with Dyke. Winn continued as the third member of the Whips' department, although Dyke was anxious not to give him a claim to a permanent appointment.[6]

The Conservative victory at the General Election of 1874 threw all these plans into confusion. Taylor now reverted to his post as Chancellor of the Duchy of Lancaster. He had some influence on the making of the minor appointments in the 1874 Government, particularly on those in the Whips' office and in the Household.[7] He continued to take an interest in questions of party discipline although no longer officially associated with the Whips' office.[8] On the resignation of the Government in 1880, Taylor expected a further reward for his long services, presumably a peerage. He wrote bitterly to Beaconsfield when he received no recognition.[9] It is perhaps not too much to assume that Taylor was never amongst Disraeli's most enthusiastic followers. Most of his service as Chief Whip was under the fourteenth Earl of Derby and in the early seventies he would have preferred the fifteenth Earl as leader.[10] He was a Tory of the old school.

Noel was unable to resume the duties of Chief Whip when the Conservatives came to power in 1874. As he was in need of an official salary, he asked Disraeli for an appointment as a Lord Commissioner of the Treasury, with a lighter part in the Whips' duties.[11] The Prime Minister was unable to meet his

[5] See below, Chapter V.
[6] Hughenden Papers. B/XXI/Dyke, to Disraeli, 24 Dec. 1873.
[7] Ibid., B/XII/A.   [8] Ibid., B/XX/T.
[9] Ibid., B/XX/T., Taylor to Beaconsfield, 14 Apr. 1880.
[10] Ibid., B/XX/T, Taylor to Disraeli, 14 Mar. 1873.
[11] Ibid., B/XII/A, Noel to Disraeli, 18 Feb. 1874; also B/XXI/Noel.

wishes immediately, but in 1876 he was rewarded for his services to the party by being appointed First Commissioner of Works in succession to Lord Henry Lennox. It was therefore left to Sir William Hart Dyke to carry out the functions of Chief Whip while the Conservatives were in office. Dyke again conformed very much to type: a county member, heir to an old baronetcy, and very popular especially amongst the country gentlemen in the party. He was a great racquets player and one of the initiators of lawn tennis. Few of his letters survive amongst the papers of the party leaders; it is not likely that he had much influence on policy or appointments. Yet he was not lacking in ability: when he had been chosen to move the address in reply to the Gracious Speech in 1867 Disraeli wrote to the Queen of his grace, good looks, ability and popularity;[12] and Sir Henry Drummond Wolff, looking back on Dyke's career, wondered why he had not risen higher.[13]

Dyke in his turn retired from the duties of Chief Whip soon after the General Election of 1880, ostensibly on grounds of health. His management of the election was much criticized, even from within the party organization. There was talk of bringing back Noel especially for the work of party management. Winn, however, had a strong claim to become Chief Whip and was willing to take the job on for a year or two.[14] The change-over was a somewhat delicate operation, as Northcote explained to Beaconsfield:

> Then comes the question of the best way of putting the matter to Dyke, and I had thought of writing you a letter which you could send on to him, putting the case before you, and speaking handsomely of him as a man who ought next year to take his place on the Front Bench and take part in debate. Winn, however, mentioned that Dyke had been asking him where I was to be found and has been saying that he wanted to come and see me. If he does, that will give me the best opportunity of saying something to him and arriving at an understanding. If I cannot find such opportunity I shall write to you as I propose. I am inclined to think that Charles Dalrymple would be a good man to enlist on the staff. He is sensible and popular, and I think he might be willing.[15]

12 Buckle, ii. 305.   13 Sir H. D. Wolff, *Rambling Recollections*, ii. 127.
14 Iddesleigh Papers, Add. MS. 50063A, Northcote's Diary, 21 and 29 May, 5 June 1880.
15 Ibid., Add. MS. 50018, Northcote to Beaconsfield, 7 July 1880.

Rowland Winn had become associated with party management soon after 1870. His appointment as a Lord Commissioner of the Treasury was recommended to Disraeli by Taylor in 1874 on the grounds that it would 'please all Yorkshire and Lincolnshire, and gratify our friend Chaplin greatly'.[16] Thus it was Winn's appeal as a county member in a specific part of the country, and his friendship with one of the more conspicuous leaders of the Tory country gentlemen that marked him out in Taylor's judgement for the task of Whip. He was hardly the ideal choice for Chief Whip, and at the very moment of his appointment Northcote wrote in his diary:

There was no Whip at the House of Commons for the greater part of Saturday and men were grumbling. The truth is, that Winn does not like staying at the House more than he can help, and his wife's influence is against his doing so. She looks on our position as hopeless, and is probably sore at her husband's not having a peerage, and she is fond of society.[17]

Winn was a Tory of the old school, accustomed to working in a medium of small electorates and aristocratic influence, afraid of the advance of democracy and determined to resist its progress. In his correspondence with Salisbury during the protracted Reform Bill battle of 1884, he emerges as an advocate of all out resistance to the threatened change.[18] When the battle was lost he, far more than his leader, was plunged into gloom and despair about the future.

It is impossible to be certain about the identity of the secondary figures connected with the Whips' department. Even when the party was in office not all Whips were office holders, while some of the offices usually associated with that of Whip were at times separated from these functions. A glance at the personalities of a few of those who composed the circle of Whips will confirm, however, that they constituted a socially very homogeneous group. Lord Henry Thynne joined the circle in 1874 on the recommendation of Taylor and Lord Abergavenny.[19] It was thought that his appointment would please

[16] Hughenden Papers, B/XII/A, Taylor to Disraeli, no date.
[17] For Chaplin, see below, p. 64.
[18] Salisbury Papers, correspondence between Winn and Salisbury, September and October, 1884.
[19] Hughenden Papers, B/XII/A, Abergavenny to Disraeli 17 Feb. 1874. Abergavenny was an influential party manager (see below, Chapter V).

Lord Bath, Thynne's brother and one of the most prominent Tory High Church Peers. Bath had a long record of antagonism to Disraeli, and was a thorn in his leader's flesh during the Reform Bill struggle in 1866 and 1867, along with men like Knightley and Beresford Hope.[20] It was a political fact of some importance that he was now, in 1874, prepared to work with the new ministry, and he was himself mentioned for the post of Lord Chamberlain. His brother sat for South Wiltshire, was the typical county member of high aristocratic origin, and often the mouthpiece for the opinions of country members. Lord Harry Thynne's prejudices are well illustrated by a warning he sent to Corry about a minor reform the Government was intending to introduce in the Session of 1874:

I wish you would call the attention of the Prime Minister to Sclater-Booth's Valuation bill. It is very unpopular with English county members and with the farmers, and if it is gone on with in its present form I am very much afraid we shall be beaten on it. What they dislike especially is the calling-in of the Government Surveyor of Taxes. The same bill or very nearly so was brought in formerly by Hunt and defeated and again by Goshen when it met the same fate. The real promoter of the bill is Mr. Lambert, the Permanent Secretary of the Local Government Board, who has got the length of Sclater-Booth's foot to a nicety. I know him well as he comes from my county and has always been one of my most active opponents. He is a great Radical and a member of the 'Red Club' at Salisbury. Nothing would please him so much as to get the Government into a mess and I have been privately and confidentially informed that at the beginning of the session he gave notice to certain members of the Opposition of the nature of this bill with his own view as to its popularity, but as that was told me under the promise of secrecy I cannot prove the truth of it.[21]

Viscount Holmesdale, who like Dyke and some other party managers sat for a part of the county of Kent, held no ministerial post but was associated with the Whip's office as well as with party management outside Parliament and with the National

[20] See Maurice Cowling, 'Disraeli, Derby and Fusion', *Historical Journal*, VIII, 1 (1965), p. 67; F. B. Smith, *The Making of the Second Reform Bill* (1967), p. 124. Bath's hostility was revived by Disraeli's policy on the Eastern Question; see R. T. Shannon, *Gladstone and the Bulgarian Agitation 1876*, p. 152.

[21] Hughenden Papers, B/XIV/B, Thynne to Corry, 8 Mar. 1874.

Union of Conservative and Constitutional Associations.[22] Lord Crichton, who was made a Lord of the Treasury in succession to Viscount Mahon in 1876 was, according to Drummond Wolff, mainly concerned with Irish affairs.[23] Viscount Barrington, an Irish Peer, held a special position; he had been private secretary to the fourteenth Earl of Derby, was a close personal friend of Disraeli, and therefore could look back upon a long political career. During the last few months of Beaconsfield's life Barrington took Corry's place as the former Prime Minister's private secretary. He had great social influence; his association with the Whips' office went back to 1886, when he worked with Taylor and Noel, and he was a member of a small committee of influential men set up by Disraeli in 1873 to ensure that county seats were properly contested.[24] As Vice-Chamberlain of the Household from 1874 to 1880, Barrington performed a useful service, whenever Disraeli was prevented from doing so, in writing the traditional daily reports on the proceedings of the House of Commons for the Queen.[25]

Some of the considerations governing the recruitment of junior Whips are set out by Northcote in a letter to Beaconsfield.

Sir W. H. Dyke having now resigned his position, Mr. Winn takes the duties of First Whip and Lord Crichton and Lord H. Thynne will continue to give him their assistance. I feel that, excellent as this start is for the present purpose, we ought to be training one or two of our younger men with a view to the future. It is an unattractive duty and one which rather severely tests the physical and mental powers; but I am happy to say that we have in our ranks several gentlemen, very well qualified, who are not only willing but even, as I am told, desirous to take the work; and I believe we should do wisely to enlist two of them for training under Mr. Winn. I feel of course that, in asking gentlemen to give us their kind assistance in opposition, we incur some obligation which must not be forgotten when we, or if we ever return to office; and it is on this account especially that I wish to have your own decision. The names I submit to you and which I submit in order of their election to Parliament are those of:

---

[22] Hughenden Papers, B/XII/A/51. Also *Minutes of the National Union Conferences.*
[23] Sir H. D. Wolff, op. cit., ii. 127.   [24] Buckle, ii. 591.
[25] Sir H. D. Wolff, op. cit., ii. 249.

Lord Folkestone	Elected	1874
Mr. Thornhill	,,	1875
Mr. Sidney Herbert	,,	1877
Sir Richard Musgrave	,,	1880

They are all men of ability, energy and devotion to the party; and I know that Mr. Winn would be most happy to act with any of them. I should myself have much difficulty in making a selection from so good a list, but I am inclined to think that the balance of considerations is in favour of Mr. Thornhill and Mr. Sidney Herbert.[26]

The political rewards for being a Whip were not great. No major political figure of this period had been a Whip at any stage of his career, nor did any Whip achieve major stature. Among the Chief Whips, Jolliffe and Winn received peerages. Taylor may have expected to be similarly rewarded, while Noel was probably prevented by financial reasons from aspiring to such an honour; both ended up in offices which were below Cabinet rank but above junior posts. Dyke, who had become Chief Whip at the comparatively early age of thirty-seven was appointed Chief Secretary for Ireland in 1885 and might have achieved a career of high office. Lord Barrington and Lord Holmesdale received peerages in 1880, but since one was an Irish Peer and the other heir to a United Kingdom peerage these honours were of limited significance. The Whips' office was the preserve of country gentlemen of great social standing for the very reason that it was not an avenue of high political advancement; only men with an assured position would be tempted into this field.

Little evidence of the parliamentary activities of the Whips survives. Most of it, so it must be assumed, was informal and by word of mouth. Letters from the Whips are not plentiful amongst the papers of the party leaders. Most of them follow the lines one might expect; they convey warnings of dangers arising from front bench policies, they deal with the attitude of groups of members, or with matters of organization and appointments. A typical example is the following letter from Dyke to Disraeli, written at the time when the Public Worship Regulation Bill had just reached the Commons and when the Prime

[26] Iddesleigh Papers, Add. MS. 50018, Northcote to Beaconsfield, 8 Jan. 1881.

Minister was about to declare the Government's attitude towards it:

The latest intelligence I have to offer you, upon the Public Worship bill question, is that the opponents of the bill have determined not to divide against the Second Reading of the measure; (a letter has been sent to Mr. B. Hope at Hatfield asking him to concur). Lord Bath is the moving spirit and he has been, I find out, using great exertions to-day to prevent a division on the Second Reading. I have seen many of our friends since our interview; there is a very strong feeling in favour of passing the bill this session: from many who are anxious to pass the bill for its own sake, but from a much larger number, who dread the idea of leaving the question open until another year and who fear the Government may be forced to take it up.[27]

This intelligence may have reassured Disraeli that he had little to fear from the High Church Tories, and that he could safely appeal to the strong Protestant sentiment that was being reported to him from inside and outside Parliament.

From this and similar examples it is evident that the Whips had to be well placed for gathering information and that therefore it was important to be part of the network of family connections still so important in the Tory party. The Whips would hardly bring any direct pressure to bear on members. They therefore depended on persuasion, human relationships, wide connections and full information. Thus it is not surprising that the Whips were during this period all men of a similar stamp; county members closely connected with the aristocracy, who were yet from their situation and ability disinclined to pursue the highest political ambitions. Men of this kind were required both for the intra- and extra-Parliamentary work which fell to the Whips; men who could talk to gentlemen as gentlemen, who could move easily in the great political world, who could negotiate with local men or influence and potential candidates, and who would be content to enjoy influence unobtrusively.

The Whips were drawn from the landed gentry because the rank and file of Tory members in the Commons came from the same social class. Some two-thirds of Conservative members were still connected with the land throughout this period. On

[27] Hughenden Papers, B/XII/F, Dyke to Disraeli, 10 July 1874. For Taylor's activities in 1866–7 see F. B. Smith, op. cit.

the Liberal side, however, only half the members were so linked, and by 1880 the proportion had dropped to less than half.[28] It is true that ownership of land did not necessarily indicate connection with the traditional landed gentry, while many landed proprietors also had interests in commerce, finance, or railways. Nevertheless, a detailed analysis of a small sample, the fifty new Conservative members elected in 1880, shows that thirty-seven of them genuinely belonged to or were closely connected with the landed gentry, while only thirteen belonged entirely to the commercial or professional classes.[29] Most of the Tory landed members held county seats, and the county members were the largest single group in the Conservative party. There were nearly 200 county members amongst the 350 Conservatives in the 1874 Parliament, nearly 150 of them sitting for English counties. County electorates had not changed drastically since 1832. The 1867 Reform Bill had enfranchised the £12 occupiers and by 1883 these formed more than a third of all county voters. In general the occupiers were similar in type and party affiliation to the £50 tenants who had had the vote since 1832. County electorates were comparatively large, little open to corruption, but liable to influence. Party organization had hardly touched them as yet. County members were therefore highly independent and, in so far as they were beholden to anybody, it was to the greater landed proprietors in their territories rather than to the party leaders. It was still a mark of high social distinction to be a county member.[30] They were not, however, difficult to manage from the party point of view: they were the backbone of the Tory party and the alternative of turning to the Liberal party was not open to them. In fact the much smaller number of Whig county members to be found on the Liberal benches were increasingly uncomfortable there. The position of the Tory county members had not fundamentally changed since the days of Peel and the Corn Laws.

[28] For an analysis of the personnel of the House of Commons, see J. A. Thomas, *The House of Commons 1832–1901; A Study of its Economic and Functional Character* (1939); also William Saunders, *The New Parliament* (1880). See also John Vincent, *The Formation of the Liberal Party 1857–1868* (1966), p. 3.

[29] Based on their biographies in *The New House of Commons* (1880), published by *The Times*.

[30] See also H. J. Hanham, *Elections and Party Management*, Chapters I and II.

The county members were not the only representatives of the agricultural interest. Most of those sitting for the smallest boroughs and even the representatives of a few larger ones were also primarily concerned with agriculture.[31] Some two-thirds of all Conservative members were elected by voters connected with the land, and when the party was in opposition before 1874 and after 1880, the proportion was higher still. The agricultural interest could speak on most issues with one voice: owners of land and occupiers, from large tenants to small yeomen farmers, all held similar views. Problems of local taxation, the malt tax, and cattle disease were the kind of perennial questions which united the representatives of the land.[32] Occasionally a matter could cause embarrassment to the party by dividing the owners from the occupiers of land. The so-called Hares and Rabbits Bill of 1880, mentioned earlier, was an example.[33] On education, a matter frequently discussed in Parliament in the 1870s, Tory agricultural members were above all annoyed by the penetration of school boards into county districts: they tended to regard education for agricultural labourers as unnecessary or even harmful, and Sandon was sometimes exasperated enough to call them 'our backward friends'.[34] The Conservative social reform programme which occupied the sessions of 1874 and 1875 did not touch the agricultural and county members closely: they supported it because it came from their side. On foreign affairs, particularly on the Eastern Question, some prominent county members were amongst the leading supporters of a spirited policy.[35] If there was a collective opinion among the country gentlemen in the Tory party, this was mainstream Toryism. The country gentlemen were prepared to

[31] Several borough constituencies with a population of more than 20,000 were, in fact, rural in character, for instance, Aylesbury, Retford, Shoreham, and Wenlock.

[32] See below, p. 70. Robert Lowe said in 1868 that the Tory country gentlemen displayed greater zeal over the Cattle Plague than over Reform. (Sir H. E. Grant Duff, *Notes from a Diary 1851–1872* [1897], 1 Mar. 1868).

[33] See above p. 26. See also *Hansard*, vol. CCLIV, col. 1681, 29 July 1880, and col. 1793, 30 July 1880.

[34] Harrowby Papers, LV/136, Sandon's Memorandum for the Cabinet on the proposed Education Legislation, 26 Oct. 1875. See also above, p. 18.

[35] See *Hansard*, vol. CCXXXVII, col. 868, 1 Feb. 1878, speech by G. W. P. Bentinck on the Supplementary Estimate, and col. 1000, 4 Feb. 1878, speech by H. Chaplin.

tolerate certain divergencies from this main stream, or had been taught to accept them by their leaders.

Some country members stood out from amongst their fellows and established an independent reputation. Sir Massey Lopes, the member for South Devonshire, was the chief advocate of the policy of transferring certain burdens from the local rates to imperial taxation. In his view this was where they properly belonged. In almost every session before 1874 he moved a resolution that the matter should be enquired into. In 1872 he succeeded in carrying, by a majority of a hundred, a motion against the Government that £2,000,000 of charges connected with justice, the police and lunatics should be transferred to the Consolidated Fund.[36] This pressure for the reduction of rates, widely supported amongst Tory country gentlemen, made it difficult for the Conservative Party to propose social reforms that might increase the rate burden.

Clare Sewell Read, the member for South Norfolk, and Albert Pell, member for South Leicestershire, were the most generally recognized spokesmen of farming as an industry. Whenever there were debates in the Commons on matters touching the farmers and the countryside, these two men were bound to be heard. Read's resignation from the Government in 1875 and Pell's motion for the abolition of unnecessary school boards in 1876 have been described.[37] On the Hares and Rabbits Bill in 1880, Pell and Read were against all moves from the Conservative side which would have amounted to a rejection of the Second Reading. They identified themselves on this measure with the point of view of the tenant farmer rather than of the landlord.[38] Read was the more consistent of the two in taking the farmers' side when it conflicted with that of the landlords.

Henry Chaplin, another prominent spokesman of the agriculturalists, was more specifically a representative of the country gentlemen. He appeared in racing dress straight from Newmarket to make his maiden speech on the Irish Disestablishment Bill. It was hoped that he might continue the

---

[36] Buckle, ii. 541. Also above, p. 51.

[37] See above, p. 51 and p. 18. For Pell, see *The Reminiscences of Albert Pell, sometime M.P. for South Leicestershire*, ed. by Thomas Mackey (1908), also T. E. Kebbel, *Lord Beaconsfield and other Tory Memories* (1907), p. 110.

[38] Iddesleigh Papers, Add. MS. 50018, Northcote to Beaconsfield, 12 June 1880.

time-honoured tradition of combining the Turf with politics, but he did not find this entirely compatible with the pursuit of a serious political career. Chaplin created for himself a position of remarkable influence among the country gentlemen, perhaps because he was one of the few in their ranks who had sufficient ability for the attainment of high political office.[39] Colonel Barttelot, the member for North-West Sussex, was an even more independent spokesman of the country gentleman than Chaplin. His views on such subjects as the abolition of purchase of commissions, school boards and the ballot, were openly hostile to change and innovation and often inconvenient for the party leaders. Barttelot expressed these views, which could easily earn the label 'reactionary', without fear or favour. Although he was often out of step with the leaders of his own party he never pursued them with persistent hostility. On the other hand he gained in authority as an independent member by having no aspirations to office. His standing was recognised by the conferment of a baronetcy in 1876.[40]

Amongst the general body of country gentlemen several groups are further distinguishable by their special attitudes or interests. A number of members were conspicuous for their irreconcilable hostility to the Reform Bill of 1867, to the whole trend of policy known as Tory Democracy, and to Disraeli personally. Sir Rainald Knightley, member for South Northamptonshire for over forty years, and George Bentinck, member for West Norfolk and known as 'Big Ben', were prominent in this group. Sir Rainald had been offered the post of Under Secretary at the Foreign Office by Derby in 1866, but refused to enter the Government because of his dislike for Disraeli.[41] The events of 1867 further embittered him. As we have seen, Knightley, and those who thought like him, looked chiefly to Lord Salisbury as their leader, but after 1872, when Salisbury and Disraeli were gradually reconciled, their resentment also began to mellow.[42] In 1874 Knightley would still have pre-

[39] Sir T. Wemyss Reid, *Politicians of To-day*, 'Mr. Chaplin'. Also Marchioness of Londonderry, *Henry Chaplin: A Memoir* (1926).
[40] Sir H. W. Lucy, *Peeps at Parliament taken from behind the Speaker's Chair* (1903), section on Barttelot. For Barttelot's influence when Northcote's leadership first came under criticism in 1880, see A. J. Balfour, *Chapters of Autobiography*, p. 144 (his name is misspelt 'Bartlett' by the Editor).
[41] *Journals of Lady Knightley*, p. 174.   [42] See above, p. 13 and p. 41.

ferred Salisbury to stay out of the Government and he rejected all attempts at bringing about a *rapprochement* between himself and the Prime Minister.[43] Knightley was more formidable as a politician than Bentinck, but the latter, as his nickname indicates, was something of a parliamentary character. Like Knightley he was suspicious of Disraeli: for instance in 1869 he spread the rumour that Disraeli was preparing to reverse the party policy on the Irish Church Bill as he had done on the Reform Bill two years earlier.[44] Bentinck continued to be a sharp critic even after 1874.[45] Some Tories similar in outlook to Knightley and Bentinck were given office in 1874, among them James Lowther, Selwin-Ibbetson and Lord Eustace Cecil.[46] This was to prevent the formation of a 'cave' among back benchers. The weakness of the group most persistently opposed to Disraeli was that they lacked a leader of the first rank. They looked to Salisbury, but in spite of his strong dislike of Disraeli he was not working systematically towards an overthrow of the party leader.

Some of Disraeli's irreconcilable opponents also belonged to the High Church party, for example Beresford Hope. The Church Party, as it was commonly called, was very active and vocal over a narrow range of issues, but virtually non-existent as an organized force over a wider political gamut. On religious and ecclesiastical matters their party loyalty could be seriously strained. The best example of this situation is the passage of the Public Worship Regulation Bill in the session of 1874. Efforts were made to get the Prime Minister to spare the feelings of High Church Conservative members as much as possible, as the following letter shows:

I believe you wish as I do that the Public Worship bill should pass. I am told that much will depend on Mr. Disraeli's speech to-morrow, that if he asks Hall to withdraw his motion, speaking highly of the exertions of the High Church party as a body and

---

[43] *Journals of Lady Knightley*, pp. 257–8.

[44] Lord Malmesbury, *Memoirs of an Ex-Minister* (1884), ii. 387, 5 Dec. 1868.

[45] H. W. Lucy, *A Diary of Two Parliaments*, i. 30, 13 June 1874. Bentinck was then criticizing the Navy Estimates. On the other hand he tried to induce Knightley to vote for the Royal Titles Bill in 1876 (*Journals of Lady Knightley*, p. 298, 17 Mar. 1876).

[46] *Letters to Lady Bradford and Lady Chesterfield*, i. 55, 27 Feb. 1874 to Lady Bradford.

regretting the excesses of a few who had imperilled the Church and made such a measure necessary, then Hardy, etc. will not feel obliged to vote against the bill. A strong speech such as that made by the Archbishop of Canterbury would arouse violent opposition which would very likely be fatal to further progress. You must take this for what it is worth.[47]

The pressure of High Church opinion outside Parliament was felt even by members who were not High Anglicans, such as Drummond Wolff.[48] Education was a matter of concern to High Church members, but their views on denominational teaching were not very different from those of the majority of Conservatives. It is well known that many High Anglicans were opposed to Disraeli's Near Eastern policy and the ill feeling caused by the Public Worship Regulation Bill is often held to be partly responsible for this attitude. This opposition was, however, carried on mainly outside Parliament by such men as Canon Liddon and found little echo amongst the Tory High Church party inside the House.[49] Only Carnarvon seemed to lend the movement some support.[50] Apart from a few specific issues the High Church party did not make itself felt much as a group. It consisted mainly of leaders and there were few followers; a set of individuals whose religious principles were, on certain occasions, decisive in determining their political attitude.

A. J. Beresford Hope, who sat for Cambridge University after 1868, was one of those members who combined adherence to the High Church party with a long record of antagonism to Disraeli. He was a man of great wealth, which he spent freely in order to further his Anglo-Catholic principles. After 1846 he was a Conservative free-trader and opposed to the protectionism of Derby and Disraeli. In the economic and social field his views were often quite liberal; 'Toryism rightly understood, and not as caricatured by Dizzy and mistaken by the Squires, is patient of being the most Liberal of systems, inasmuch as having faith

[47] Hughenden Papers, B/XII/F, Kennaway to Corry, 14 July 1874. On religious questions Sir Rainald Knightley was in full agreement with the Prime Minister and thus his isolation was further increased. (*Journals of Lady Knightley*, p. 269, 1 Nov. 1874). See also above, p. 61, letter from Dyke to Disraeli.

[48] See below, p. 216.

[49] R. T. Shannon, *Gladstone & the Bulgarian Agitation 1876*, pp. 189–90.

[50] See Sir Arthur Hardinge, *Life of Carnarvon*, ii. 339. Also G. C. Thompson, *Public Opinion and Lord Beaconsfield 1875–1880* (1886).

in the super-plebeian it can afford liberty *quantum suff*, while more materialistic systems have to devise secondary checks'.[51] Disraeli seems to have reciprocated his dislike and in a letter to Derby in 1861 called him 'one of a coterie who hate us and think they have a monopoly of Church championship'.[52] In 1867 Hope was one of the leaders of the Conservative malcontents and supported the stand taken by Cranborne, his brother-in-law and later third Marquis of Salisbury. Yet he claimed to have advised Salisbury to join the Government in 1874 and over the Public Worship Regulation Bill his attitude was relatively moderate. He ceased to be a freelance and espoused party orthodoxy, and when the Government went out in 1880 he was rewarded with a Privy Councillorship.

Beresford Hope's counterpart at Oxford was Sir John Mowbray. He had first helped to back Hardy against Gladstone at Oxford in 1865 and had himself joined Hardy in representing the University in 1868.[53] Mowbray was much more conformist than Hope, and ambitious for office. He became a Church Estate Commissioner, but was profoundly shocked to find himself left out of the 1874 Government.[54] Perhaps he had not proved himself sufficiently troublesome to force Disraeli to give him office. In 1880 he was given a baronetcy, became quite an influential supporter of Northcote and ended up as Father of the House. The comparison between Mowbray and Beresford Hope makes evident the great political diversity of the High Church group outside the ecclesiastical and religious field. Sir William Heathcote was the Grand Old Man of the group and his country seat at Hursley in Hampshire was a frequent meeting place for his political friends. He had retired from the House when Mowbray had succeeded him as representative of Oxford University in 1868, but he continued to be consulted. Other prominent members of the High Church Party in the Commons included J. G. Hubbard, Lord Henry Scott and J. W. Henley.

Many of the country gentlemen in the Tory party had at one time or another served in the Army, and some continued to make Army affairs their special interest. For this reason Cardwell's

[51] H. W. Law and I. Law, *The Book of the Beresford Hopes* (1925). In an earlier phase, Beresford Hope was a Peelite.
[52] Buckle, ii. 92.
[53] Sir John Mowbray, *Seventy Years at Westminster* (1900).
[54] Hughenden Papers, B/XII/A., Mowbray to Corry, 5 Mar. 1874.

Army Reforms and the abolition of the purchase of commissions caused such bitter opposition in the Conservative ranks. The obstruction of the 'Colonels' went much further than the party leaders, notably Disraeli, would have liked. Prominent among these army officers was Colonel Loyd-Lindsay, one of the members for Berkshire. He belonged to the younger branch of the Lindsay family, of which the Earl of Crawford was the head, and had won the V.C. in the Crimean War.[55] Most of his property was in Berkshire, but when the minority clause was introduced in 1867, he was thinking of withdrawing from Berkshire and standing with Sir Rainald Knightley in Northamptonshire. Loyd-Lindsay had some support from the Tory front bench, notably from Sir John Pakington, in his stand against Cardwell's reforms, but Disraeli was lukewarm in his attitude and tried to make Loyd-Lindsay tone down his opposition.[56] Cardwell had friendly contacts with Lord Overstone, Loyd-Lindsay's father-in-law, and gradually the latter's attitude to the reforms mellowed. By 1874 Loyd-Lindsay had some expectation of becoming Under Secretary for War, and Disraeli went to the length of explaining why he was unable to appoint him.[57] He undertook a Red Cross journey to the Balkans in 1876, and supported Disraeli's policy by his eye-witness reports that many of the atrocities were carried out by Serbs and not by Turks. He entered the Government in August 1877 as Financial Secretary to the War Office in succession to the Hon. F. A. Stanley. Loyd-Lindsay came from the ranks of Tory country gentlemen, but he was also a man of wider outlook and greater ability than many of his colleagues. His wife reports, in his biography, that amongst the Conservative leaders he felt himself closest to W. H. Smith and Disraeli. Amongst the army group of Tories, Colonel Gilpin, the member for Bedfordshire, ran truer to type. He represented his county for some thirty years in the House of Commons and over six general elections only had to fight two contests. In 1867 he fought actively to keep county electorates uncontaminated by new

[55] *Lord Wantage, V.C., K.C.B., A Memoir*, by his Wife, (1907).
[56] Lady Wantage, op. cit., pp. 206 ff. See *Hansard*, vol. CCIV, col. 1397, 6 Mar. 1871, for Second Reading of the Army Regulation Bill. Also Sir Robert Biddulph, *Lord Cardwell at the War Office* (1904), pp. 113–28; 'The Commons and the Colonels', *Spectator*, 17 June 1871, p. 124.
[57] Lady Wantage, op. cit. p. 217. Also Hughenden Papers, B/XII/A.

borough voters, who might threaten the Tory position.[58] Others belonging to the military group were Colonel the Hon. C. H. Lindsay, member for Abingdon, and Loyd-Lindsay's cousin, Major Arbuthnot, member for Hereford City,[59] and Major-General Sir Percy Herbert, member for South Shropshire.

Over against the serried ranks of the Tory squirearchy, stood the much smaller body of Conservative borough members. It is difficult to find a politically useful definition of a borough member. A man might sit for quite a large borough and still belong in background and attitude to the squirearchy. James Lowther, for example, sat for York, which in 1874 had a population of 50,000 and an electorate of nearly 10,000, yet he clearly was one of the Tory country gentlemen.[60] When the party leaders and Whips talked of borough members, they meant the representatives of the larger industrial towns and of some small boroughs of a predominantly industrial character, mainly, though not entirely, in the North. Amongst these they thought, in particular, of those members who in background and social status did not belong to the landed gentry. This way of thinking is well brought out in a letter from Northcote to Beaconsfield on the Cattle Plague Bill of 1878. Ever since the disastrous rinder pest of 1865–7, the agriculturists had been pressing for restrictions on imported cattle, for suitable quarantine and slaughter-house facilities at the ports, and for compensation for cattle compulsorily slaughtered. On the other hand, such demands could be represented as an interference with the freedom of trade and as a threat to people's food supplies. It was an issue which divided town and country. The first major enactment on the subject, The Contagious Diseases (Animals) Act of 1866, had been a notable triumph for the agriculturalists, and Ward Hunt had made his reputation on it.[61] The Bill of 1878 was one in a series of subsequent regu-

---

[58] *Sun*, 30 Jan. 1874; F. B. Smith, op. cit., p. 218.

[59] Arbuthnot drew up a scheme for the organization of the Conservative Party locally and centrally, which he twice sent to Beaconsfield, in 1877 and 1880. He was in favour of taking office in March 1873. (Hughenden Papers, B/XXI/Arbuthnot). He lost his seat in 1874.

[60] Lowther was an extreme Tory and is sometimes credited with being the originator of obstructive tactics, first used on the Army Regulation and Ballot Bills. (Lord George Hamilton, *Parliamentary Reminiscences and Reflections 1868–1885*, p. 46; Sir H. Maxwell, *Life of W. H. Smith*, i. 176).

[61] See H. J. Hanham, op. cit., pp. 33–35.

lations and statutes. The reference in Northcote's letter to Hermon, the member for Preston, and Tennant, member for Leeds, as typical of borough members is significant:

The great debate on the Second Reading of the Cattle bill (four days) ended last night in a division of 319 to 162. The majority was I think rather inconveniently large; and we are somewhat embarrassed by it for it will make concessions more difficult and yet I imagine that we shall find it necessary. Forster's position was a very ill-chosen one. He professed to approve the general provisions of the bill, and only to desire a minute, though of course an important, alteration in one of its details; yet he put his supporters in the position of voting against the Second Reading of the bill and this they would not do. But when we are in Committee and have to deal with alteration itself, moved as it will be by one of our own men, C. Ritchie (Tower Hamlets), we shall find the great bulk of the Liberals, and not a few of our own party ready to vote against us. The amendment that will be proposed will be, to empower the Privy Council to except from the compulsory slaughter clause cattle coming from any country in which it may at any time be proved that the diseases do not exist, and where laws have been passed which adequately prevent their introduction. It is difficult to refuse this; and not only our Hermons and Tennants, but even our Pells and Barttelots support it. At the same time H. Chaplin, C. S. Read, and others are strongly against any modification.[62]

The party leaders were aware of the importance of the representatives of the larger towns and of the mass of voters behind them. There are frequent references to the necessity of taking their opinions into account. On the other hand the typical borough members, with their urban commercial background, had not yet gained full acceptance into the body of the parliamentary Tory party. As has been noted, none of them achieved office at this stage, except Smith. The highest parliamentary distinction any of them ever attained was to be asked to move or second the motion for the Address in reply to the Gracious Speech.[63] Some of the borough members were am-

[62] Iddesleigh Papers, Add. MS. 50018, Northcote to Beaconsfield, 2 July 1878. See *Hansard*, vol. CCXLI, col. 133, 24 June 1878, for Second Reading of Contagious Diseases (Animals) Bill; also col. 331, 27 June 1878, and col. 513, 1 July 1878.

[63] Callender in 1874, Torr in 1877, and Tennant in 1878. Northcote and Dyke recognised the latter's claims with considerable reluctance (Iddesleigh Papers, Add. MS. 50053, Northcote to Tennant, 6 Jan. and 5 Nov. 1877, 7 Jan. 1878; Add. MS.50018, Northcote to Beaconsfield, 3 Dec. 1877).

bitious for general political advancement, and even for office, and this made them sometimes into better party men than the more independent county members. They were well aware of the opinions of their constituents, but they also realized that often the best way of pleasing their supporters, especially the most important of them, was to build up a position of influence with the party leaders.[64] Deep rooted habits of deference between social classes were still at work.

Some of the topics on which borough members were in opposition to the county members have been mentioned. In the field of education Conservative borough members tended to support the school boards. Several of them worked actively on the boards and were deeply interested in educational advance.[65] Borough members were closely concerned with the various aspects of Conservative social reform, and of them were the spokesmen for specific interests in these matters. Callender of Manchester spoke for the Nine Hour Movement and Wheelhouse of Leeds for some of the Friendly Societies. On religious issues most of the borough members were robustly Protestant in outlook.[66] Many of them supported the ballot because they felt it would make the lower-middle-class voter and the 'shopocracy' freer to support the Conservatives. The borough members were susceptible to the humanitarian feeling of the time. Even when they represented the shipping interest or a great port, like Bates of Plymouth or MacIver of Birkenhead, they could not ignore the Plimsoll agitation.[67] In 1876, the incident of the Fugitive Slave Circulars caused uneasiness among many of them,[68] and the humanitarian aspects of the Near Eastern crisis touched

[64] See below, Chapter VIII.
[65] W. H. Smith was a member of the London School Board and friendly with Forster (Harrowby Papers, XXXIX/189; Sir H. Maxwell, *Life of W. H. Smith*, i. 179; Sir T. Wemyss Reid, *Life of W. E. Forster*, [1888]); Birley (Manchester) and Hamond (Newcastle) were members of the school boards in their cities. See also the debates on the Education Act of 1876, *Hansard*, vol. CCXXX.
[66] Hughenden Papers, B/XII/F, the bundle on Public Worship Regulation Bill, contains much material on the Protantism of the boroughs.
[67] See the debates on the Merchant Shipping Acts Amendment and Unseaworthy Ships Bills, 1875, *Hansard*, vols. CCXXII–CCXXVI, 18 Feb. to 2 Aug. 1875.
[68] Hughenden Papers, B/XX/T, Taylor to Disraeli, 24 Feb. 1876; *Hansard*, vol. CCXXVII, col. 685, 22 Feb. 1876, and col. 820, 24 Feb. 1876.

them closely. In the various phases of this crisis the representatives of the larger boroughs, like the commercial classes in general, desired above all a peaceful settlement. They were sensitive to the argument that war and crisis was disturbing to commerce and trade. Tennant for Leeds, for example, assured the Leeds Chamber of Commerce in January 1878 that no one in the Government wanted war.[69] His speech seconding the motion for the Address in reply to the Gracious Speech, at the opening of the 1878 session, contrasted strongly in its peaceful tenor with some of the speeches from the Tory benches in the debate.[70]

The Fair Trade movement received increasing support from borough members at the end of the 1870s and in the 1880s and Wheelhouse (Leeds), Eaton (Coventry), MacIver (Birkenhead) and Ritchie (Tower Hamlets) were among those sponsoring parliamentary action in this cause. Farrer Ecroyd, who represented Preston from 1881, was the leading publicist of the League. During a visit to Sheffield in September 1881, Northcote found audiences very responsive to protectionist sentiments:

'Fair Trade' is a spell which seems to work upon popular audiences here: but I am rather confirmed in my belief that many who shout for it don't very well know what they want. I had some quiet talk yesterday with two or three leading Conservatives, who told me they thought the fair traders were simply uneasy and dissatisfied with the present state of things, had no clear views how it was to be amended, and were looking out for guidance. They themselves were distinctly against taxes on food, and against taxes on the raw materials of industry. They said matters were very bad with them, though not quite as bad as they had been. They were quite in favour of an enquiry; and I believe we shall do well in supporting Ritchie's move. We must, however, communicate with Ritchie before long on the line he is to take. Lord Grey's letters will be useful as an attack on the treaty system, which is in fact a departure from the pure doctrine of the early free traders, and which is now proving very much of a failure. I am not myself in favour of retaliating duties, varying with the duties imposed by foreign countries. But I think we might make use of the revenue derived from them to

[69] *The Times*, 16 Jan. 1878.
[70] *Hansard*, vol. CCXXXVII, col. 68, 17 Jan. 1878.

lighten the burdens on agriculture and other great branches of industry.[71]

The spread of the Fair Trade doctrine among borough members and their constituents, combined with the agricultural demands for measures of protection, made a considerable impression on the party leaders.

The borough members had thus recognizably distinct attitudes on a considerable range of topics, adding up to a Conservatism that differed materially from the Toryism of the landed gentry. Amongst the principal party leaders, Derby and Northcote were closest to this moderate Conservatism of the boroughs; Disraeli appealed to it often, but did not belong to it. The similarity between moderate Conservatism and moderate Liberalism struck many contemporary observers and gave rise to frequent speculations about a re-alignment of parties.[72] The Conservative borough members did not, however, form a party within a party. The natural community of interest between them often led them to act in concert, but reasons of organization, the activities of pressure groups, and personal ambition made them, in general, more dependent on the party and more loyal to the leaders than many county members. Much of Conservative domestic policy after 1867 was designed to appeal to the urban electorates, for with them lay the difference between victory and defeat for the Tory party. The borough members, in the sense defined here, had therefore little occasion or desire to be anything other than loyal party men.

The number of borough members who created a personal position for themselves in the House of Commons was relatively small. Outstanding among them was Samuel Graves, a wealthy shipowner and great local figure at Liverpool. He was elected in 1865 and Sandon became his running mate in 1868. In that year Graves was considered for ministerial office at the Admiralty. As a great shipowner, however, he often entered into contractual relationship with that department, and this

---

[71] Salisbury Papers. Northcote to Salisbury, 3 Sept. 1881. See also below, p. 89 and p. 214. For the debate on C. T. Ritchie's motion, see *Hansard*, vol. CCLXVII, col. 1823, 24 Mar. 1882. See also Benjamin H. Brown, *The Tariff Reform Movement in Great Britain 1881–1895*.

[72] See, for example, 'The Attitude of the Conservative Party', *The Economist*, 5 May 1870, p. 156.

was used as an argument against his appointment.[73] When he died early in 1873 the *Spectator* called him 'the representative of a class never too numerous—local business notabilities equal to high political work' and considered that he would have made an excellent President of the Board of Trade.[74] It is significant that Graves' successor at Liverpool, Torr, considered that the appointment of two country gentlemen, Adderley and Cavendish-Bentinck, to the Board of Trade in 1874 was highly unsatisfactory; he reported much discontent about it from the port.[75]

W. R. Callender, an influential borough member, represented Manchester from 1874 to 1876. He was personally acquainted with the Prime Minister, since he had been Disraeli's host during the Lancashire visit in 1872. He refused the suggestion that he should stand for a county seat, on the ground that it was too high a social distinction for him; he managed to win a second seat for the Conservatives at Manchester in 1874.[76] Callender used his personal contact with Disraeli on a number of occasions.[77] The following letter shows him exerting his influence explicitly on behalf of Lancashire borough members and borough members in general. The point at issue was the clause limiting infant insurance in the Friendly Societies Bill of 1875. The working classes were angered by allegations that infanticide was often resorted to in order to secure benefit;

It is with very great reluctance that I venture to trespass upon your attention and I should hardly have presumed to do so but from the fear that the position which the Government appears to be taking with reference to the Friendly Societies bill is likely to produce widespread and permanent dissatisfaction not only among the Lancashire constituencies but in many other towns and districts where such societies exist. The first complaint which affects all the Societies alike is the great delay which is taking place—a bill introduced last session was reprinted and finally withdrawn—there

[73] Hughenden Papers. B/XX/Co., Corry to Beaconsfield, 23 Sep. 1868.
[74] 'The Late Mr. Graves', *Spectator*, 2 Jan. 1873, p. 102. *The Economist*, 25 Jan. 1873, p. 91, called him a consummate manager and manipulator of men.
[75] Harrowby Papers, L/221, Torr to Sandon, no date.
[76] Hughenden Papers, B/XIII/Election Matters, Callender to Disraeli, 2 Aug. 1873.
[77] See also below, p. 213.

appears little probability that the House will go into Committee before Whitsuntide . . .

The second cause of complaint is I fear more serious because so far as I can learn it will have to be debated in the House and if so it will place at least 30 to 40 members of the Government under the necessity of taking an active part in opposition. The point I refer to is that of the 'infant insurance'. The present law which was passed in 1855 permits the insurance in 'one or more than one society for the funeral expenses of a child under 5' of a sum not exceeding £6. Acting, as I presume, on the report of the Commission the original bill of last year entirely prohibited infant insurance—the bill as reprinted allowed the sum of 30/—and the bill now before the House extends the sum to £3—i.e., *one half* of the amount which for 20 years has been permitted . . . if the clause pass in its present shape it will have a most serious effect on our future political prospects. Yet as matters stand now—we are to have a discussion in which we must speak out and probably nearly all the representatives of the great constituencies which at all events assisted to place the present Government in office will be compelled to walk into the same lobby with the Opposition who will hardly fail to take advantage of such an opportunity. I venture to think that the Government cannot be unaware of the very strong feeling against the 27th clause, but the fact is that we have kept down the opposition as much as possible in the hope of receiving an assurance that our wishes may be complied with. Not only is the parliamentary strength of the Lancashire Liberals small—but a reference to the division lists will show that they are not particularly attentive to Parliamentary duties and our Conservative supporters are not likely to appeal for Radical support unless they become convinced that we are unable to help them. I may claim a knowledge of local politics of many years standing not only in Manchester but throughout the district and I am not overstating the case by saying that nearly every Lancashire borough seat will be endangered if its representatives vote for this 27th clause as it now stands. All we ask is that the law may remain as it has stood for nearly a generation—I trust the importance of the issue involved may plead a sufficient excuse for addressing you.[78]

Callender, the son of a Liberal cotton manufacturer, had reacted strongly against the doctrines of the Manchester school, and had become the champion of Trade Unions and Co-operative Societies.[79] Through his father-in-law, Samuel Pope,

[78] Hughenden Papers, B/XXI/Callender, to Disraeli, 29 Apr. 1875.
[79] See W. R. Callender Junr., *Trades Unions Defended* (Manchester 1870). Also Hanham, op. cit., p. 315.

the honorary secretary of the United Kingdom Alliance he had also become a strong temperance man. Disraeli selected Callender for the honour of seconding the Address at the opening of the 1874 Parliament and a baronetcy was offered to him in 1875, but he died before it could be gazetted.

Edward Bates, the member for Plymouth, was the only other borough member with a commercial background who had the territorial title of a baronetcy conferred upon him by Disraeli. Bates was one of the country's principal shipping magnates, reputedly of enormous wealth, and was the victim of the famous Plimsoll incident in the House of Commons in July 1875.[80] He had not the political standing of Graves or even Callender, but was probably of greater industrial eminence than either. The New York Herald Tribune wrote of him:

> Mr. Bates is a Conservative of the new type—a wealthy, one ideaed merchant, who feels he has a stake in the country and that he must protect his interests. The House of Commons is just now swamped with such as these . . . Mr. Disraeli . . . cannot afford to irritate the plutocrats, shippers, merchants, and others who are the backbone of the Conservative party.[81]

Hugh Birley, Callender's colleague in the representation of Manchester, came from a family for a long time distinguished in the public and commercial life of the city. An ancestor of his had helped in the preservation of law and order at the Battle of Peterloo, and the family were Tory supporters by the 1840s, when this was still a rarity amongst manufacturers and mill-owners.[82] Birley and his two brothers, Herbert and Thomas, were great philanthropists; the former was particularly interested in Church affairs. He was Chairman of the National Education Union and a member of the Manchester School Board.

Hermon (Preston) and Tennant (Leeds), mentioned by Northcote as typical borough members, had their main interests in the textile industry, but were also connected with coal-mining. Both of them could be taken as fairly typical

---

[80] *Hansard*, vol. CCXXV, col. 1822, 22 July 1875.
[81] *New York Herald Tribune*, 8 Aug. 1875.
[82] See A. Redford and I. S. Russell, *The History of Local Government in Manchester* (1939), i. pp. 301 and 344.

examples of the provincial bourgeoisie, recently arrived to great wealth, which used to find its political inspiration on the Liberal or Radical side. Charley (Salford), Wheelhouse (Leeds), Whitley (Liverpool), and Hamond (Newcastle) were all of them lawyers and representatives of the professional classes. Charley was a prominent figure in Lancashire Conservatism, noteworthy for his strongly Protestant views and his keen interest in ecclesiastical affairs.[83] He received a knighthood in 1880. Wheelhouse held one of the Leeds seats in the Conservative interest in 1868 and 1874, but he failed in the General Elections of 1880 and 1885. He was a fairly frequent parliamentary performer; he applied unsuccessfully to Disraeli for the post of Chairman of Committees in 1874, became a Q.C. in 1877, and received a knighthood from the Liberal government in 1882.

Whitley entered the House of Commons after the by-election at Liverpool in February 1880, a striking Tory success which undoubtedly contributed to the Cabinet's decision to dissolve Parliament in the following month. A solicitor, and the son of a Liverpool solicitor, he had been a prominent figure in local politics for a long time and had been Mayor in 1868. He was one of the chief figures in the Conservative organization in the town and wrote frequent reports on it to Sandon.[84] He did not work very harmoniously with another leading Liverpool Conservative, A. B. Forwood. The latter became in the late seventies a strong exponent of the methods and aims of Tory Democracy, and in the 1880s one of Lord Randolph Churchill's most faithful supporters.

Hamond of Newcastle was another borough member who took much interest in education and was a member of the Newcastle School Board. Knowles, who sat for Wigan from 1874 to 1883, was probably the only Conservative M.P. of working-class origin. His father was an overman at a colliery at Ince and he started work as a collier boy. He became chairman of a coal and iron company. In the debate on the Educa-

---

[83] Charley was active in building up working men's associations in Lancashire; his address to the electors in 1868 is friendly to the trade unions. See also William White, *Inner History of the House of Commons*, ii. 169, for his Protestantism.

[84] Harrowby Papers, vol. L.

tion Bill of 1876 he declared himself in favour of compulsion.[85] Alderman Cawley, who became Charley's colleague in the representation of Salford in 1868, described himself as a civil engineer, while Alderman Nicholson, who was elected for Newark in 1870, called himself an agricultural engineer.[86] The Conservative borough members were thus drawn from a great variety of backgrounds: there were self-made business men, members of patrician urban families, industrial magnates of great wealth, lawyers of greater and lesser standing, and representatives of other professions.

In spite of the borough members and their importance in the estimation of the party leaders, the Conservative party in the Parliaments of 1868, 1874, and 1880 was still predominantly the party of the landed gentry. It was not much changed by the second Reform Bill, either in composition or in its mode of operation. Powerful extra-parliamentary movements did not impinge upon it, as they did upon the Liberal party, nor was there on the Tory side anything like the cleavage between Whigs and Radicals.[87] The dissident groups, the Knightleys, Bentincks, the High Church party, were mainly on the right wing of the party, which made them ultimately less dangerous. The borough members, while capable of acting together on a number of issues, were not an organized section, and personal ambition and a conformist outlook made them into good party men. Thus the absence of organizational pressure outside Parliament and the independent position which many Tory members continued to enjoy did not lead to a lack of coherence in parliament; in fact party unity, after 1867, was reinforced by the emergence of powerful leaders and clear-cut issues.[88]

[85] See Second Reading of Elementary Education Bill, 1876, *Hansard*, vol. CCXXX, col. 15–101, 19 June 1876.
[86] *The New House of Commons* (1880), published by *The Times*.
[87] J. Vincent, op. cit., Chapters I and II.
[88] See S. H. Beer, *Modern British Politics* (1965), p. 257, Table on Party Unity 1860–1908.

IV

THE CONSERVATIVE APPEAL
TO THE VOTERS

I N the 1870s the parliamentary Conservative party was, as we
have seen, still mainly based on the landed gentry. In order to
build up a parliamentary majority, however, the leaders of
the party had to gain support from a much wider section of the
country at large. They had to appeal to a broad range of public
opinion in conditions that were new, and whose effects were
incalculable. The task of building up a connection that could
win a general election was partly one of mobilizing influence
and organization, partly one of political appeal. Organization
and influence are discussed in later chapters of this study. This
chapter traces the sources of Conservative support in the
country and describes the policies and appeals through which
the leaders tried to consolidate their following.

The three general elections of 1868, 1874, and 1880 were
fought on the same distribution of seats and this makes a comparison between them meaningful. The following tables[1] show
the composition of the Conservative party in the three Parliaments by categories of seats.

It is clear, from these tables, that the Conservative majority
of 1874 was largely achieved through gains in the more
populous English boroughs, outside Lancashire and Cheshire.
Out of the eighty-six additional seats won in that year, thirty-
five were won in these boroughs, although they accounted for
less than a quarter of all parliamentary seats. In 1868, when
the £12 occupier franchise was first applied, the Tories had
already consolidated a remarkably strong position in the
English counties and their predominance was further empha-

---

[1] These tables are based on F. H. McCalmont, *The Parliamentary Poll
Book*, 1880 edition; *The New House of Commons* (1880), published by *The
Times*; Alfred Frisby, 'Has Conservatism increased in England since the
last Reform Bill?', *Fortnightly*, vol. 30, Dec. 1881, p. 118, and 'Voters *Not*
Votes: The Relative Strength of Political Parties as shown by the Last Two
Elections', *Contemporary Review*, vol. 38, Oct. 1880, p. 635.

TABLE I

	1868	*1874*	*1880*	*Totals in each Category*
English Counties	115	129	110	154
English Industrial Counties	10	15	8	18
English Boroughs under 20,000 population (1871)	52	60	41	118
English Agricultural Boroughs over 20,000	5	5	3	8
English Boroughs over 20,000	34	72	36	159
All English seats	216	281	198	457
Welsh, Scottish and Irish Counties	29	45	19	111
Welsh, Scottish and Irish Boroughs	13	15	13	81
Universities	4	7	5	9
Total	262	348	235	658

TABLE II

English Boroughs over 20,000 Population (1871)

	1868	*1874*	*gains*	*losses*	*1880*	*gains*	*losses*
Lancashire & Cheshire	16	19	6	3	9	0	10
London	2	10	8	0	8	1	3
Others	16	43	32	5	19	4	28
Total	34	72	46	8	36	5	41

TABLE III

English Boroughs with more than 17,500 registered electors (1880):

	1868	*1874*	*1880*	*Total*
Conservatives:	10	24	13	57
Liberals:	47	33	44	

sized in 1874. After 1868, however, the scope for further gains in the English counties was too limited to have produced a working majority without the great advance in the larger boroughs. The Conservatives required a big English majority in order to outweigh their opponents' advantage along the Celtic fringe. In 1880 the Tories dropped below the 1868 level in all categories of seats, except in the larger English boroughs (outside Lancashire and Cheshire), where they held some of their gains of 1874. Disraeli's gamble of extending the franchise to the urban masses was, therefore, justified in the interests of his party: it won the victory of 1874, and in the longer term strengthened rather than weakened the electoral position of the Tories. This conclusion is even more strikingly confirmed if, instead of seats, the number of voters is considered. The following tables are compiled on the assumption, which is approximately correct, that, where there is more than one candidate for a party, the number of voters is equal to the gross vote cast for that party, divided by the number of votes each elector is entitled to cast:[2]

TABLE IV

Results in 182 English Constituencies contested in 1868 and 1880:

1868

Conservatives: 131 seats: 439,863 voters = 44.3%
Liberals: 173 seats: 553,227 voters = 55.7%

1880

Conservatives: 114 seats: 607,303 voters = 45.9%
Liberals: 190 seats: 714,579 voters = 54.1%

TABLE V

Results in 29 English Constituencies, with more than 17,500 registered electors in 1880, contested in 1868 and 1880:

1868

Conservatives: 17 seats: 172,518 voters = 37.5%
Liberals: 45 seats: 287,224 voters = 62.5%

1880

Conservatives: 19 seats: 290,966 voters = 44.3%
Liberals: 43 seats: 365,770 voters = 55.7%

[2] Quoted by Alfred Frisby, op. cit., *Fortnightly*, Dec. 1881. Frisby's method is also adopted by J. P. D. Dunbabin, 'Parliamentary Elections in Great Britain, 1868–1900', *English Historical Review*, vol. LXXXI, no. cccxviii (Jan. 1966), pp. 82–99, and similar conclusions are reached. See also J. Cornford, 'The Transformation of Conservatism in the late Nineteenth Century', *Victorian Studies*, VII, 1 (1963), pp. 35–66.

The Conservative proportion of the poll in large constituencies therefore rose by nearly 7 per cent in 1880, compared with 1868, and this rise was sufficient to outweigh losses in the smaller constituencies and still leave the Tories with a gain of 1·6 per cent in England as a whole. In the light of these figures, the Tories would seem to have had less to fear than many of them imagined from a redistribution of seats based on population, such as was eventually introduced in 1884.

The Conservative position in the English counties was less happy. The following table represents a further break-down of Table IV:

TABLE VI

Results in 29 English County Constituencies with less than 17,500 registered electors, contested in 1868 and 1880:

1868
Conservatives: 40 seats: 99,387 voters = 53.4%
Liberals: 17 seats: 86,797 voters = 46.6%

1880
Conservatives: 34 seats: 107,532 voters = 50.8%
Liberals: 23 seats: 104,077 voters = 49.2%

The decline of 2·6 per cent in the Conservative portion of the poll was, no doubt, a reflection of the severe depression that had begun to affect the countryside before 1880.

An even greater drop in the Tory percentage took place in the medium-sized English boroughs where the electorate number between 7,400 and 17,500. But, both numerically and proportionately, these losses were compensated by the gains in the large urban and industrial constituencies in England. To complete the picture the following table compares the elections of 1874 and 1880 in the large constituencies:

TABLE VII

Results in 28 English Constituencies, with more than 17,500 registered electors in 1880, contested in 1874 and 1880:

1874
Conservatives: 32 seats: 225,696 voters = 49.6%
Liberals: 27 seats: 230,544 voters = 50.5%

1880
Conservatives: 14 seats: 258,014 voters = 43.4%
Liberals: 45 seats: 335,888 voters = 56.6%

The Conservatives, even if they were gaining in the industrial areas, could thus barely equal the Liberals in such places, even in a year when they were winning. Their great reserve strength in the English counties was essential to them, and they might well be afraid of the unpredictable effects of household suffrage in the counties on their position.

The task which faced the Conservative leaders in gaining a parliamentary majority emerges clearly from these electoral facts. The basis of Tory strength lay in the English counties and in the agricultural areas in general. The preponderance of the party here was, however, so great and it was so easy to be complacent about it, that the Tory leaders were at times tempted to neglect this section of their followers. Moreover, influence was in this category still as important or even more so than genuine voting strength. Preponderance in the rural areas was not, however, sufficient to furnish the Conservatives with a parliamentary majority. For this they had to look to the English boroughs, especially the larger ones. Particularly striking was the Conservative advance in the largest urban constituencies, but this category was still so under-represented in the House of Commons that the immediate utility of these gains in terms of seats was limited. This urban accession of strength might become very important if, in the future, there was to be further enfranchisement and redistribution of seats. It is doubtful, however, if such long-term considerations entered greatly into the calculations of practising politicians. Thus the ingredients of Tory strength in the country at large were very similar to the composition of the parliamentary Conservative party. There was, however, this difference between the management of the party in the House of Commons and in the country; in the House social homogeneity facilitated the achievement of unity; in the country a very different appeal had to be made to such divergent elements as the squirearchy, on the one hand, and the urban artisan, on the other. The increasing pre-dominance of national over local issues in politics, made the appeals and moves of the party leaders all the more important in the struggle for the allegiance of voters.

Some of the special concerns of the squirearchy and the agricultural community have been mentioned in the previous chapter. The identity of interest between the Tory party and the farming community was so much hallowed by tradition and taken for granted, that the party leaders had to do little by way of positive appeal and policy to reinforce it. This was especially so while the party was in opposition before 1874. The assiduous wooing of the electorate that went on during those years was rarely addressed to the landed interest: for instance Disraeli's great policy speeches of 1872 and 1873 contain only passing references to matters concerning the land, and these were not regarded by contemporary opinion as the significant portions of those speeches.[3] Some of the legislation of the Gladstone government did, however, enable the Conservative leaders to take up a position as the special guardians of the land. Gladstone's Irish Land Act, to take one instance, was deeply disturbing to landlords in England as well, but, in securing for tenants the benefit of improvements, it took a line which Disraeli himself was to follow later in England. The Conservative stand on the Land Bill of 1870 was therefore carefully selective; no outright opposition, but insistence on safeguarding the rights of landlords, emphasis on moral rather than legal ties between landlord and tenant, and firm adherence to the principle of freedom of contract.[4] The latter point was of significance not only to landlords and tenants, but to all property owners, already disturbed by some of the activities of the Gladstone government, and it was not irrelevant even for doctrinaire Radicals. The selective Tory stand on the Irish Land Bill was partly dictated by the need to appeal to landlord and tenant alike, and to allow nothing to disturb the apparent harmony of interest between them. In addition it gave an impetus to the drift of Whig landowners into the Tory camp and this was particularly noticeable in the House of Lords.[5] On the

[3] See *Selected Speeches of the Earl of Beaconsfield*, ed. by T. E. Kebbel, ii. 490 (Manchester speech) and p. 523 (Crystal Palace speech).

[4] 'Mr. Disraeli and Free Contract', *Spectator*, 19 Mar. 1870, p. 367. Salisbury's attitude to the Irish Land Bill was much more hostile, see Lady G. Cecil, *Life of Salisbury*, ii. 25, and 'Lord Salisbury on the Land Bill', *The Economist*, 18 June 1870, p. 755.

[5] Lord Granville's biographer speaks of a slow but steady reduction in the number of Government supporters in the House of Lords after the Irish Land Act (Lord E. Fitzmaurice, *Life of Second Earl Granville*, ii. 3). Lord Russell was drifting towards the Tories on several issues (see above, p. 16; also Richmond Papers, especially bundle 1872, for Russell's attitude on the Ballot Bill; S. Walpole, *Life of Lord John Russell* [1889], ii. 443). An analysis

question of the ballot, the strongest opposition to the Liberal proposals came from the spokesmen of the landed interest on the Conservative side. The leaders of the party were, however, not able to follow them to the extremes of opposition, partly because the ballot was favoured by many Tories in urban areas and in small boroughs.[6]

Once the Conservatives were in power, they were in a position to benefit their landed followers more directly. After six years in office, however, their record was disappointing and this must have contributed to the fall in the rural vote in 1880, mentioned earlier. Immediately after coming into office, they had an opportunity to meet the long-standing grievances of the landed interest over taxation. Northcote's first budget used over £1 million, out of an available surplus of over £5 million, for the relief of rates: it gave a contribution of 4s. a head to the Unions for each lunatic, costing £480,000 in a full year, and another £600,000 for the police. Removal of the duties on horses helped the farmer-breeder. Representatives of the rural areas welcomed these measures, but also expressed regret at North- cote's inability to deal with the malt tax.[7] This tax, which had for many years been the subject of motions in the House of Commons moved by rural members, was never abolished during the Conservative period in office and the budget sur- pluses from which this might have been done soon vanished.

---

of parties in the House of Lords for the session of 1872 gives, excluding bishops, 222 Conservatives, 193 Liberals and 21 doubtful (Richmond Papers, 26 Feb. 1872); for the Session of 1874, 231 Conservatives and 218 Liberals, 10 of the latter doubtful (Hughenden Papers, B/XXI/Lathom, Skelmersdale to Disraeli, 4 June 1874). See also D. Southgate, *The Passing of the Whigs* (1962), Chapter XIII.

[6] Conservatives at Rochester and in South-East Lancashire favoured the ballot (Hughenden Papers, B/XXI/Gorst, to Disraeli, 25 July 1870, and A/IV/58–96, Lancashire visit). The Conservative candidate in the York- shire (West Riding, Northern Division) by-election, F. S. Powell, also favoured the ballot (Richmond Papers, Cairns to Richmond, 23 Jan. 1872); he won this seat from the Liberals, just when the Ballot Bill was on its second passage through Parliament in 1872. On the other hand, Carnarvon wrote to Richmond (Richmond Papers, Carnarvon to Richmond, 15 May 1872), '. . . I like the measure less and less . . . my dislike is strengthened by . . . agitation among the agricultural labourers. I have very little faith in our gaining any *real or permanent* advantage from it as some people believe and if things should turn out badly our hold on the counties, which after all is the real source and centre of our strength, might be affected.'

[7] A. Lang, *Life of Northcote*, ii. 52–64.

From the fiscal point of view, a Conservative government was thus of limited benefit to the farmers.

In 1875, a parliamentary session which saw the peak of Tory legislative activity in the domestic field, one major piece of legislation was brought in for the special benefit of tenant farmers, the Agricultural Holdings Act. As has been mentioned it was designed to secure for tenants some of the value of unexhausted improvements, but its provisions were on a permissive, not on a compulsory basis. A demand for a measure of this kind had been in the air for some time and had been voiced by Chambers of Agriculture. Thus the ball had been set rolling 'across the path of the Conservative Ministry', as *The Times* put it.[8] Disraeli personally introduced the bill in the Commons and made much of his long-standing desire to pass such a measure. The spokesmen for tenant farmers, for example Read, objected to the permissive principle in the bill; on the other hand the landlords did not like any interference with their property rights or with the relationship between themselves and their tenants, and this feeling was voiced in the debate by Barttelot and others.[9] The Act was not of great practical importance in subsequent years, because of its permissive character. The demand for a compulsory bill was of some significance in the General Election of 1880.

Apart from the Agricultural Holdings Act, the Tories brought in some other legislation favouring the landed interest, such as the Cattle Plague Bill of 1878.[10] On minor matters the Conservative government was sensitive to that great section of its followers which lived on and by the land. From an electoral point of view, these initiatives were less important than the growing economic depression in the rural areas. British agriculture now began to suffer the fate which many had feared might have overtaken it thirty years earlier when the Corn Laws were abolished.[11] There was a succession of bad harvests but instead

[8] *The Times*, 19 May 1875. 'The Tories and the Land', *Spectator*, 14 Nov. 1874, considered that a measure to deal with land tenure was to be expected from the Government.
[9] *Hansard*, vol. CCXVIII, 16 Apr. 1874. See above, p. 20 and p. 64.
[10] See above, p. 70.
[11] See J. H. Clapham, *An Economic History of Modern Britain* (1932) ii. 279; H. L. Beales, 'The "Great Depression" in Industry and Trade', *Economic History Review*, vol. v, 1934–5, p. 65.

of their effect being mitigated by rising prices to the farmers, as used to happen, prices now fell. The depression was general, but the farmers were the worst hit, and from their crisis there was to be no real recovery. In many quarters the Government itself was being blamed for bad trade, on the ground that it disturbed the economic equilibrium through its foreign adventures. Whatever might be the truth of this, the Conservative government seemed unable or unwilling to do anything to relieve the distress of the farming community, their most loyal followers. Northcote, as Chancellor of the Exchequer the minister most immediately responsible for economic affairs, wrote to Beaconsfield from his home near Exeter as early as December 1878, when the worst of the depression had not yet arrived:

About distress: beware of another coup manqué . . . Down here for instance there is nothing to call forth the charity of England. Yet there are a good many local claims, for example the sufferers by the West of England Bank failure. Then I don't quite understand how we are to act as a government in the matter, except in the collection of information, which indeed I think might be useful as enabling us to lay the ground for action should it be thought desirable. At present we do not have any that would justify our moving. . . . I don't think it wise to hoist a flag of distress when there has been no visible calamity to account for it,—no cotton famine, no bread or meat famine, no convulsion of nature. We have bad trade, and our workmen themselves aggravate the misfortune by their disputes with the employers of labour. We want peace and confidence, and then we may hope for a return of better times. If there were deeper causes at work we must take care not to encourage the idea that they are to be met by national subscriptions. Think of the danger of having a relief committee sitting en permanence; yet that is what it might easily come to if the movement were started without great care.[12]

Northcote was evidently far too much inclined towards *laissez faire* to have contemplated, with anything but alarm, the acceptance of responsibility by the Government for the consequences of bad trade. In the meantime there was a growing demand for reciprocity or protection, from the landed interest, whatever the exact meaning of these terms. The reciprocity

[12] Iddesleigh Papers, Add. MS. 50018, Northcote to Beaconsfield, 23 Dec. 1878; Beaconsfield repeated these sentiments almost verbatim to Lady Bradford (*Letters to Lady Bradford and Lady Chesterfield*, ii. 200).

agitation had first appeared in 1870, but had then come mainly from trade, industry and the towns and had received little encouragement from the Conservative leaders.[13] Now the cry became much more insistent and organized, and came equally from town and country. Beaconsfield took issue with the various demands of the landed interest in two speeches in the House of Lords, in March and April 1879.[14] He argued that his Government had already done all that could be done to relieve real property of its tax burden; as for reciprocity, there was not enough left now on which it could be negotiated. To those who had dug up his old speeches in favour of protection he replied that this question was long ago closed and that it was not practical politics to reopen it. Beaconsfield was probably right in assuming that, in spite of the growing clamour for protection, taxes on food were still so profoundly unpopular that it would have been electorally damaging to saddle the party with a fair trade programme. Thus the Prime Minister seemed unable to hold out any hope to the landed interest, and left the field wide open for his opponents to propose their own remedies. The only concrete action of the Government, in response to repeated parliamentary demands, was the appointment of a Royal Commission on Agriculture under the chairmanship of the Duke of Richmond. To counteract the effect of Radical agitation, Beaconsfield went out of his way, in two major speeches in the next few months, to praise the agricultural system of England and to proclaim its superiority to systems of peasant proprietorship.[15]

All this could not prevent considerable Liberal inroads into the solid Conservative strength in the counties in the General Election of 1880. The Farmers' Alliance played a significant part in bringing about Liberal gains in the rural areas.[16] This organization was founded in July 1879 and its chief demands

[13] 'The Conservative Party and Reciprocity', *The Economist*, 22 Jan. 1870. Derby and Northcote publicly repudiated reciprocity at this time. See also above, p. 73 and below, p. 214.

[14] *Hansard*, vol. CCXLIV, 28 Mar. 1879, col. 1976, and vol. CCXLV, 29 Apr. 1879, col. 1388. See also R. Blake, *Disraeli*, p. 698.

[15] At the Mansion House on 6 Aug. 1879 and to the Royal Bucks. Agricultural Association at Aylesbury on 18 Sep. 1879. See Buckle, ii. 1370–2.

[16] See W. E. Bear, 'The Revolt of the Counties', *Fortnightly*, vol. 27, April 1880, p. 720. Also H. J. Hanham, *Elections and Party Management*, pp. 30–32.

were: compulsory compensation for unexhausted improvements, prohibition of limited ownership in land, simplification and cheapening of land transfer, the right for tenants to kill ground game, and the abolition of the law of distress. The Conservative Central Office regarded the Farmers' Alliance as hostile and, while many Liberal M.P.s joined it, not a single Conservative did. Liberal candidates in the elections were generally much more positive in answering the questionnaire sent round by the Alliance than Conservative candidates. After the Liberals had come to power they lost no time in meeting one of the demands of the Farmers' Alliance with the Ground Game Bill of 1880, finally passed in 1881. This bill, also known as the Hares and Rabbits Bill, caused Beaconsfield and Northcote considerable anxiety, as has been mentioned, because it brought into the open again the division between landlord and tenant already observable in the election.[17] The Gladstone government also abolished the malt tax in 1880.

Thus, by 1880, the Conservative position in their traditional rural strongholds had been considerably weakened. The actual turnover of votes to the Liberals was not sufficient to have justified undue alarm, but the loss of seats in the counties made the Conservative position appear worse, and was in fact greater, than the turnover of votes would have warranted. A small turnover of votes usually produces a much larger turnover of seats under the British electoral system, but in this instance this effect was aggravated by the larger number of contested seats as compared with 1874 and 1868. If therefore the Conservative position in the rural areas in 1880 was not as much shaken as appeared on the surface, it was nevertheless serious, particularly in the light of the fact that household suffrage in the counties had now become an imminent possibility. The Conservative leaders had taken the loyalty of the landed interest and the absence of divisions within it too much for granted, and when the great depression came they seemed as much under the spell of the 'dry bones' of political economy as their opponents. On 17 April 1880 Salisbury wrote to Richmond; 'Before this Parliament is over the country gentlemen will have as much to do with the government of the country as the rich people in America have. . . .'[18]

---

[17] See above, p. 26.   [18] Richmond Papers, 17 Apr. 1880.

After 1868 the strengthening of the party in the boroughs was a more pressing concern with the Tory leaders than appeals to the landed interest. The new voters in the boroughs were the Great Unknown which had to be mastered if the Tories were to achieve power. Except for Lancashire they had had little success among the newly enfranchised voters in 1868. The task was not merely to gain adherents among the artisans but also to build up enough middle class support in the boroughs to provide the Conservative party with local leaders.[19] The great organizational effort directed towards the working classes, especially after 1870, is discussed in subsequent chapters. The Conservatives were less successful in finding and presenting new policies to appeal to these voters. The disorganization of the leadership for some years after the General Election of 1868 has been emphasized in these pages. As long as such conditions prevailed there was no possibility of the leaders making a bold approach to the new classes they had to win. In addition, the Liberal government firmly held the initiative for a time, and the course of parliamentary affairs offered the Conservatives few opportunities to make a fresh appeal.

Many of the Tory leaders felt that the party must seek support among the working classes even if it meant striking out along quite unprecedented lines. This is well illustrated by the curious episode of the New Social Movement in 1871. This affair caused a sensation at the time, but was later forgotten because it had no immediate and direct consequences. It was an attempt to give concrete shape to Disraeli's vision of a union between the upper and the working classes. Some of those who took part in this venture may have seen in it a means of 'dishing the Whigs' yet again. The chief exponent of the enterprise was John Scott Russell, an engineer, who had a record of achievement in his own field and had been associated with the Great Exhibition of 1851. He was a protégé of Sir John Pakington, who, as Secretary of State for War, was one of Disraeli's less distinguished colleagues in the 1868 government. Russell's scheme was to form a 'Council of Legislation' (consisting of Peers) and a 'Council of Workmen' (consisting of Labour leaders). Negotiations were initiated, through Russell, between

[19] This is the recurring theme of the party organizers. See, for example, Gorst's letters to Dyke quoted below, Chapter VI.

certain Conservative Peers on the one hand and some Labour leaders on the other, which led eventually to the signing of a memorandum of a purely exploratory kind. It stated that at the request of Scott Russell, as chairman of a council of representative working men, the signatories had consented to consider in a friendly spirit whether and how they could help to remove the disadvantages which affected the well-being of the working class. They did not underestimate the difficulties, they could only agree to legislation consistent with the real interest of all classes and they reserved full freedom of action. The signatories on the Conservative side were Carnarvon, Salisbury, Lord John Manners, Pakington, Northcote, Hardy, and Sandon; on the Labour side they included Applegarth, Howell, the secretary of the Reform League, Potter, and Latham, the chairman of the Labour Representation League.

On 5 October 1871 Sir John Pakington made a somewhat indiscreet speech to the Social Science Congress in Leeds, in which he alluded in expansive terms to the needs of the working classes and advocated parliamentary action to secure better housing, cheaper food, and more education. He made very flattering references to Forster. As *The Times* said in a leader on the following day, it was not easy to see how the demands voiced by Pakington could be satisfied by parliamentary action. The speech did, however, lead to speculation about a *rapprochement* between the Tories and the working classes. On the Labour side there were many who strongly disliked the contacts with the Tories into which some of their leaders had entered, and it may have been from some such hostile source that the premature disclosure of the whole scheme came. The *Daily News* blazoned forth the story of a contact between Conservative Peers and representatives of the working men and their agreement on a seven-point programme:

1. Workmen to be moved out of dismal alleys into the wholesome air of detached homesteads. 2. Perfect organization for self-government of counties, towns, and villages, with power of acquisition and disposal of land for the common good. 3. A day's labour to consist of eight hours of honest work. 4. In addition to schools for elementary education, establishment of schools for technical education and practical knowledge. 5. Places of public recreation, knowledge, and refinement as parts

of the public service. 6. Public markets in every town for the sale of best quality goods at wholesale prices. 7. Great extension and reorganization of the public service on the model of the Post Office. Parts of this programme were fanciful and others, like point seven with its overtone of nationalization, so far ahead of their time as to be wholly out of touch with reality.

Immediately denials came from several Conservative participants in the alleged scheme: Salisbury wrote to the *Daily News* that, while he sympathized with the demand for better dwellings, he had not assented to any of the resolutions mentioned and objected strongly to some of them. Denials followed from Derby and Richmond, who with Disraeli had been mentioned as sympathizers, though not signatories, and from Carnarvon, Hardy and Northcote. *The Times* discussed the whole affair in terms of ridicule, but stated that mystery was to be expected of Disraeli and that the inclusion of Lord John Manners' name allowed the inference that the former Premier might have had a hand in it. Pakington on the other hand would be quite willing, so *The Times* said, to take office on a pledge to make everyone happy. The *Spectator* also held Disraeli to be the real author of the scheme, but wrote; 'The hill squirearchy of England will never be dragged behind the triumphal car of their viewy and literary chief.'[20] Behind the scenes, some of the Tory leaders mentioned were seriously perturbed by the disclosure.[21] They were, above all, anxious to prove that the initiative had not come from them but from the working men, while the Labour leaders tried to make it appear that they had been approached in the first instance, and that their demands had eventually been met after long negotiations. The affair thus petered out amid a welter of mutual recriminations. In some ways it was too absurd an episode to be regarded as very important, but even Gladstone took it sufficiently seriously to utter a public warning against the Tory machina-

[20] 'Mr. Disraeli's Flank March', *Spectator*, 14 Oct. 1871; for this episode see *The Times*, *Daily News*, *The Economist*, and *Spectator*, for October and November 1871. Also W. H. G. Armytage, *A. J. Mundella, The Liberal Background to the Labour Movement* (1951), pp. 98–100; H. J. Hanham, op. cit., Chapter XV.

[21] See Harrowby Papers, XXXIX/272, Sandon to Pakington, 18 Oct. 1871; Cairns Papers, Hardy to Cairns, 29 Oct. 1872.

tions.[22] Since so many of the leading figures of the Conservative party were implicated in the negotiations, it is difficult to believe that Disraeli did not know of them, and until they miscarried he did nothing to discourage them. Scott Russell's seven points give a clue to what the leaders of the working classes considered to be their practical aims for the period immediately ahead. The Tory leaders were at least prepared to toy with these ideas and some of them, in milder and adapted form, were taken up by the party.

The portion of Disraeli's Manchester speech of April 1872 concerned with public health undoubtedly owed something to the New Social Movement. There are links between the Tories and the Nine Hour Movement, and a new Factory Act was passed in the session of 1874. Once the Tories were in power, the bulk of their domestic legislative activity was in fact directed towards the urban working classes.[23] In the labour legislation of 1875 the Tory government showed itself more sensitive to the opinions of the trade unions than the Gladstone government had done with the Criminal Law Amendment Act of 1871. This is not the place to examine how effective and important this legislation was, but it cannot be disputed that it helped to maintain the image of the Conservatives as the party concerned with the needs of the working classes and less bound by the harsh doctrines of the Manchester School than the Liberals. It cannot be denied that the articulate working classes and their leaders made their political home mainly with the Liberal party. Nonetheless, links between the Tories and the leaders of Labour can be found: for example among the founders of the British Socialist movement in the 1880s Hyndman and Butler-Johnstone were men with a Tory past.

[22] In a speech to his constituents at Blackheath on 28 Oct. 1871. For the background, see S. Maccoby, *English Radicalism, 1853–1886* (1938), p. 177 The Liberals had made similar efforts to enlist the support of working-class leaders during the election of 1868 (see Royden Harrison, 'The British Working Class and the General Election of 1868', *International Review of Social History*, V [Pt. 3, 1960], pp. 424–55, and VI [Pt. 1, 1961], pp. 74–109).

[23] For a contemporary assessment, see, for example, Prof. Hunter, 'Mr. Cross's Labour Bills', *Fortnightly*, vol. 18, Aug. 1875, p. 217. Also P. W. Clayden, *England under Lord Beaconsfield* (1880), written from a Radical point of view. For some of the background, W. H. G. Armytage, op. cit.; *Thomas Burt, M.P., An Autobiography*, with supplementary chapters by Aaron Watson (1924), pp. 254 ff.

For the strengthening of urban Conservatism it was of almost equal importance to build up the position of the party among the middle classes, the employers, the traders, and the professional men. There were some families among the textile employers in Lancashire, like the Birleys of Manchester or the Hornbys of Blackburn, who had a long tradition of loyalty to the Tory party. More recently many Conservative politicians and organizers, in Lancashire and elsewhere, were reporting a growing trend towards the party among employers, especially amongst the younger generation. The desire for social equality with the gentry may have played its part in this movement. In general, however, these classes were still regarded as the preserve of the Liberal party, especially the large proportion of them who were Nonconformists.[24] In the years before 1874 the Gladstone government gave the Conservative leaders an opportunity to appeal to the middle classes as the party protecting property and the freedom of contract. Such Liberal policies as the Irish Land Act, the abolition of purchase in the Army, and the Licensing Act were exploited to the utmost from this point of view: they could all be regarded as examples of 'plundering and blundering', as Disraeli put it in the Bath Election Letter. Salisbury, in an unsigned article in the *Quarterly* in October 1872, also foresaw the well-to-do classes moving increasingly over to the Conservative side, as a result of Liberal attacks on property and vested interests.[25] This line was even of use in appealing to the working classes: the Conservative argument was that they had a great deal more to lose than their chains and that they would be the first to suffer from a disturbance of trade and capital.[26] To the middle classes the Conservatives could furthermore appeal as the party of modera-

[24] See R. C. K. Ensor, 'Some Political and Economic Interactions in Later Victorian England', *Transactions of the Royal Historical Society*, 4th Series, vol. XXXI (1949).
[25] 'The Position of the Parties', *Quarterly Review*, Oct. 1872.
See also 'Lord Salisbury on Tory Prospects', *Spectator*, 19 Oct. 1872, p. 1320.
[26] See, for example, Derby's speech to the Conservative Working Men's Association at Edinburgh, 17 Dec. 1875 (*Speeches of the Fifteenth Earl of Derby*, ed. by T. H. Sanderson and E. S. Roscoe, i. 261); also Disraeli's Manchester Speech; 'The Political Future of the Working Classes, or Who are the real friends of the people?', *Publications of the National Union*, No. VII, 1872.

tion and sound government, while Gladstone and his colleagues could be represented as reckless adventurers. It was not easy to sustain this image, for among the middle classes there was great trust in Gladstone, especially as a financier, while Disraeli still inspired distrust. Another difficulty was that lesser Conservative leaders often made public pronouncements which were not moderate in tone and Disraeli's Bath Election Letter itself came under criticism for this reason.[27]

The more active imperial policy, which Disraeli put forward from 1872 onwards, was also likely to appeal to that middle-class opinion which had backed Palmerston, especially when it stood in contrast to the weaknesses and failures, real or alleged, of the Gladstone government.[28] On the other hand, solid middle-class opinion was made to feel uneasy in turn when the Conservatives had a chance to carry out their foreign and imperial policies in office. The amount paid for the Suez Canal shares was seen as excessive, and the Royal Titles Bill was regarded as a useless and flamboyant gesture. The Tory government seemed to be insensitive to humanitarian feelings, so important to the middle classes, in its attitude to the Plimsoll agitation and on the issues of the Fugitive Slave Circulars. Such matters caused, as we have seen, uneasiness even among Conservative borough members.[29] The impact of the Near Eastern crisis on public opinion was very profound, and to some extent cut across the more permanent ties of interest and party already discussed here. In 1879 that moderate middle-class opinion which had been turning increasingly to the Conservatives was affronted by the expensive involvements in South Africa and Afghanistan.[30] To many observers, foreign policy was the key

[27] 'Mr. Disraeli and the Bath Election', *The Economist*, 11 Oct. 1873, p. 1231, considered that the letter was the most foolish a Conservative leader ever wrote and that the reluctance of his party to have Disraeli as leader would be increased tenfold by this extravagance.

[28] Among Disraeli's colleagues, Carnarvon and Adderley had taken the closest interest in imperial affairs. See, for example, C. B. Adderley, *Review of the Colonial Policy of Lord John Russell's Administration and of Subsequent History* (1869).

[29] See above, p. 72 and footnote 68.

[30] See R. T. Shannon, *Gladstone and the Bulgarian Agitation 1876*; also G. G. Thompson, *Public Opinion and Lord Beaconsfield, 1875–80* (1886), a study of public opinion on the Eastern Question, and R. W. Seton-Watson, *Disraeli, Gladstone and the Eastern Question* (1935).

issue of the election of 1880 and if so, this must have had an effect in turning moderate middle-class opinion away from the Conservatives.[31] Nevertheless, important though the impact of foreign affairs was between 1876 and 1880, in the longer term strong economic and social currents were moving the middle classes towards the Conservative party. They had now achieved, in the main, their entry into the citadel of social and political privilege. Having attacked the *status quo* they now began to defend it, and their mood became increasingly conservative. The gradual conversion of Goschen to Conservatism shows this tendency at work in a leading figure. For the time being, middle-class conversion strengthened the position of the party in the boroughs.

Just as the Conservative leaders had to contend with different factions and viewpoints inside the parliamentary party, so the attempt to court different sections of their followers in the country caused some tension and stress. There was no great basic divergence of interest between town and country that need have made it difficult for the Conservative leaders to appeal equally effectively to both these sections. Issues like local taxation or the cattle plague were not of sufficient importance to cause any deep division. Town and country suffered equally from the depression and both rural and urban Tories were looking in the direction of protection, reciprocity, and fair trade for a remedy. The difficulty arose not from agriculture as an economic section, but from the country gentlemen whose influence was still so pervasive in the party. For them the crucial point was their survival as a governing class and the Conservative party was to them ultimately only a means for discharging their mission of ruling the country. Their battle had really been lost in 1867, but since the consequences of this defeat were not immediately as obvious as many of the country gentlemen in their bitterness had feared, they took fresh heart. The continued strength of the country gentlemen as a class may be gauged from the fact that in 1871 even the Liberal government was constrained to move Goschen from the Poor Law Board to the Admiralty, because he had given mortal

[31] See, for example, editorial comment in the *Fortnightly*, May, 1880, 'Home and Foreign Affairs'; 'The Elections', *The Economist*, 10 Apr. 1880, p. 406.

offence to the squirearchy by attempting to pass an ambitious bill for the reorganization of local government. Cardwell told Goschen a little later: 'Nothing has gone right with us since you alienated the country gentlemen with your rating bill and Bruce alienated the licensed victuallers by his licensing bill'.[32] The country gentlemen were therefore not in a mood for fresh surrenders. This was the attitude of Salisbury and Carnarvon for some years after 1867, as we have mentioned earlier, and it remained the attitude of the Knightleys, Bentincks, and those in the country who thought like them. To the latter it still seemed the worst possible policy for the Tory party to 'try a little Liberalism'.[33] They were out of sympathy with the appeal to the masses which their leaders felt it necessary to make, and instinctively disliked what came to be known as Tory Democracy.

In practice, however, the social reforms of the Disraeli government, in 1874 and 1875, were so carefully selected and mild that the country gentlemen had no difficulty in accepting them. What would really have aroused them to the strongest opposition would have been another flanking march in the manner of 1867, perhaps on the county franchise and equal electoral districts, but this was not within the realm of practical politics up to 1880. Thus the Conservative leaders had no undue difficulty in making country gentlemen and urban artisans run in harness in their voting allegiance. The middle classes in the towns, especially the employers, were not yet so numerous in the Tory camp that this was a barrier to working-class Toryism; on the contrary the party could still gain working-class adherents through the antagonism inspired by many Liberal employers. It was not until after 1880 that the growing conversion of the middle classes to the Conservative party made it difficult at times to appeal to the workers, and thus Forwood, the great Liverpool champion of Tory Democracy, was blamed by other Tories for using the accents of class warfare too stridently at a by-election in the city in 1882.[34] The strength of Radicalism was greater and its aims so much more advanced

---

[32] A. D. Elliot, *Life of George Joachim First Viscount Goschen* (1911), i. 126.
[33] 'Mr. Disraeli's Position this Session', *Spectator*, 20 July 1872, p. 904.
[34] Harrowby Papers, L/265, Lord Claud Hamilton to Viscount Sandon, 14 Dec. 1882, see below p. 170.

after 1880 that the stakes were higher in the bidding for the working-class vote.

We have so far considered the electoral problems facing the Conservatives mainly in terms of social and economic class divisions. Religious and ecclesiastical issues and affairs were hardly less important and these to some extent cut across the politics of economic interest and class. In the period of fluctuating party alignments between 1852 and 1867, a period which has been called the era of good feeling in British party politics, religious issues were frequently predominant. Church and State, the influence of Catholicism, the Ritualist movement, Modernism, Church schools, matters such as these were again and again in the forefront of public controversy. The 1868 election was dominated by Gladstone's proposal to disestablish the Church of Ireland. On the whole the Conservative party could do little to make itself attractive to organized Nonconformism, although the party may well have been benefited incidentally from the disenchantment of nearly all shades of Nonconformism with the Gladstone government arising mainly out of the Education Act of 1870. The Conservative leaders were faced with a more immediate electoral problem in the Ritualist movement. Soon after coming to power the Tories had to declare their attitude to the Public Worship Regulation Bill, promoted by the Archbishop of Canterbury. The popular policy, especially for the urban voters, was to emphasize the Protestantism of the Church of England by supporting the bill. This was bound to antagonize the High Church Party, which would cause difficulty not merely in Parliament and in the Cabinet, but also with the electorate. An authoritative view from Liverpool stressed the Protestant argument:

I wrote a very strong letter to Cross and represented to him the difficulty I have had on the hour question in the Licensing bill; that if the Government allowed the Worship bill to fall through we should be charged with giving way to the beer interest in the one case and the Ritualists in the other and the consequences would be most serious and that in fact no member should be returned for any division of the county or any borough on our side of the House who voted against the bill. This is my sincere conviction. I also pointed out the difficulties which might arise if the Archbishop gave up the bill another session and placed the onus upon the Government.

That made it a Cabinet question which might cause serious divisions in the party which might be avoided if the bill passed this session and then concluded by saying you may assure Mr. Disraeli that no member in this part of the country who votes against the bill can hope to be returned.[35]

Gorst, the Conservative party agent, was more concerned with the damage done to the party electorally by offending the High Anglicans, and forwarded to Disraeli this interesting letter from a supporter in Derby:

Then of course this Public Worship bill has caused many to declare openly that they will not again support a Conservative unless he is also a strong Churchman. You know better than I do how difficult it was at the last General Election to induce High Churchmen (although Conservatives) to vote against *Gladstone*. I did something myself in that way, but I can now count nearly a score of influential electors in this constituency (South Derbyshire) who will certainly not *again* vote for any supporter of the ministry. This is serious, for it only cuts *one* way. *I* have never heard of a Liberal Low Churchman voting against the Liberal party, and I don't believe half a dozen can be found in all England. I know many Low Church Whig clergymen who detest Gladstone's ecclesiastical appointments but are always ready to support his political friends at the polling booth. Though we have a large majority in the *House*, yet most of the seats were secured by narrow majorities of the electors. Take the three divisions of this county, parties are very evenly balanced even in the north, where there was no contest last time. Forty or fifty influential men would make a great difference. The clergy have now, under the Household and Twelve Pound franchise, more *personal influence* than before. Twenty clergymen going wrong, represents at *least*, on an average, eighty votes.[36]

The antagonism which developed over the Public Worship Regulation policy between the Disraeli Government of 1874 and the High Church Party became an even deeper rift over the Eastern question. The only wing of Anglicanism fully represented in the agitation against the Bulgarian atrocities were the Anglo-Catholics. Men like Liddon, R. W. Church, Malcolm MacColl, and others were prominent among the organizers of the protest movement against the Government's pro-Turkish

[35] Harrowby Papers, L/59, Whitley to Torr, 15 July 1874.
[36] Hughenden Papers, B/XII/F, Borough to Gorst, 26 July 1874. John Borough had been a Conservative agent.

policy. The attitude of the High Church party on the Eastern question was no doubt due to the merits of the case, as they saw it, and owed a great deal to religious sympathy with Greek Orthodoxy.[37] On a lower plane, however, many Anglo-Catholics were disgruntled by the Public Worship Regulation Act and harboured long-standing suspicions of Disraeli. The Premier, whose upbringing was remote from Anglicanism, perhaps never developed a really organic relationship with the Church of England; but from his public actions it could be assumed that his sympathies lay with the Low Church. Among his ecclesiastical appointments the Low Church had the lion's share and it was usual to talk of 'Derby-Dizzy bishops'. In spite of the fears of Gorst and others, however, a staunchly Protestant line was at all times electorally more rewarding than any concessions to the High Church party.

On many issues of the day the internal divisions of Anglicanism were of little significance and the Tory party could, without difficulty, appear as the party pledged to uphold the Established Church. This theme occurred in Disraeli's policy speeches of 1872 and 1873. In the great controversy about denominational and secular education after the passage of the Education Act of 1870, the Conservative party stood squarely behind the Church schools: the Education Act of 1876 was based on the denominational principle and to safeguard the future of the Church schools was one of its main purposes.[38] The educational controversy did more than anything else to keep alive and nourish the political and class-consciousness of the dissenters. There must have been many middle-class non-conformists who for political and economic reasons might have drifted towards Conservatism, but who remained tied to the Radical wing of the Liberal party because of their views on education and, to a lesser extent, licensing. Gladstone's attitude on foreign affairs made its strongest appeal to this section.[39] Nevertheless the gradual drift of a man like Roebuck towards Conservatism shows that even among Radicals the Tories might

[37] See R. T. Shannon, op. cit., pp. 171ff.
[38] Harrowby Papers, LV/136, Memorandum for the Cabinet on the Proposed Education Legislation by Lord Sandon. Also Sir T. Wemyss Reid, *Life of W. E. Forster* (1888).
[39] See G. C. Thompson, *Public Opinion and Lord Beaconsfield;* S. Maccoby, *English Radicalism 1853–1886* (1938), Chapters XIV and XV.

make converts and this movement might well in time extend to middle-class dissenters.[40] In any case the questions which had most strongly influenced the political attitude of dissenters moved somewhat into the background in the later 1870s. The religious currents became less important than the social and economic ones in determining party allegiance.

The task of leadership in the Conservative party of the decade 1870 to 1880 had much in common with the problems of leading the party in more recent times. Even today the party has its zealous adherents and active workers whose opinions differ widely from those of the great mass of politically semi-conscious voters, whose support has to be canvassed for winning elections. The leaders have to take account of both groups; in appealing to the second, the mass electorate, they have frequently to display a political agility which their more ardent or extreme followers find difficult to understand or to accept. In the 1870s the country gentlemen were the largest group of party activists. They also controlled the county electorates, partly through influence, partly through the sense of common interest that still existed throughout the farming community. The support of the country gentlemen and the landed interest was, however, not sufficient. The leaders had to appeal to the commercial and professional middle classes and to the urban artisans. This courtship met with little understanding and sympathy from their traditional followers. Nevertheless, the Tory leaders of 1870 and 1880 were not unsuccessful in enlarging the electoral base of the party. In so doing they enabled the Conservative party to play its part in the orderly transition towards full political democracy.

[40] See R. E. Leader, *Life and Letters of J. A. Roebuck* (1897), pp. 309 ff. W. H. Smith was a Methodist by birth; Sir Robert Fowler, Tory M.P. for the City of London from 1880 to 1891, had been a Quaker before his conversion to the Church of England.

PART TWO

THE PARTY ORGANIZATION

V

THE CENTRAL PARTY ORGANIZATION
1867–74

IT is a frequently made historical generalization that the Reform Bill of 1867 entailed important changes in the party system, and that these changes were mainly due to the growth of party organization. It is the purpose of this chapter to examine in detail the story of the Tory party organization in the years after 1867. The broad picture is well known; the foundation of the National Union of Conservative and Constitutional Associations in 1867 and of a central party office in 1870 are the two salient developments. These, paralleled as they were on the Liberal side, are generally thought to have been an important factor in the growth of a clear-cut two-party system, based on strict parliamentary discipline. A closer view tends to blur the clear definition of this picture. In its early years, the National Union was not an influential body and additional evidence from private papers of the period confirms this view. Under closer scrutiny the Conservative Central Office also looks less of an advance on the type of organization existing in the 1850s and 1860s. The period between 1867 and 1885 represents a transitional phase in electoral conditions and methods: in many constituencies, local issues still predominated, and influence and sometimes corruption were still prevalent; in the larger constituencies, however, more modern means of electoral organization and propaganda were being introduced.[1] These transitional conditions were one of the main sources of tension inside the parliamentary Conservative party: the gulf between county and borough members, the disagreement between Tory aristocrats and Tory democrats, all spring from this root. The party organization, in daily contact with electoral

---

[1] See Norman Gash, *Politics in the Age of Peel: A Study in the Technique of Parliamentary Representation* (1953), for a comprehensive picture of the politics of the period after the first Reform Act. Also Samuel H. Beer, *Modern British Politics*, pp. 43 ff.

problems, was particularly prone to friction for the same reasons: traditionalists amongst the party managers continued to cling to old methods and ideas, while some of the men in party management had an outlook conditioned by the problems of mass electorates and political democracy. The friction resulting from these differences reacted back on the party as a whole, particularly after 1880 when the Conservatives were once more in opposition. The story of the party organization is an integral part of Conservative politics after 1867 and helps our understanding of it.

In 1868 the central management of the Conservative party was shared between the Whips, the party agency and federal bodies, such as the National Union, which had affiliated associations in the country. The National Union was, however, only one, and by no means the most important, among a number of such federal bodies. The Whips, in their capacity as party managers, dealt with the selection of candidates and with the collection and expenditure of the central party fund. In most of these matters they were aided by the party agent, on whom fell the bulk of the daily work of party management. The development of the party agency, its relations with the party leaders and Whips an the one hand, and with the constituencies on the other, is therefore one major strand in the story. The other major issue of interest concerns the place which the federal bodies, chiefly the National Union, assumed in the general scheme of party management. By the 1860s the Conservative clubs in London, the Carlton and the Junior Carlton, were no longer playing an important role in the party organization.

Until 1870 the central agency of the party was in the hands of Markham Spofforth, a member of the London firm of solicitors Baxter, Rose, Norton & Co. Spofforth had begun his connection with Conservative party management in 1853 as assistant to Sir Philip Rose. Rose was a partner in Baxter & Co. and besides acting as party agent, was also Disraeli's lawyer, confidential agent, and eventually one of his executors. At the time of the General Election of 1859 Spofforth succeeded him as principal agent.[2] Spofforth's virtues and failings as a party organizer were summed up by Disraeli when he wrote; 'Mr. Spofforth served

[2] Robert Blake, *Disraeli*, p. 352.

us for years, and years of adversity—if not always with perfect judgement, with great talent, honour and devotion. He was not well used by us, but he has never murmured.'[3] The remaining traces of his activites give the impression of a faithful, industrious, and active party worker, who was sometimes led astray by his enthusiasm and lack of shrewdness. In a medium which demanded exceptional tact and judgement Spofforth was a heavy-handed practitioner. Nonetheless, the position he occupied in party management outside Parliament was at least as important as that of the Whips, and he had direct access to the party leaders. On occasions he played a role, if a minor one, in the political game at a level much higher than the world of Tadpoles and Tapers that was party organization. Thus he took part in Conservative contacts with the Adullamites during the Reform Bill crisis of 1866.[4] His tasks and methods were not essentially different from those of Bonham who had been party agent in the days of Peel.[5]

The ordinary routine of Spofforth's work can best be seen in the evidence he gave at the trial of election petitions and at enquiries into corrupt practices. Before the Bridgwater Commission he explained, though perhaps not with complete frankness, the part he played in the selection of candidates.[6] When leading party supporters in the constituency were looking for a candidate and were unable to find one locally, he put them in touch with men who had their names down as candidates at the Carlton or for whom the party was anxious to find a seat. Spofforth denied before the Commission that he kept a noted-up register about the character of the constituencies, and said 'when an election is likely to take place I write down to

[3] Cairns Papers, Disraeli to Cairns, 13 Jan. 1875.
[4] Maurice Cowling, 'Disraeli, Derby and Fusion, October 1865 to July 1866', *Historical Journal*, VIII, 1 (1965), p. 52. See also F. B. Smith, *The Making of the Second Reform Bill* (1966), p. 215, for an example of Spofforth's activities during the Reform Bill debates.
[5] N. Gash, 'F. R. Bonham: Conservative "Political Secretary", 1832–47', *English Historical Review*, Vol. LXIII (1948), p. 502.
[6] *Report on the Existence of Corrupt Practices at Bridgwater. Parliamentary Papers*, 1870, (10, 11, and 12), vol. XXX, p. 802. See also Spofforth's evidence at the Totnes enquiry, *Parliamentary Papers*, 1867 (3776), Vol. XXIX, p. 979, where mention is made of a lithographed letter from Colonel Taylor, the Chief Whip, to all Conservative agents, referring them to Spofforth for information. For a reference to Spofforth's earlier activities as election agent, see A. E. Gathorne Hardy (ed.), *Gathorne Hardy, A Memoir*, i. 99.

the leading Solicitor or agent, or leading Conservative of the place, to ask whether there is a good chance, and he replies to that, but I keep no register'. Where it was decided that a candidate should be supported from the central party fund Spofforth would normally be, as he reluctantly admitted, responsible for giving this support. The party fund itself was, however, ultimately under the control of the Whips, headed by Colonel Taylor, the Chief Whip; Lord Nevill, who became the fifth Earl of Abergavenny, played an important part in the collection and management of it.[7] Although Spofforth worked under the supervision of the Whips he was also in a position to correspond and consult directly with the party leader:

> I want much to see you about Dockyard patronage. If we cannot induce a change in the present mode—we shall not return one Conservative for a Royal Dockyard Borough at the General Election. The Comptroller Chief Constructor and all their subordinates are virulent antagonists and their present masters banded together prevent anyone of Conservative politics being promoted and the system of competitive examination enables them to monopolise for their protégés the whole patronage.[8]

During the 1868 Election, Spofforth was assisted by an *ad hoc* committee of Whips and others, chiefly Taylor, Gerard Noel, Abergavenny, and Montagu Corry. The committee's work consisted in helping the constituencies to find candidates and giving financial support where necessary. Constituencies were kept under constant review. In some cases the committee might attempt to stimulate local effort in order to prevent a seat from remaining uncontested; more rarely they might try, in the interests of general party tactics, to prevent a contest. The ability of the central committee to achieve results in the constituencies was limited. It could only work by persuasion, had few means of bringing pressure to bear, and its interference might merely cause friction. Such authority as the party managers in London enjoyed in their dealings with the constituencies was due to the fact that they were known to be acting on

---

[7] According to Lady Dorothy Nevill, Lord Abergavenny was known as the 'Tory Bloodhound'. She quotes a letter from Disraeli to Spofforth highly praising Abergavenny. See Ralph Nevill (ed.), *The Reminiscences of Lady Dorothy Nevill* (1906), p. 70.

[8] Hughenden Papers, B/XXI/Spofforth, to Disraeli, 24 Oct. 1866.

behalf of the leaders of the party. This authority was slightly reinforced by the lure of honours and preferment. The complexity of local influencies in many constituencies made the exercise of any initiative by the centre a matter of great delicacy. The information at the disposal of the committee seems to have lacked precision, as the following report from Corry indicates:

Though we have not been idle I have no general result to report to you of our meeting to-day at Victoria Street. Our time was chiefly spent in 'posting up' Taylor in what has passed. As much depends on the impressions conveyed to his mind, I felt it very important that I should remain, to check—and occasionally contradict—the Spofforthian version of past transactions. . . . Thursday is to be our great day, when Noel and Nevill will join us. I shall attempt after that to give some idea of our general prospects; all I can say at present is that *we* have increasing hopes in the new electors: that *I* have every hope in your address.[9]

Gladstone's main challenge to the Government in the 1868 Election was the proposal to disestablish the Irish Church, and the activities of Spofforth were much concerned with the mobilization of a religious front on this issue. In April 1868 Spofforth played a part in the formation of a Central Board for the defence of the Irish Church. Various organizations devoted to the support of Protestantism and the Church of England, such as the Church Institution and a number of Protestant Defence Associations, were represented on this Board. The Wesleyans had been traditionally attached to the Conservative party, but these links had grown perceptibly weaker over the last decade.[10] Spofforth was convinced that the emphasis which Tory propagandists were laying on the defence of Protestantism in the 1868 election would make most Wesleyans support the Conservative cause.[11] This view was shared by some other competent observers, such as Graves, the member for Liverpool.[12] The Wesleyan Conference, however, remained officially neutral, and the majority of Wesleyans probably supported the Liberals. Spofforth sent the following estimate of the line-up of religious groups for the election to Disraeli:

[9] Ibid., B/XX/Co., Corry to Disraeli, 22 Sept. 1868.
[10] H. J. Hanham, *Elections and Party Management*, p. 212; John Vincent, *The Formation of the Liberal Party 1857–1868*, p. xxii.
[11] Hughenden Papers, B/XXI/Spofforth, to Disraeli, 8 and 9 April 1868.
[12] Ibid., B/XX/Co., Graves to Corry, 7 Nov. 1868.

1. As to Dr. Pusey and the Tractarians—it is only a small and extreme section of the Ritualists who are desirous of separating themselves from the establishment. They represent no material influence or voting power.
2. The High Churchmen and the Guardians. I cannot say anything as to the Guardians but will answer for the High Churchmen generally being in favour of Church and State—I don't hear of any even small section of High Churchmen going with Mr. Gladstone.
3. The Jowetts and Kingsleys are not numerous enough to be called a class. The Broad Church are generally with you.
4. The majority of Dissenters.
5. The Whigs and Peelites.
6. Mr. Bright and the advanced Liberals.
7. Mr. Beales and the Reform League are of course with Mr. Gladstone but the last may and I think will be a source of weakness in dividing the constituences—they have been useful and will be again.[13]

Spofforth was responsible for the organization of a great Church meeting of protest which was held at St. James's Hall in May 1868. Churchmen of all shades of opinion came together for this meeting, and it was hoped to counter the enthusiasm generated in the Gladstonian camp by the disestablishment policy. From the first, Shaftesbury was critical of the arrangements for this meeting and considered that insufficient attention had been paid to arousing the interest of the laity; afterwards he emphasized to Disraeli that it had been a failure as far as its effect on public opinion was concerned, for the country could no longer be 'be-bishoped and be-duked'. Spofforth was, as usual, optimistic and claimed success.[14] His over-sanguine reports on this and other occasions may have unduly raised Disraeli's hopes for the election.

Another sphere in which Spofforth and his office developed considerable activity was the dispensation of ecclesiastical patronage. During Disraeli's nine months' premiership, the number of important Church appointments which fell vacant was exceptionally large. It included Canterbury, London, and Peterborough, as well as many deaneries and canonries. The disposal of this patronage was of electoral significance, and

[13] Ibid., B/XXI/Spofforth, no date. 'The Guardians' refers to the reader of the Church paper, *The Guardian*, an organ of the High Church clergy.
[14] Buckle, ii. 366.

Disraeli was determined to use his opportunities to the fullest advantage. His knowledge of ecclesiastical personalities and prominent preachers was, however, not sufficiently intimate to enable him to act without advice.[15] For this he turned frequently to Spofforth and his helpers. Disraeli's strongest bid for the support of the Evangelicals in the Church of England was made with the appointment of Canon McNeile to the Deanery of Ripon in August 1868. Amongst Disraeli's papers there is a list of possible candidates classified under two headings; "clergy commanding the esteem of the church—suited to the office of dean—and who would be of essential use to the Conservative party' and 'clergy held in high esteem in the Church whose appointment would give satisfaction to the Evangelical party, but who, though Conservatives, have no special political talent.' Canon McNeile's name appears as the most prominent of these listed under the first heading. The information was supplied from Spofforth's office at 6 Victoria Street.[16]

The central party machinery, as it existed in 1868, was thus unsystematic and loosely organized. There was Spofforth, and his assistants, working from 6 Victoria Street; there was Abergavenny, and his committee, supervising the election; and last, but not least, Colonel Taylor and the other Whips were also closely involved. The activity of the party managers consisted partly in watching and guiding local effort in the constituencies; partly in conducting the national campaign by mobilising pressure groups; partly in serving as the eyes and ears of the leaders. The National Union, whose foundation and history are traced below, was merely one of the many bodies issuing literature and propaganda; it was a federation of local Conservative associations on paper rather than in reality.

Spofforth's tenure of office as party agent ended in March 1870. He had frequently come in for criticism. In June 1868, for example, Ward Hunt, the Chancellor of the Exchequer, threatened to resign unless Colonel Taylor was dismissed from the post of Chief Whip, and blame was put on Spofforth for exacerbating friction between the two men.[17] The 1868 Election

[15] R. Blake, op. cit., p. 507.
[16] Hughenden Papers, C/III/A, J. S. Baxter to Corry, 19 Aug. 1868.
[17] Ibid., B/XX/Hu. The election committee of 1868 may have been set up to take matters out of Spofforth's hands, cf. Buckle, ii. 414. For a further complaint about Spofforth, see Buckle, ii. 278.

Committee had felt that Spofforth could not be left to act without close supervision. The immediate reason for his resignation in March 1870 was the election of the Hon. E. W. Douglas as Secretary of the Junior Carlton Club. Spofforth and the party managers had attempted to secure the election of Major the Hon. C. K. Keith-Falconer, who, as secretary of the Central Conservative Registration Association and of the Middlesex Registration Association, also had his offices in Victoria Street. The feeling in the Club, as conveyed to Disraeli, was that this was a 'Victoria Street job' and that Spofforth had acted very injudiciously. He became increasingly unpopular with many members. On the other hand the party managers and Whips regarded the election of Douglas as a slight, and Abergavenny, Lord Colville, Noel, and others resigned from the Junior Carlton. For a moment there was the danger of a serious split between the two Clubs, and the Junior Club wrote a letter of regret to Abergavenny assuring him that there was no personal feeling against him or the Whips.[18] The quarrel was patched up, but the end of Spofforth's activities as party agent seems to have been connected with this incident. Spofforth had also been so frequently associated with corrupt practices that it may have been considered useful to get a new man. Whether his resignation was offered or exacted is not clear, but by the beginning of April 1870 Noel was looking for his successor and mentioning Gorst as a possibility.[19]

Spofforth was not given any immediate reward and since the party was out of office this was perhaps hardly to be expected. His relations with Disraeli continued to be friendly, and he occasionally wrote to him on election matters and party affairs. In January 1875 Disraeli used his personal influence to get Cairns to appoint Spofforth a Taxing Master in Chancery. Cairns was advised that these appointments should be made on a salary scale rising from £1,500 p.a.[20] For the moment, however, no appointment was made and in March 1875 Spofforth

[18] Hughenden Papers, B/XXI/W.P. Talbot, to Disraeli, 18 Mar. 1870.
[19] Ibid., B/XXI/Noel, to Disraeli, 2 Apr. 1870. According to another account, which seems not very credible, Spofforth resigned after the election of 1868 and there was no incumbent of the post of party agent until Gorst took over in 1870 (see T. H. S. Escott, *Randolph Spencer-Churchill, as a Portrait of his Age*, p. 185).
[20] Cairns Papers, Cairns to Disraeli, 13 and 14 Jan. 1875.

put himself forward for the post of Clerk of the Parliament, which had just been turned down by Corry.[21] In November 1877, by which time the Government had been nearly four years in office, Spofforth was at last made a Taxing Master. In spite of the delay he seems to have been quite satisfied and thanked Disraeli through Corry for his good offices. He continued to be in contact with circles connected with the management of the Conservative party and was sometimes consulted, but he was clearly a man without any political ambitions of his own.[22]

The resignation of Spofforth also ended the official association between the party and the firm of Baxter, Rose, Norton & Cc. The time had gone when participation in party management could be profitable to a firm of solicitors in London. Up to 1868 election petitions had been tried before committees of the House of Commons and had thus provided a substantial income for a London firm appearing in such cases. After 1868 election petitions were tried locally before a specially appointed judge and could no longer be dealt with from London.[23]

Gorst became Spofforth's successor, but it is clear, not least from the considerable difference in personality and standing of the two men, that it was intended to introduce new methods into the business of party management. John F. Gorst was a thirty-five year old lawyer who had sat in the House of Commons for Cambridge from 1866 to 1868. He had taken an interest in party organization and was in the chair at the inaugural meeting of the National Union in November 1867. He had frequently declared himself a convinced believer in the political principles of Disraeli and in the Tory working man. He had political ambitions, but his defeat at Cambridge in the 1868 election had interrupted his parliamentary career. There can be no doubt that he saw a chance of advancement in the post of principal party agent, though this does not mean that he was

[21] Hughenden Papers, B/XXI/Spofforth, Spofforth to Taylor, 12 Mar. 1875.
[22] Ibid., B/XIV/B., Spofforth to Corry, 28 Nov. 1877. There are occasional references to political activities by Spofforth in the 1880s; cf. T. H. S. Escott, *Randolph Spencer-Churchill*, pp. 128, 184, where he is mentioned as an intermediary between Beaconsfield, Northcote, and Lord Randolph Churchill.
[23] H. J. Hanham, op. cit., p. 274.

given any definite promises. Noel made it clear to Gorst that his acceptance of the appointment would mean giving up the idea of returning to the House of Commons for the time being.[24] Gorst must have thought, therefore, that the terms on which the job was offered him not merely held out hopes of eventual political promotion, but probably better prospects than a seat in the House. The real change, therefore, from the Spofforth régime, consisted not so much in any formal alteration of duties and arrangements, as in the fact that an ambitious young politician was now willing to accept the job of party agent. To some extent the change was simply a reflection of the general political circumstances: to convert the recently enfranchised electors required more systematic organization, and without many such conversions the Conservative party could not return to office. Noel, in commending Gorst to Disraeli for the appointment, spoke of him as a gentleman, with an excellent manner, a legal education and great energy, but he still regarded the post as relatively subordinate, for in case of Gorst's refusal he suggested Carnarvon's private secretary as an alternative.[25] The expectation of Disraeli and others probably was that the affairs of the party would now be run much more methodically and professionally, and by someone who understood the problems posed by the new borough electorate. Gorst established offices at 53 Parliament Street and for the next few years he operated from there in his capacity as party agent. The term Conservative Central Office or Central Conservative Office does not at this stage seem to have been used.

Gorst's methodical approach to the business of collecting information from the constituencies may be seen from one of his first reports to Disraeli, on Rochester, where a by-election was pending:

> The Conservative Party in Rochester has never polled its strength since 1859. Since the candidate in 1865 and 1868 was not acceptable to the whole party, and many of the leading men gave him merely their votes and did not work for his return: Fox, the candidate of last week, announced himself as an Independent: he was only taken up by the Conservatives on the evening of the nomination day, he had been proposed by a discharged attorney's clerk and seconded

[24] Hughenden Papers, B/XXI/Noel, to Disraeli, 22 Apr. 1870.
[25] Ibid., B/XXI/Noel, to Disraeli, 14 Apr. 1870.

by a common labourer; there was no time to bring the strength of the party to bear in his favour. The register has not been attended to for years, no Conservative agent appears at the revision court. The Mayor, the entire town council, the overseers, assistant overseers, and rate collectors are all radicals; both register and burgess-roll are no doubt affected by this circumstance. The chief employers of labour are of the same party—Foord, a large government contractor; Aveling and Porter agricultural engineers; Nayler a builder. The Radicals have an influential supporter in Levy, a man who lends money and has much house property. There are no Conservatives large employers of labour. Mr. Nicholson (a retired Banker), Mr. Manclark and other of the gentry who take interest in the county elections take little in the borough elections. Mr. Essell (the Chapter Clerk) who did use great influence is now agent to the Admiralty and private solicitor to Mr. Foord, and so remains quiet. The Chapter has been 'antediluvian' and exercised no influence at all. Mr. C. S. Fox seems to have made great way with the people during the few days he was before them. No charge was made against him at the election except that of having been a Liberal. The Conservatives propose to take him up and with his help to have the registration attended to at once. An association of working men is about to be formed to advocate what is called 'Reciprocity'. It is hoped by this means to get a hold upon the lower class of voters. The ballot is looked forward to rather as an advantage than otherwise. With a fairly prepared burgess-roll it is thought that by the help of the women voters who are Conservative a change could be effected in the Town Council. Mr. C. S. Fox has publicly announced his intention of sticking to Rochester till he wins the seat, but as I have not the pleasure of his acquaintance I cannot pronounce any opinion as to his qualities of perseverance.[26]

Gorst supplied much factual information of this kind and gave sound advice to the party leaders on many problems and situations in the years to come. If anything he was too clear-sighted for the taste of many of those with whom he had to work and he was frequently tactless. This caused much of the friction which later centred round him.

The first major organizational enterprise which Gorst helped to launch was Disraeli's visit to Lancashire in April 1872.[27] This demonstration was an important step in the re-establishment of Disraeli's position as party leader. The lengthy negoti-

[26] Ibid., B/XXI/Gorst, to Disraeli, 25 July 1870.
[27] See also above, pp. 8ff.

ations required to prepare it showed up deep rifts amongst Lancashire Conservatives, symptomatic of the general disunity in the party at the time. It took several years before the various sections of Conservatism in the County Palatine were sufficiently united to convey an acceptable request to Disraeli that he should honour a popular demonstration in Manchester with his presence. Gorst was from the beginning very eager that such a demonstration should take place. If successful, it would strongly counteract the opposition to Disraeli's leadership and confirm his hold on the popular imagination. Gorst was naturally a personal follower of Disraeli, and his own position was bound up with the fortunes of his leader. He was also a fervent adherent of the policy of building the future of the Tory party on the loyalty of the working masses, and he took this to be Disraeli's personal policy. The practical consequences of this policy were, as we have seen, greatly disliked by many Conservatives in Lancashire and elsewhere. A successful popular rally would furnish striking proof of the power of popular Toryism and its appeal to the working classes. It would, moreover, demonstrate the importance of party organization among the masses in the large towns, in which Gorst was particularly interested. He had thus every inducement to forward the enterprise, yet here, as in other matters, the Central Office could only wait for local initiative, and for opinion in Lancashire to mature.

In a lengthy letter forwarded to Disraeli by Gerard Noel in September 1870, Gorst set out the arguments in favour of a visit; he wrote what might be regarded as the motto for all his work as party agent, 'We are generally strong in counties and weak in boroughs, and we shall never attain stable political power till the boroughs are conquered. The only boroughs where we are really the stronger party are the Lancashire boroughs.'[28] Gorst went on to say that the Lancashire operatives were 'genuine *bona fide* Conservatives', though he admitted that special causes might have been at work there in the 1868 Election. He considered that the employees in large staple trades like cotton and shipbuilding were the most likely recruits to the ranks of Conservative working men; he admitted that the artisans and craftsmen in the small consumer trades producing for the well-to-do classes were more likely to be dissenters and

[28] Hughenden Papers, B/XXI/Noel, Gorst to Noel, 22 Sept. 1870.

radicals. Gorst felt sure that Disraeli would receive a great reception in Lancashire and that this might help the Conservative swing in the West Riding for which he was hoping.

Unfortunately the disunity of the different factions in Lancashire soon became evident: the Conservative working men of Manchester were by no means of the same mind as the county Tories outside the big cities. Even so Gorst remained optimistic that something could be arranged. On 19 November 1870 he wrote to Disraeli that the operatives were most enthusiastic about the visit and had wanted to move without their leaders; Algernon Egerton, member for South-East Lancashire, had now put himself at the head of the movement and he (Gorst) offered his services for the visit.[29] On 22 December he wrote again to Disraeli that there was a strong desire in Lancashire for a visit, but admitted that there had been a tepid response in rural South-West Lancashire, where Lord Derby, amongst others, had much property. Disraeli himself was only too well aware of the divisions in the party, and the antagonism which he personally inspired in some quarters, and apparently tried to check Gorst's enthusiasm. The latter, however, still thought that the difficulties had now been removed and that the working classes in the boroughs strongly desired a meeting at Blackburn or Preston and would there thank Disraeli for their enfranchisement.[30]

Gorst's optimism was decidedly premature and it was another year before preparations for the projected visit could definitely be put in hand. In making the actual arrangements, Gorst played an essential part and showed the efficiency and usefulness of the organization he had created. On 8 December 1871 Gorst, just back from Manchester, reported that there was still great support for the proposed visit. On the other hand the delicacy of Disraeli's position as leader of the party was appreciated and they were prepared to wait patiently.[31] On 24 January 1872 the *Bolton Chronicle* reported that a meeting of the Disraeli Reception Committee was to be held, at which a statement would be read that Disraeli would visit the county in Easter week and would deliver public addresses at Manchester,

[29] Ibid., B/XXI/Gorst/235.   [30] Ibid., B/XXI/Gorst/236.
[31] Ibid., B/XXI/Gorst/239.

Liverpool, and Preston.[32] By the end of January, Gorst was again in Manchester working on the arrangements. Disraeli was very anxious to address only one meeting and to have it made clear that his visit was to the county as a whole. Gorst, before leaving for Manchester, assured him that in all the letters he had written on the subject he had always stated that the visit was to the county generally and that no meetings would be addressed but such as were decided on by the entire county. He was going to do his best to persuade them to have one meeting only, but thought that, if a special meeting for the working classes became inevitable, this should also be held in Manchester.

Soon after he arrived in the city Gorst found, after consultation with Egerton and Birley, that it was impossible to hold only one meeting and that the Free Trade Hall, holding 7,000 people, was not really large enough even if those from the north of the county had been willing to go there. The Corn Exchange at Preston, which held 8,000, was suggested for a second meeting. After further consultation in Oldham with Colonel Wilson Patten and T. W. Mellor,[33] Gorst learnt that the jealousies of North and North-East Lancashire made Preston impossible. There now emerged another proposal to overcome local and sectional conflicts: a meeting in the Free Trade Hall, supplemented by a monster demonstration in the Pomona Gardens at Manchester, at which deputations from all over Lancashire would present illuminated addresses ('which these people are greatly addicted to' wrote Gorst). Even in those days the railway companies were prepared to run special trains for such an occasion, and some thirty to forty thousand people could be accommodated in the Gardens. Arrangements now went ahead for a visit in the week after Easter, with a meeting in the Free Trade Hall on Wednesday, 3 April 1872, as the climax, preceded by a demonstration on the previous day. In putting the finishing touches to the programme, Gorst was joined by Corry and by W. R. Callender, the influential Manchester Tory, with whom Disraeli stayed during his visit. The Conservative leader

[32] Ibid., A/IV/N/58–96. References to the Lancashire visit are to this bundle, unless otherwise stated.

[33] Wilson Patten and Mellor were the members for Lancashire (North) and Ashton-under-Lyne respectively. See above, Chapter I, on further reasons for the obstacles to Disraeli's visit.

must have felt himself that the whole project was very much Gorst's doing; on the back of a hostile letter telling him not to come, Disraeli scribbled 'This is not agreeable, what will Gorst say?'

The methodical way in which the Central Office collected information can again be seen from the notes, in Gorst's own handwriting, supplied to Disraeli to enable him to reply to the addresses from Conservative associations at the big rally in the Pomona Gardens.

The following are samples:

N.E. Lancashire and Blackburn.
In Blackburn about half the employers of labour are Conservative. The town smarts under Gladstone's calumny that the election of 1868 was won by intimidation. Wiles J. who tried the petition reported no extensive intimidation and none by employers (all that was proved was by fellow workmen) and he made the petitioners though successful pay their own costs. Gladstone notwithstanding repeats his assertion every session. The Hornby family is exceedingly popular. They are an old Lancashire family but have been cotton spinners for forty or fifty years.

South East Lancashire.
South East Lancashire is a continuous town—chiefly engaged in cotton manufacture, but there is also worsted in the East and coal mining and iron manufacture scattered about.
The employers of labour are generally Radical with an increasing number of exceptions. The sons usually inclining to Conservatism. The strength of our party is amongst the employed as the results of the election of 1868 show.
The South East Lancashire Conservatives are in favour of the ballot which would strengthen our position.

Oldham.
Cobbett sat for Oldham for the Reform Bill till his death (1835). His son J. M. Cobbett (once a Radical) is now the Conservative candidate.
The Conservatives were beaten by a majority of 6 only in '68 and will win both seats at the next vacancy.
Employers with one or two exceptions radical. The borough is organised by the workmen themselves, who have about 20 most admirable ward associations. Almost every man on the register is canvassed and his politics known. Ballot desired. Men very strong for 10 hrs: bill.

Gorst's part in arranging the Lancashire visit shows both the technical efficiency of the organization he had created, and his personal energy and political knowledge. On the other hand the limitations of central initiative are very evident in this case; and it can be seen that Gorst and his activities were very much bound up with a concept of Toryism which did not by any means command universal approval in the party.

Gorst, Keith-Falconer, and others regarded contact with the press as part of their work. In 1871 a business called *The Central Press Board* had been purchased, which was in effect a Conservative news agency for provincial newspapers.[34] Gorst and Keith-Falconer acted for a time as editors. At the suggestion of Noel, Gorst also entered into a connection with the *Standard*, the London Conservative paper. He acted as their political representative and supplied them with authoritative views on Conservative policy and was sometimes referred to as the 'political manager of the Standard'.[35] This soon became a cause of friction between Gorst and the party leaders and Whips. During the ministerial crisis of March 1873, Gorst thought he was voicing the general sentiment of the party in giving the editors of the *Standard* the impression that the Conservatives were ready and eager for office. He was taken by surprise when Disraeli refused the Queen's commission and angry that he had been kept in ignorance of the real intentions of the party leaders.[36] The line taken by the *Standard* during the crisis was broadly in favour of taking office, on condition that a dissolution of Parliament could speedily follow.[37] A leading article on 18 March when it had become clear that Gladstone would remain in office, showed considerable perplexity and irritation, and spoke of a great chance thrown away. This attitude in a newspaper usually so loyal was probably due to the information supplied by Gorst, who had found himself excluded from inside knowledge of the party leaders' intentions. This episode may have helped Gorst to see that the position of party agent was not as influential as he had hoped, and may have started his search for other avenues of advancement.[38]

---

[34] Hughenden Papers, B/XXI/Keith-Falconer; for the growing importance of the provincial press, see John Vincent, op. cit., pp. 58–65.
[35] Cross Papers, Add. MS.51266, Derby to Cross, 21 Mar. 1873.
[36] R. Blake, op. cit., p. 528.   [37] *Standard*, 13–19 Mar. 1873.
[38] Hughenden Papers, B/XXI/Gorst, to Corry, 17 Mar. 1873.

By the time of the 1874 Election, Gorst and his assistants had built up an efficient central party organization. The aim had been, according to Disraeli's own instructions, to have a candidate ready in every constituency offering any hope of success. As Gorst wrote at the time of his resignation in 1877, the natural leaders in each borough had been found and contacted, their active co-operation secured, and the responsibility placed upon them of selecting their own candidates and building up their own organization. Help was given when needed, yet there was no interference with local effort. Gorst's chief assistant in the work had been Keith-Falconer; on the Whips' side they were helped by Noel and later by Taylor. Disraeli, advised in this matter by Cairns, kept a close watch on the work. A report was sent to him after each borough election, prepared by a Central Office expert or a travelling agent.[39] Even Derby was aware that Gorst occupied a key position for collecting political information.[40] There is no trace of any clear-cut division of functions having been arranged between the Whips and the party agent, as was the case in 1880. The expenditure of money from the party funds was probably the preserve of the Whips, but Gorst took a large share in the selection of candidates in so far as this could be done from the centre. The only familiar name that seems to have been somewhat out of the picture during the years 1870 to 1874 was that of Abergavenny, and it is not unlikely that he was the chief of those hostile influences to which Gorst made such frequent reference later on. The scope of the Central Office was greatest in the larger boroughs; in the smaller boroughs still dominated by influence, there was little room for initiative from the centre, while for county seats Disraeli had, in 1873, created a separate Committee, composed of gentlemen of high political and social standing. In February 1873 Gorst reported to Disraeli that in the previous year 69 new Conservative associations had been formed and that 420 associations were in existence, the majority of them in good working order.[41]

By-election successes increased after 1872; the only failure was Bath, and many attributed it to the extravagant language

---

[39] Buckle, ii. 525 (to Lady Chesterfield).
[40] Cross Papers, Add. MS.51266, Derby to Cross, 21 Mar. 1873.
[41] Hughenden Papers, B/XXI/Gorst, to Disraeli, 12 Feb. 1873.

of Disraeli's Bath Election Letter. This letter was in itself something of an innovation, for there was as yet no regular system of
endorsement of candidatures by the party leaders; only very
occasionally a letter, which could be published in a local newspaper, might be sent from the leader to an influential elector.
Many regarded the tone of Disraeli's letter to Lord Grey de
Wilton as mistaken, but Keith-Falconer reassured the Chief on
this point. He attributed the failure to capture the seat to the
treachery of a section of local Conservatives, 'who availed
themselves of the ballot to desert their party without fear of
detection.'[42] Perhaps the best testimony of the vigour of Conservative organization on the eve of the 1874 Election is a list
of Conservative agents in England, Wales, and Scotland which
contains in its 186 pages a wealth of information on local
Conservative associations, clubs, registration societies, and their
secretaries. Some of the organizations listed had only a shadowy
existence and, notwithstanding Gorst's optimistic reports, there
were many gaps. Of the forty-nine boroughs with a population
of more than 50,000, thirty-three had a Conservative association,
in name at any rate; eight had only registration associations,
three were controlled by Conservative clubs, another three had
only a solicitor acting as agent, and two had no organization
at all.[43] Yet the list shows that the centre must have been
assiduous in making local contacts and there must have been
many instances where local organization was due to central
initiative. Developments since the days of Spofforth had been
swift: even so Gorst was hardly over-optimistic when the
dissolution of 1874 was announced; his estimate gave the
Conservatives a majority of only three.

The Conservative Central Office was one of the major new
features in party organization that became permanently established in the period after the Second Reform Bill. Another
was the National Union of Conservative and Constitutional
Associations. Its early history is an example of the survival of
the fittest; it emerged from a host of other similar organizations
and several times it was nearly moribund. In the month before
the Second Reform Bill was finally passed, many Conservative
and Constitutional Working Men's Associations had been

---

[42] Ibid., B/XXI/Keith-Falconer, to Disraeli, 13 Oct. 1873.
[43] Hanham, op. cit., p. 115.

founded.[44] Lord Nevill was active in the promotion of these associations. His name has already been mentioned in connection with the management of the 1868 Election; he came nearest to being the *eminence grise* of the party, and his influence was probably due to the fact that, without being a Whip, he was the only *grand seigneur* who took an interest in party management, which was otherwise the preserve of wire pullers, professional men and middle-class politicians. Helping him was a rising young politican, Henry Cecil Raikes, who in background and outlook was not dissimilar from Gorst.[45] Either Nevill or Raikes, or both, conceived the idea of organizing the growing movement of Conservative and Constitutional associations into a national body. An existing organization, the Conservative Union, was to be used as a basis. One of the earliest reports of a central gathering of Conservative Working Men's Associations appeared in the *Standard* on 30 April 1867: twenty-one local and metropolitan associations had met in London. The idea of forming a national body aroused a certain amount of opposition from some of the larger existing associations, which did not want their independence reduced; thus the Manchester association was at first hostile, and the Metropolitan Conservative Alliance, which had extensive connections in the country, remained a serious rival. From the beginning there was emphasis on getting support in the big industrial boroughs. Eventually the support of the party leaders was sought:

(T. E. Taylor to Disraeli, 8 September 1867)
I hope next week to tell you that our organisation of 'Working Men's Constitutional Associations' is established. I issued a circular a few days after the Prorogation and the answers are very generally satisfactory. Colville has not yet applied to the Peers, but will do so immediately and I have advanced for present purposes money sufficient to carry on with and propose to place its expenditure at the joint discretion of Nevill and Gerard Noel.[46]

(Sir James Ferguson to M. Corry, 24 October 1867)
Mr. Leonard Sedgwick, a Yorkshire gentleman, has undertaken at Lord Nevill's desire to organise the various working men's Con-

[44] R. T. McKenzie, *British Political Parties* (1955), pp. 150 ff.
[45] H. St. J. Raikes, *Life and Letters of H. C. Raikes* (1898), 2 vols.
[46] Hughenden Papers, B/XX/T.

servative associations throughout the country—and Mr. Colleton Rennie, son of Sir John Rennie and a barrister, is helping him. They want one or two questions as to the constitution of their union decided, the chief of which at present is whether members of the Government will countenance the scheme—I think it would be well if you saw Mr. Sedgwick.

(H. C. Raikes to M. Corry, 25 October 1867)
My friend Mr. Sedgwick is going to call upon you to-day with a letter from Sir J. Ferguson and wishes to ascertain, (if you can give him any information) what part, if any, members of the Government are likely to take with regard to the proposed Conservative demonstration at the Crystal Palace.
Mr. Sedgwick is acting in the matter for Lord Nevill, and I have had the pleasure of consulting with him on several occasions with reference to this subject.
I am sure Ministers will not fail to recognise the importance of making such a demonstration successful; and I need scarcely add how important an element of success would be supplied by the presence of any, even subordinate member of the Government.[47]

The party leaders were, however, very cautious in their support of the project, in spite of the fact that it had the goodwill of Nevill and Spofforth. Disraeli especially was very reluctant to see the Government in any way committed, and when some of his colleagues allowed their names to appear as Vice-Presidents of the National Union, Spofforth nearly stopped this move. The Crystal Palace demonstration never took place and no member of the Government attended the opening meeting of the National Union in the Freemason's Tavern on 12 November 1867. It had even proved impossible to secure a Peer as chairman and thus Gorst, at this time a young and relatively insignificant M.P., had to take the chair. There were delegates from fifty-five cities and towns. The discussion as this and subsequent conferences was recorded in minute books which are still available at the offices of the National Union.

Discussion at this opening conference was concerned mainly with the objects, the name, and the rules of the new Union. As regards the objects, the emphasis was on the carrying of Conservative principles to the working masses. The question of the

---

[47] Ibid., B/X/B/20a and 20b. See also B/IX/D/32, letters from Nevill, Noel, Sedgwick and Raikes to Corry and Spofforth.

name of the Union provoked an argument whether it was expedient to use the word 'Conservative'; as a compromise it was decided to use the word 'Constitutional' as well. The contention that the word 'Conservative' might scare off the working-class voter has been advanced from time to time in the history of the party.

As for the rules of the Union, it was decided that every association subscribing one guinea or more per annum might, by vote of the committee, be admitted a member of the Union. There was a good deal of discussion on this rule about the position of the large associations in the industrial towns, with many affiliated ward associations. The example of Leeds was mentioned, with fourteen affiliated ward associations. Were they all to be entitled to separate membership? Finally it was decided that a branch must have at least a hundred members in order to join the Union. This debate may be an echo of the difficulties which faced the Union from the beginning in its relations with some of the big borough associations. The Council of the Union was to consist primarily of twenty-four members to be elected annually by the conference from the officers and delegates of subscribing associations. There was also provision for co-opting members.

The election of officers and the Council gave rise to an interesting discussion: some of the delegates were against having any or many working men in prominent positions and emphasized the necessity of having the support of men of influence and prestige. These remarks highlight the dilemma of the National Union, and perhaps of the whole concept of the Tory working man at this juncture: it was desired to attract the support of the masses, yet preserve and accept the supremacy of the upper classes, a feat easier to accomplish in literature than amid the harsh realities of political life.

At the opening conference of 1867 there was finally some discussion of the ways and means by which the Union might be made effective: it was suggested that the Union should hold meetings to supply information; that it should settle disputes, supply speakers and funds, and, if necessary, candidates to associations in Radical boroughs; defend the policy of the Conservative government, increase the influence of the Conservative press, popularize the party through annual meetings.

Of this multitude of suggestions only two, had they become concrete, would have been of major importance in the party constitution: the supply of funds and of candidates. The National Union, in practice, never came near to carrying out these two functions.

During the 1868 Election the National Union was of very minor importance. It figures as one of the organizations represented on Spofforth's central Board.[48] A pamphlet issued by the National Union on its aims and objectives gives the statistical information that while Gladstone's Irish Church resolutions were being debated, the National Union sent out 37,000 letters and circulars from its offices and that 864 petitions, bearing 61,792 signatures, were presented through it. At its annual Conference of 1869 the National Union claimed the credit for the Conservative victories in Lancashire. This was an entirely specious claim, for in so far as these victories were helped by organization they were due to the work of local associations. The 1868 annual conference of the National Union gave a picture of a practically moribund organization, with an attendance of only seven.

The year 1869 saw a new departure in the formation of a General Consultative Committee, which had a string of impressive names on it, and was an obvious attempt to revive the flagging fortunes of the Union.[49] These names included Abergavenny, Taylor, Keith-Falconer, Lord Sandon, Noel, and others. It is interesting to find Lord Henry Scott included in the list, since he was the only member of this committee who was not either a party manager, a Whip, or a borough member, but a county member closely associated with the High Church party. In view of the general cleavage about the policy of the Reform Act of 1867 running through the party at this time, it was, however, difficult to popularize the National Union amongst the general run of Conservatives and not much more was heard of this consultative committee. A similar step was the creation of a new classification of honorary officers of the Union—one patron and not more than ten vice-patrons. By this means it was hoped to associate prominent Conservative statesmen with the work of the Union without involving them, especially when

[48] Hughenden Papers, B/XXI/Spofforth, to Disraeli, 16 Apr. 1868.
[49] *Publications of the National Union*, No. I, 1872.

the party was in office, in any responsibility for the Union's activities and publications. Lord Derby was elected the first patron.

Gorst's appointment as party agent in 1870 increased for the time being the difficulties of the National Union. Gorst also became secretary of the Metropolitan Conservative Alliance, from the beginning a rival of the National Union, and used its connections in the country to make contact with leading Conservative supporters. The complications that arose are described by him in a letter to Raikes on 8 March 1871:

> The difficulty is this: Sedgwick (the secretary of the National Union) and I are both in correspondence with country associations and agents. We sometimes ask simultaneously for the same information, and sometimes give answers on the same subjects not exactly in the same sense. This method of proceeding is not calculated to create confidence on the part of the country associations in the central organisation of the party.[50]

These difficulties were soon overcome by Gorst's appointment as honorary secretary of the National Union in 1871 and by the removal of the headquarters of the National Union to his office in 53 Parliament Street, now definitely referred to as the Central Office. Sedgwick resigned. Thus came about the housing of the two organizations under one roof, which has continued to the present day and only once, in 1884, threatened to be disrupted. Before 1868, the Central Conservative Registration Association was the most important of the organizations in London which were in correspondence with local registration associations, and this body was also housed in close proximity to the party agency in Victoria Street. The arrangement was now repeated with the National Union. The relative decline of the Metropolitan Conservative Alliance and the Central Conservative Registration Association was, no doubt, due to the fact that the older type of local registration association was becoming less important compared with the new type of working man's association, particularly in the boroughs. The Conservative Central Office could do all the work the former two bodies had been doing, while the National Union was much better placed to form the organizational and propaganda front now required. Keith-

[50] Raikes, op. cit.

Falconer, Gorst's chief assistant, who, as has been mentioned, had been secretary of the Central Registration Association, was now also associated with his colleague in the secretaryship of the National Union.

The year 1872 saw an upward turn in the fortunes of the National Union. The Lancashire demonstration showed the importance of the Conservative constituency organizations. The speech which Disraeli delivered at the Crystal Palace in June 1872 was addressed to the National Union, as the body to which Conservative and Constitutional associations throughout the country were affiliated. In fact the co-operation between the National Union and the Central Office became so close that their identities, with Gorst in the lead on both sides, were virtually merged. The National Union was simply the Central Office in its capacity as a propaganda agency. Thus when Disraeli was anxious, in the autumn of 1873, to drive home the advantage he had gained over Gladstone, he suggested to Gorst that pamphlets should be issued through the National Union.[51] In reply Gorst enclosed two pamphlets already issued, one on Gladstone's administration from 1869 to 1872[52] and another on 'The Wasted Session of 1873'.[53] He promised to have another paper prepared, if Disraeli wished it, along the lines of 'The Wasted Session', to be ready as soon as a dissolution was announced. The National Union was thus being used by the party leader as his mouthpiece. This to some extent fitted in with the conception some of the leaders of the National Union had of their organization, and which had made them place their headquarters under one roof with the Central Office.[54]

On the other hand the National Union was hardly functioning yet as a channel of communication from the rank and file to the leaders. This function had been envisaged by Lord George Hamilton at the 1872 conference when he spoke of the circulation of opinion between the country associations and the leaders of the party. Raikes had made a similar point when he said at the 1873 conference that without the National Union and the local associations 'the leaders of the party would not

[51] Hughenden Papers, B/XXI/Gorst, to Disraeli, 11 Nov. 1873.
[52] *National Union Publications*, No. XVII.
[53] *National Union Publications*, No. XXII.
[54] *National Union Publications*, No. XV.

have had the same or any adequate means of knowing what were the sentiments of their followers'. As far as the National Union was concerned, there was little substance in this claim, for hardly any notice was taken of the occasional bursts of criticism at the annual conferences. The heavy spate of resolutions from constituency associations, which became so wearisome a pre-occupation for the party leaders in the 1880s, were not yet a feature of political life at this stage, except perhaps on occasions such as the Lancashire visit.

An early series of National Union publications, numbered I to XXVII, is available at the British Museum. The earliest publication date is 1872, but some of the pamphlets are reprints of literature in circulation during the 1868 Election. At first the emphasis is strongly on the Tory party's care for and appeal to the working class. Pamphlet No. V, which originally appeared in March 1868, is entitled 'Practical Suggestions to the Loyal Working Men of Great Britain on Points of Policy and Duty at the Present Crisis'. It speaks of the Reform Act of 1867 as having given the industrial working classes their just place in the exercise of political power. The author speaks of the many Conservative statesmen risen from the ranks, and points to Disraeli, the man of ability, recognized by Lord Derby, aristo-crat of aristocrats. Pamphlet No. VI details Conservative legislation for the working classes, up to 1867, making much of Shaftesbury's Factory Acts. Pamphlet No. VII poses the question 'Who are the Real Friends of the Working Class?' Not the stale spouters of sedition, says the author, a member of the committee of the London and Westminster Working Men's Conservative Association; the working classes are dependent on capital and confidence. What must have been one of the earlist publications of the National Union, No. IV, 'The Tory Reform Act', written apparently in December 1867 and in-tended for publication as a magazine article, gives some interest-ing advice on local organization and on the keeping of voters' lists in counties and boroughs. The publications of the National Union from 1873 onward, that is after the removal of its offices to 53 Parliament Street, are less strongly concerned with the working-class voter and take on more the character of general party propaganda. The speeches of Disraeli and other party leaders are reprinted in pamphlet form and the reports of the annual conference are issued. In addition we have brochures on the Alabama Claims, the Irish Education Question, and Gladstone's Foreign Policy, as well as the two pamphlets mentioned by Gorst to Disraeli.

Reviewing the history of the National Union during the first seven years of its existence from 1867 to the Election of 1874, it can be said that it owed its existence to the initiative of the official party managers, principally Abergavenny, as well as to the enthusiasm of several young middle-class Conservative politicians such as Raikes and Gorst. The attitude of the party leaders was from the first lukewarm, while the official party managers soon lost interest. The influence of the Union on the 1868 Election was slight and mainly confined to circulating literature. Various attempts made in the next few years to revive the fortunes of the Union by enlisting the interest of prominent Conservatives all failed. The appointment of Gorst as party agent in 1870 faced the National Union temporarily with a nearly fatal crisis, for Gorst, as secretary of the Metropolitan Conservative Alliance, used that organization for promoting his contacts in the constituencies, thus by-passing or duplicating the work of the National Union. This state of affairs was happily resolved in 1871 by the appointment of Gorst in place of Leonard Sedgwick as the secretary of the Union and the establishment of the Union's offices under the same roof with the Central Office. From this time until the General Election of 1874 the National Union was an integral part of the Central Office organization and was used by the party leaders as a mouthpiece and as an organizational front for popular demonstrations. Never, throughout these first seven years, was there any sign that the National Union had even the remotest influence on party policy, though the claim was beginning to be heard that it should act as a channel of communication between the rank and file and the leaders. The early development of the National Union had little in common with the almost simultaneous rise of the National Liberal Federation. On the Liberal side the organization grew out of a broadly based popular movement against Forster's Education Act, and owed nothing to initiatives from the established parliamentary leaders.

The foundation of the National Union and the Central Office thus represented the two major developments of the period leading up to the electoral victory of 1874 in the field of Conservative party organization; but neither of these two bodies produced for the time being any fundamental change in the structure of the party. Both were concerned mainly with the larger boroughs and the newly enfranchised electors. They largely owed their existence to and were taken seriously by the professional politicians among the leaders, men like Disraeli, Hardy, or Cairns. They were ignored or treated with hostility by the more traditional elements. The appearance of these organizations is symptomatic of a parliamentary, aristocratic party having, somewhat reluctantly, to adapt itself to new electoral conditions and reaching out to organize new support. The contrast with the Liberal party at this period is considerable: The Liberal party was a parliamentary group finding itself under pressure and propelled in new directions by a multitude of extra-parliamentary associations, and in this process party organization was of minor importance.[55] On the Conservative side there were not the movements of the deliberate social and political purpose, such as the Liberation Society, the Reform League or the National Education League, to have an impact on the parliamentary party. Organization, even if many Tories were as yet unaware of it, was a way of creating a popular extension of the party.

[55] J. Vincent, op. cit.

VI

DECAY AND REORGANIZATION
1874–85

ELECTIONS are never won by organization, but the history of party organization is dominated by the rhythm of elections. Up to 1874, Conservative party organization was on the upswing; it was attuned to putting the party into power and the party leaders took it seriously. After the victory of 1874 it deteriorated and, partly as the result of personal bickerings, soon virtually disintegrated. With the advent of the Conservatives to office Gorst's official engagement as party agent ended. He devoted himself for the time being to his legal practice, but was on the look-out for a chance to resume his parliamentary career. He remained, however, unofficially available for party management until some new arrangement could be made. This vague and increasingly unhappy state of affairs continued for no less than three years.

Major Keith-Falconer, Gorst's assistant, left the service of the party altogether. In February 1874 he applied to the new Prime Minister for appointment as Secretary to the Board of Works and his application was strongly supported by Gorst. Disraeli had other plans for rewarding him and by the end of March was recommending him to the Queen as Commissioner of Inland Revenue.[1]

Thus the two men in professional charge of party management since 1870 faded, completely or partially, out of the picture and the making of new arrangements was not regarded as urgent. There could be no clearer indication that the set-up of 1870 was seen not as a deliberate new departure, but merely as a practical attempt to obtain greater efficiency in preparation for the next election. Some time in 1874, the Central Office was moved to new premises in St. Stephen's Chambers, Westminster Bridge.

[1] Hughenden Papers, B/XXI/Gorst, to Disraeli, 26 Feb. 1874. R. Blake, *Disraeli*, p. 684.

Gorst's own history in the next three years illustrates the decline of Conservative organization. At the very moment when Disraeli was forming his administration, Gorst was complaining to Corry that, as political representative of the *Standard*, he was being given less information than *The Times*.[2] In particular he resented that the news of Lord Salisbury's adherence to the Cabinet was not given through the *Standard*, and demanded a clear answer to the question whether he was to have the same information as *The Times*. Soon more serious grievances arose. In May 1874 Gorst could have had the vacant parliamentary seat at Midhurst, if the appropriate recommendation by the party leaders had gone to the local magnate, whose support was decisive.[3] Instead, Dyke, now Chief Whip, offered the party interest to Ward Hunt, the First Lord of the Admiralty, on behalf of Admiral Hornby. Gorst was indignant at being thus passed over for an outsider, and cited a previous promise by Noel (presumably made when he was appointed in 1870) which, he claimed, was confirmed by Disraeli. Soon a harsher note crept in; on 19 November, Gorst wrote at length to Dyke complaining about misdirection of patronage and citing three cases, one involving Lord Cairns.[4] The cause of all this venom was Gorst's feeling that he and his brother had been insufficiently rewarded. Dyke's letter to Disraeli forwarding Gorst's complaints is instructive.

I am obliged to trouble you now with some letters from Gorst which I have kept for some time to show you and their tenor will throw light on the later remarks in his last letter to you. I dissected with him many of the cases he cites in his letter to me of November 19th and they crumbled away. I did *not* touch upon the violent language he uses, or even point out there is not a *single* instance quoted of a Minister appointing a relation—had I done so I must have spoken strongly and so let it alone: he says to his friends that we get on admirably together: he is I am bound to say of great use to me with all his crotchets and since our talk the other day he writes me a cheerful letter and he is working hard now at the St. Ives Election. The Standard people are always at him and they will

---

[2] Hughenden Papers, B/XXI/Gorst, to Corry, 19 Feb. 1874.
[3] Ibid., B/XXI/Gorst, to Disraeli, 7 May 1874.
[4] Ibid. B/XXI/Dyke/463b, quoted in full by H. J. Hanham, 'Political Patronage at the Treasury, 1870–1912', *Historical Journal*, III, 1 (1960), p. 78.

never forgive me. The case of his brother he quotes. He wished him made joint Examiner of Bills on behalf of the Treasury worth barely £100 a year: this is always given to first-class solicitors. His brother is *not* a solicitor, but a barrister without chambers or brief—the appointment would have damaged Smith and myself irretrievably. He refers to my opinion, but on what grounds he quotes it I know not: except by my not referring to his 'strong language' he may have thought I acquiesced. Things are so quiet now that I am much disposed to keep Gorst in hand crotchets and all. I am delighted with Monty's account of you. I send you my exact thought as I know you wish.[5]

Gorst's anger was particularly directed against Cairns because the Lord Chancellor, who had previously been so closely connected with party management, had probably made promises to him and had not kept them: a letter of June 1874 indicates the postponement till the following year of hopes held out to him.[6] He continued to press the claims of his brother and in March 1875 recommended him as Clerk of the Parliament, a post refused by Corry and desired by Spofforth.[7] When not pestering the party leaders for rewards Gorst was warning them about the electoral dangers of their policies and the decay of the organization. He complained about the lack of interest taken by the party leaders in provincial speaking engagements:

I hear from Ford that the Bristol people are in great consternation as Northcote has thrown them over at the last moment and they have *nobody* to speak at the Dolphin dinner on the 13th. Last night at the Guildhall there were twice as many Cabinet Ministers as were wanted and Lord Derby was reduced to proposing the 'Ladies'. So unequally are our forces applied. The Radicals always put in a good appearance at this great Bristol day and last year Goschen, Stansfeld, Henry James and Winterbottom all held forth—we were nowhere and I suppose shall abandon this year also Bristol to the enemy. It is just the same case as Sheffield and really someone ought to be told off to go down.[8]

The results of the municipal elections of November 1874 gave rise to some interesting if gloomy reflections from Gorst. He

[5] Hughenden Papers, B/XXI/Dyke, to Disraeli, 8 Dec. 1874.
[6] Cairns Papers, Gorst to Cairns, 27 June 1874.
[7] Hughenden Papers, B/XXI/Gorst, 12 Mar. 1875; see also above, p. 113.
[8] Hughenden Papers, B/XIV/B, Gorst to Dyke, 10 Nov. 1874.

appeared to be feeling his way towards a theory of the swinging political pendulum. The reaction against the Conservatives in the municipal elections seemed to be strongest in the boroughs which had swung to the party in the parliamentary elections earlier in the year, while the party was still gaining ground in places 'where the movement of repulsion [against the late Government] had spent itself in a Parliamentary victory'. Gorst went on to emphasize the importance of 'creating a permanent Tory faction' in the boroughs, groups of middle-class leaders, without whom a Conservative mass movement was impossible. The Liberals had such a staff of borough leaders and, when in office, had used their patronage to encourage them. Gorst once again complained that Disraeli's colleagues, none of whom were borough members, had no understanding of the position.[9] Dyke shrugged off these complaints when they were referred to him.[10] The municipal elections of the following year brought further Conservative losses and gave rise to an inquest at a conference of party agents. Gorst reported to Dyke:

The meeting to-day did not pass any formal resolution on the subject of municipal elections, but wished me to represent to you the conclusion at which they generally arrived. They think that in those places where municipal elections are not conducted on political grounds it is for the interest of the Conservative party to leave things as they are and not attempt to introduce a political element into municipal affairs, but in those places where contests are conducted on political grounds the organisation of the party should be used to the utmost to promote the return of Conservative candidates for all local offices. With regard to our losses during the last two years, they do not think that these losses are to be attributed to any general failure of confidence in the party leaders, but that they may be attributed to two causes:

(1)   The increased activity of the Radicals to which they have been stimulated by a desire of revenging the losses of 1874 and

2nd   To what your friend Dr. Monckton called 'the rascally apathy' of the upper classes of the Conservative party, who will neither themselves discharge the duties of municipal offices nor take

[9] Hughenden Papers, B/XXI/Dyke, Gorst to Disraeli, 2 Dec. 1874. This letter was sent to Dyke for comment; it is quoted in full by H. J. Hanham, *Elections & Party Management*, p. 389.

[10] Hughenden Papers, B/XXI/Dyke, to Disraeli, 8 Dec. 1874, the second part of the letter of 8 Dec. 1874 quoted above. This part is reproduced in H. J. Hanham, op. cit., p. 390.

the slightest trouble to secure the return of candidates of their own party.

They think that the losses in the municipal elections afford no reason to believe that we should lose at the present moment in a General Election.

Some very strong remarks were made as to the importance of the leaders of the Conservative party taking a more active part in Conservative demonstrations; and a desire was especially expressed that some Conservative movement should be made in the towns of Birmingham and Sheffield and the attendance of one or more of the prominent party leaders should be secured. After the discussion of the subjects named in our paper the question of School Board Elections and the present position of elementary schools was brought forward and some very strong remarks were made, in particular by gentlemen from Birmingham in favour of the Government undertaking some measure of relief for voluntary schools. The following resolution was passed unanimously: 'That in the opinion of this meeting it was desirable that the Government should introduce a measure in the ensuing session, which will relieve the present denominational schools in the destructive competition which they have to bear against rate-aided schools.'[11]

In February 1875 Gorst at last entered Parliament as member for Chatham. His son states that his candidature was opposed by the party managers.[12] By becoming an M.P. Gorst must have lost, in the eyes of the party leaders, most of his usefulness as an organizer. The rule that the party agent should not be an M.P. had hitherto always been observed, and was applied again in the 1880s. As an M.P. Gorst soon fell foul of the party and on one occasion divided the House against the Government. His hold on party management became tenuous, though this impression may be partly due to the lack of interest in the organization among the party leaders, now that they were in office.

In November 1875 Gorst was offered the post of Secretary to the Local Government Board under Sclater-Booth, in succession to C. S. Read.[13] After some hesitation he turned down the

[11] Hughenden Papers, B/XXI/Dyke, Gorst to Dyke, 21 Dec. 1875.

[12] H. E. Gorst, *The Fourth Party* (1906), p. 22. There are also some useful references to Conservative Party organization at this period in *The Earl of Beaconsfield* (Victorian Era Series, 1900) by the same author, especially in Chapter XIII.

[13] Hughenden Papers, B/XXI/Gorst, to Disraeli, 20 Nov. 1875, B/XII/A/168a and 169. For the circumstances of Read's resignation, see above, p. 51.

offer, because he felt that with his chief in the Commons it would not give him much scope. The only concrete reward he seems to have succeeded in securing was a minor post for his brother. In March 1876 rumour had it that a vacancy was about to occur at the Treasury and Gorst again applied to Disraeli for appointment. He pointed out that he was still the only party manager not rewarded.[14] Correspondence between Gorst and Corry early in 1876 indicates that his connection with the *Standard* was still causing friction and that he was still complaining that other papers were being given more information. The final break came in March 1877, and caused Gorst to write to Disraeli a letter, which was deservedly marked important by Corry:

Sir William Hart Dyke has informed me last Thursday evening, that with the concurrence of the party leaders he has arranged for someone to assist him in the management of elections in my place. Having thus at last dropped from the position in which you placed me in 1870, and of which the functions have since the election of 1874 been gradually abstracted, I should like as an independent member of the Party, while my experience is still fresh, to give you my views upon the subject of our organisation. You will remember that from 1870 to 1874 Major Keith Falconer and I with the help first of Mr. Noel and afterwards of Col. Taylor established a system of electoral management for the Party. The principle on which we proceeded was to find out in each Borough the natural political leaders, to evoke their zeal and active co-operation, and to throw upon them the responsibility of selecting their own candidates, and organising their own machinery. We helped but never interfered. Our work was tested in 1874, and you will I think admit that our system was not on the whole unsuccessful in its results. My own official engagement with the Party ended with the General Election and has not since been renewed, but I consented, at Sir W. Dyke's request and out of personal regard to him, to remain in a sort of undefined position until some fresh arrangement could be made. During this period I have found myself without any power and with continually decreasing influence, having had little or no voice in the selection of candidates and the management of elections, and I have had the misfortune to witness the whole system, to establish which so much trouble was taken, gradually fall into decay. Our organisation in 1877 is greatly inferior to what it was in 1874; and the attempt to renovate and improve it has not come a day too soon.

[14] Hughenden Papers, B/XXI/Gorst, to Disraeli, 30 Mar. 1876.

But to succeed in the attempt you must put a stop to that which has been the chief cause of all the mischief that has occurred—the system which Sir W. Dyke has been required to follow of managing elections at the Treasury. I always thought this a most unwise policy on the part of the late government, and since we have been in office, experience has justified that opinion. Instead of the management being vested in my office, under Sir W. Dyke's control, I have been consulted intermittently, in certain elections only, and at certain stages only of the elections: money has been spent against my advice and without my knowledge; and I have had a mere fragmentary and imperfect acquaintance with what has been going on. The established principle of non-interference with local leaders has in many instances been neglected; and those leaders have been constantly offended and alienated both in the distribution of patronage and in other matters. I trust therefore that one part of the new arrangement may be to separate entirely and for ever the electoral management of the Party from the Government Department of the Treasury.[15]

Gorst went on to advise Disraeli to appoint an 'independent M.P. in the Government's confidence' as his successor, and offered to put his experience at his disposal. He suggested Plunket as a possible successor. He also recommended that no single person should have the power to spend money in elections and that this task should be entrusted to a finance committee consisting of men like Taylor, Noel, and Dyke. There is no reason to doubt that Gorst's strictures were substantially correct and this is borne out by the story of his gradually loosening control of party management. The Central Office practically ceased to exist except as a clerical agency. The management of elections reverted to the Whips and the set-up was therefore similar to what it had been before Gorst and his office became a strong centre of activity. On the other hand Gorst does not seem to have realized that his own parliamentary ambitions increasingly disqualified him from holding a position in which he had to keep out of the limelight.

The termination of his duties as party agent still left Gorst as the honorary secretary of the National Union. Lord Claud Hamilton seems to have had the intention of moving a motion, probably in the council of the Union, that the party agency and the secretaryship of the National Union should continue to be

[15] Ibid., B/XXI/Gorst, to Beaconsfield, 3 Mar. 1877.

vested in the same person. Gorst took offence at this and North-cote was required to send him a calming letter:

I am very sorry that the motion should have been made without notice being given to you; and I am sure that all of us, who know what good work you have done for the party, must regret that your feelings should have been in any way hurt. At the same time I feel that it is important that our machinery should be kept in good working order; and I cannot but fear that such a delay as you suggest would prove inconvenient to the interests of the party, which I know you value as highly as anyone can. The National Union has been worked so much in connection with the party agency, and there is so much difficulty in keeping them distinct while they remain under the same roof and employ the same staff of clerks, that it seems to be very desirable to maintain the connection which you yourself estab-lished by making the same person party agent and secretary of the union.[16]

The incident was hushed up by the withdrawal of Lord Claud's motion, but it faintly foreshadows the serious strife which could be caused by the separation of the National Union from the Central Office.

Nine months later, at the time of the Cabinet reshuffle of March 1878, an exchange of letters with Beaconsfield took place, in the course of which Gorst regretted that, when he refused office in 1875, he had not sought an interview with the Prime Minister. According to Gorst's son, Beaconsfield re-proached him for this later and admitted that in consequence he had been badly treated. This was Gorst's parting shot:

I am sorry that my letter of Saturday last was so ill-expressed as to convey anything like a 'reproach'. I have never supposed that you were either responsible for, or even cognisant of, the way in which the party managers have since 1874 behaved towards me: and I have regarded *their* hostility as the natural consequence of my stead-fast adherence to those popular principles in politics, which you taught me, which won the boroughs in 1874, and which though for the time being in discredit must ultimately prevail.[17]

Thus ended, for the time being, Gorst's connection with Conservative party management. His successor was Mr. W. B.

[16] Iddesleigh Papers, Add. MS. 50053, Northcote to Gorst, 9 July 1877.
[17] Hughenden Papers, B/XXI/Gorst, to Beaconsfield, 4 Apr. 1878.

Skene, who proved to be entirely unsuitable for the post of party agent.[18] He was a Scottish landowner and had the social standing which Gorst lacked, but in matters of party organization was entirely an amateur. When, after three years in the job, he was thinking of retiring he still called himself a novice and wrote to Beaconsfield; 'How much I long to get out of my present position which I feel I was an idiot to have assumed. I do hope you will be able to find me something more congenial and which I shall be better fitted to undertake with credit and satisfaction to myself.'[19] Communications between Skene and the party leaders were infrequent, but the new agent, like Spofforth and Gorst before him, worked for the Prime Minister on ecclesiastical patronage, finding out the background and affiliations of potential candidates for preferment. A letter to Corry, of November 1877, evokes memories of the Lancashire demonstration: Skene hoped Lord Beaconsfield might be prevailed upon to visit Sheffield and stay with Mr. Mark Firth, which might induce the latter to stand for the borough and turn out Mundella.[20] But by this time Lord Beaconsfield had little stomach for provincial appearances of this kind. Skene gave advice on finding the right moment for a dissolution in 1879 and 1880. His comments in July 1879 seem, in the light of subsequent knowledge, quite perceptive:

Have you noticed the paragraph at the end of the first leader in to-day's Times with reference to the ground given by the conduct of the Opposition leaders for an appeal to the country? It seems to me to be worth notice.

Besides I fear there is little or no chance of prosperous times coming back in time to help us, and the Protectionist argument is a very awkward one, is daily gaining strength and in spring there will be the bill to pay for the Zulu war. It may also be considered that time will efface the recollection of our successful policy in Europe and Afghanistan and that it is not impossible that before spring fresh complications may occur. I do not think we stand nearly so well as we did last autumn when I think our real chance of a great victory

---

[18] A brief sketch of Skene's career appears in *Who Was Who 1897–1915*, see Glossary of Names. According to T. H. S. Escott, *Randolph Spencer-Churchill*, p. 186, Skene was nominated as a paid official and Gorst gradually withdrew from party management.

[19] Hughenden Papers, B/XXI/Skene, to Beaconsfield, 16 Feb. 1880.

[20] Ibid., B/XIV/B, Skene to Corry, 8 Nov. 1877.

was missed, but I should imagine we may hold our own now and no-one can say how we should stand in the future especially if the harvest is a failure as seems probable.[21]

A long memorandum of 16 February 1880, which probably contributed towards the decision to dissolve Parliament, was decidedly amateurish. Here there is little of that acute analysis of the electoral position which Gorst used to supply to the party leaders. Instead there are a great many guesses about the possible course of events at home and abroad which could have been much more competently made by the Prime Minister himself. Skene's main points were:

(1) Feeling on foreign policy is in favour of the Government, so our travelling inspector reports. The Liverpool and Suffolk Elections point in the same direction.
(2) Parliament has gone on longer than usual and leading members of the opposition have taunted us with the fact.
(3) The revival of trade is now an accomplished fact. We have benefited from this revival as far as we are likely to profit by the more hopeful feeling of all classes.
(4) The danger of a reverse in Afghanistan or elsewhere.
(5) The Liberals in consequence of their by-election defeats will perfect their organization.
(6) Unfavourable conditions in the House will make measures of importance impossible this session.
(7) Members will from this time to the General Election be subject to continual demands on their resources and a speedy dissolution would be a great saving of expenses.
(8) It would be very desirable in case of any European complications that the Government should be able to say that they had the renewed confidence of the country.

Skene went on to say:

With regard to the prospects of the party in case of a dissolution it is very difficult to give a reliable opinion but I should be inclined to predict that we should lose six or seven seats in Scotland, five or six in Ireland and say five on the boroughs in England which would still leave us a working majority which would probably be increased after the Election were the verdict of the country in our favour. Even were the Seats bill not carried before the Election we should have a

[21] Ibid., B/XXI/Skene to Beaconsfield, 19 July 1879.

substantial advantage in those constituencies for which we propose giving an additional member were our proposals known.[22]

Beaconsfield did not blame the party managers for their advice over the timing of the dissolution, but thought that some of the subagents in the country might have held out unjustifiable hopes.[23] On the other hand Balfour reported to Salisbury after the elections that much blame was being put on Skene and the Whips for their bad management.[24] Cranbrook, writing to Cross after the magnitude of the defeat had become clear, wondered 'why in fact the indications were all the other way and our experts at the Central Committee up to the first day of polling were so favourable'.[25] Beaconsfield himself, in his quizzical way, wrote to Salisbury on 2 April, while the elections were still in progress: 'The Committee with their wonderful organization, and vast resources, and great preparation and experience appear to be quite demoralized, and have scarcely sent me a telegram, tho' they promised to do so every half hour.'[26] The Committee referred to was the informal committee of Whips, party managers and others who were in charge of the election in 1880 as on previous occasions. Dyke had become ill through overwork late in 1879, and his absence no doubt contributed to the confusion among the party managers. In the summer of 1878 he had been against dissolution, saying 'it would be like throwing up a rubber at Whist whilst holding nothing but good cards', but a year later he was in favour of dissolving as soon as possible after the introduction of the new electoral register in January 1880.[27]

While the Central Office was languishing under Skene's inexpert guidance, the National Union also failed to display much activity between 1877 and 1880. It continued to issue pamphlets; thus Lord Claud Hamilton in October 1879 asked Lord Sandon, as an ex-Vice-President of the Committee of Council on Education, for his views on two papers on the education question. He explained that the system was that such

[22] Ibid., B/XXI/Skene, 16 Feb. 1880.   [23] Buckle, ii. 1396.
[24] Salisbury Papers, Balfour to Salisbury, 7 Apr. 1880.
[25] Cross Papers, Add. MS 51267, 8 Apr. 1880. Also Richmond Papers, Cairns to Richmond, 2 Apr. 1880.
[26] Salisbury Papers, Beaconsfield to Salisbury, 2 Apr. 1880.
[27] Hughenden Papers, B/XXI/Dyke to Beaconsfield, 19 July 1878 and 28 July 1879.

papers were submitted to the Literature Committee of the National Union Council before publication as pamphlets.[28] A deputation from the National Union was received by Lord Beaconsfield after his triumphal return from Berlin and exhorted not to cease from their electoral labours. But the National Union seems to have played little part in the preparations for the next general election.

The General Election of 1880 and the Conservative defeat set off a new phase in the affairs of party management. As Skene was on the point of resigning even before the dissolution, new arrangements were becoming necessary. The generally accepted view of the parties and their electoral prospects had been fundamentally changed by the Liberal landslide. The importance of organization, of appealing to the masses, was obvious to all and there was a real prospect of an extension of household suffrage to the counties. At the last meeting of the Conservative Cabinet it was decided to take 'some serious steps to improve our organization', and W. H. Smith was appointed chairman of a standing committee on which it was suggested Salisbury should also serve.[29] On 19 May 1880, a meeting of 500 Conservative Peers and M.P.s took place at Bridgwater House and was addressed by Lord Beaconsfield. In analysing the causes of the party's defeat he referred to the 'new foreign political organization' of the Liberal party and told the meeting of the committee under W. H. Smith which had been appointed to investigate a system which demanded 'the most minute criticism and consideration.'[30] *Blackwood's Magazine*, an ultra-Conservative journal, carried an article in its issue of June 1880 calling for an overhaul of Conservative party organization. Lack of contact between the metropolitan headquarters and the provincial agents was described as the fundamental fault. The article advocated the creation of three central committees in London, Edinburgh and Dublin, and the formation of area committees of two and three counties, with trained staffs of election managers, to keep in touch with the centres. The London agent should be a man of high social position, the equivalent of the Chief Whip, so that he could mix with the

[28] Harrowby Papers, L/139, Lord Claud Hamilton to Sandon.
[29] Iddesleigh Papers, Add. MS. 50063A, Northcote's Diary, 20 Apr. 1880.
[30] Buckle, ii. pp. 1447–9.

wealthy supporters of the party. The area committees should send monthly reports on the state of feeling in their part of the country and more attention should be paid to the provincial press.

Against this background of criticism Smith's committee carried on its inquest into the Conservative defeat. All the men connected with party management and the Whips' office, including Gorst, took a hand in the proceedings and among ex-ministers Northcote, Salisbury, Stanhope, as well as Smith himself, were frequently present.[31] A good many general complaints were heard, for example, about the negligence of members in looking after their seats; but attention was also given to more specific problems, such as the tendency to employ too many solicitors as local agents, and the usefulness of voluntary canvassers. There was a good deal of criticism of Dyke, in particular of his handling of finance; 'Claims come in for £1000 here, or £500 there, of which there is no kind of record; and all that Dyke can say is: that it is impossible to remember all the promises that were made'.[32] The two main results which emerged from this inquest were a decision to re-engage Gorst as party agent, and the creation of a permanent committee to supervise party organization. This new permanent body grew out of Smith's committee of investigation, and became known in due course as the Central Committee. It was in essence the successor of the election committees which had existed in 1868, 1874, and 1880. It was a slightly more formalized version of that group of Whips and party officials, seasoned by a few front-rank politicians, who had always kept an eye on party management and on the administration of the party fund. The difference was that the Central Committee now became a more clearly defined institution, frequently referred to as such even by persons outside the inner circle of the party. Even so membership of the committee was somewhat shifting. Smith and Stanhope were the Conservative frontbenchers most closely associated with it.

When Gorst was re-engaged as party agent in July 1880, an attempt was made to define on paper his exact relationship

[31] Iddesleigh Papers, Add. MS. 50063A, Northcote's Diary, 5, 21, and 26 May 1880.
[32] Ibid., Add. MS. 50063A, Northcote's Diary, 5 June 1880.

with the Central Committee and the Whips, since it was this relationship which had caused so much friction earlier on:

(1) An Executive Committee consisting of Mr. W. H. Smith as Chairman, the Whip, Edward Stanhope as Vice-Chairman, Gorst and Raikes or other as representative of the National Alliance with power to appoint a secretary.

(2) Mr. Gorst to be charged with the primary responsibility of securing candidates for seats but not to be at liberty to promise any money (marginal comment: Mr. Gorst or some other members of the committee should be head of the office and the secretary and clerks should take orders from him only). If assistance of this nature is required the Whip must undertake the responsibility of giving or refusing it: but the Whip will not promise any such contribution without communicating with Mr. Gorst in the first instance: and on the other hand Mr. Gorst will keep the Whip and the members of the committee informed of all proposals and arrangements as to candidates. (marginal comment: I think Mr. Gorst should in all cases initiate proposals to spend money though he should have no power to do this without the sanction of the committee).

(3) It will be the duty of this committee to ascertain the existing state of the party organisation in every constituency and to suggest improvements where-ever they may appear to be necessary.

(4) It will probably be requisite that members of the committee shall visit many of the constituencies with a view to stimulate the exertions of the local leaders: and experienced agents will be required to supply practical information and advice on the spot as to the best kind of organisation which would be adapted to the particular constituency.

(5) A Secretary to the Committee should be appointed who should be capable of conducting the correspondence of a confidential character which would pass between the Committee and the constituencies or candidates, but it is not desirable that he should have the position or the authority of Agent.[33]

The main point of the new arrangement was that the primary responsibility for selecting candidates was to rest with Gorst; while for the spending of money the ultimate sanction of the Whip and those assisting him was required. But on both these

[33] Hambleden Papers, Series I, packet A, Memorandum on Party Organization by Smith, undated. See also Viscount Chilston, *W. H. Smith*, pp. 159–65.

matters there was to be regular inter-communication between the two sides. All this had never previously been so clearly stated. The National Union was to be represented on the new Committee, and this representation later became of political significance when Lord Randolph Churchill and his supporters made it one of their demands. Gorst was now appointed despite the fact that he was an M.P. of considerable and increasing standing, and also had to look after a large legal practice. The old principle that the party agent should not be an M.P. was thus disregarded, and this was the cause of considerable future difficulties. Gorst had so many other commitments that complaints were soon heard that he was not giving enough time to the party. An attempt was also made to clear up another earlier cause of friction, namely what political reward was to be given to Gorst for his services. Smith recorded a conversation between himself, Northcote, and Gorst:

> I stated to Mr. Gorst that if he gave his assistance in reorganising the electoral machinery of the constituencies, and the party were successful, his services would be recognised by the offer of office for which he might be eligible.
>
> He remarked that a similar statement had been made prior to the Conservative Government coming in, and the only offer he got was an Under-Secretaryship with the Chief in the Commons, thus practically shelving him. Hence he declined.
>
> I rejoined that he would be eligible for a Law Officer's appointment only, if he had practice and position at the Bar which would justify it and he fully accepted this view; but he contended that if an offer was made, it should be one which would not silence him in the House or deny him the chance of showing his own ability and claim for further political promotion.
>
> Mr. Gorst undertook to give his cordial assistance and all the time his own profession did not require to the working out of the reorganisation required.[34]

Yet the old antagonisms between Gorst and some of the Whips and party managers soon cropped up again. One of the bones of contention was the method of spending money. Gorst had always claimed that it was one of his major principles not to countenance corrupt practices and certainly to prevent the

[34] Hambleden Papers, Series I, packet A, Notes of an interview between Northcote, Smith, and Gorst, 7 July 1880.

Central Office from getting involved in them. Disraeli himself, in building up the party organization after 1870, had made it one of the cardinal points that corrupt devices should be avoided[35] The inquiry into corrupt practices at Oxford during the by-election of May 1880, caused by the appointment of Harcourt as Home Secretary, showed the Conservative party managers very careless in the spending of money and negligent about where it went.[36] Gorst's letter to Smith of September 1880 shows the continuance of this problem:

I will do what is possible to prevent an appeal for funds from the National Union. We used to appeal in our general circular and give the subscriber the option of giving his money to the Central Fund, National Union, or Registration Association as he pleased. People won't subscribe to more than one central fund, and if several independent authorities apply it is an excuse for not giving at all. I will do my best to 'menager' Winn and his protégé Shaw. My objection to the latter is more complex than the former supposes. Chiefly he is prone to corrupt practices, which accounts for his being in such request among corrupt constituencies. What Winn's phrases about not appreciating the money etc. spent at Birmingham come to is that I won't fight corruption by corruption. To this I plead guilty: it is our policy to force the Government to pass an Act that will stop as much corruption as possible, and if Harry Thynne and his friends will have corrupt practices on our side we must have them locally not fostered and organised from headquarters by Mr. Shaw or anybody else. . . . I am quite in favour of treating Winn and the old identity with consideration, but they can hardly expect us to take their modus operandi as our model or accept Dyke's judgment of character as infallible. There is a regular intrigue going on on the part of Bourke and others against Lord Randolph Churchill, Wolff and myself. They tried to detach Balfour from us but failed. We mean to stick together and we shall be loyal to Northcote if he is loyal to us. But self-preservation is the first law of politics as well as of nature, and contingencies may happen which will end in your being obliged to take the place of leader in the Commons whether you like it or not.[37]

Rowland Winn, an Assistant Whip since 1874, had just suc-

[35] Buckle, ii. 526.
[36] *Shorthand Writer's Notes of Evidence of the Trial of the Oxford Election Petition, Parliamentary Papers*, 1880 (349—Sess. 2), vol. LVIII, p. 557. Also *Parliamentary Papers*, 1881, vol. XL (Chester) and XLIV (Oxford).
[37] Hambleden Papers, Series I, packet A.

ceeded Dyke as Chief Whip.[38] Shaw had the title of Inspector of Registration Associations and was later referred to as 'travelling agent'. He had been agent at Sheffield and had also worked in other boroughs, but some of his claims evidently had a slender basis in fact.[39] Gorst's letter reflects the tension which had arisen inside the House of Commons between Northcote and the Fourth Party. By implication the letter also shows how unsuitable as party agent Gorst, for all his experience, had become. His position as an M.P., increasingly independent of the official leadership, interfered with his duties as a party official. His relations with Northcote were, however, still reasonably friendly at this stage. There was an exchange of letters between them in which gossip about the party organization was interwoven with somewhat ominous sparring about the activites of the Fourth Party. Northcote wrote to Gorst:

> I shall be very glad by and by to have a little talk with you about our organisation and our present prospects. We shall need both courage and care . . . I am inclined to think the 'Fourth Party' has done enough for its fame and that it will be the wiser course for its members to take their places in the main body where they will have work enough and to spare . . .[40]

Gorst replied:

> . . . I like Fitzroy Stewart our new man at St. Stephens' Chambers very much. He is vivacious and industrious and pleases everyone who comes into contact with him. . . . Our little association, to which enemies to sow dissension among us have given the name of the 'Fourth Party', will I am sure prove one of your best instruments of political warfare. Each of us feels stronger for the support and wiser for the counsels of his fellows; and we are all determined to back you up loyally in fighting the battle of the Conservative cause against the combination of Whigs and Radicals who oppose us.
>
> You may rely on my letting you know anything which occurs in connection with our organisation. I think we ought next session to force the Government to pass a strong Corrupt Practices Act. It will not be a popular measure. The boroughs in their hearts love corruption. But pure and inexpensive elections in boroughs would be all in

---

[38] See above, p. 56.
[39] Iddesleigh Papers, Add. MS. 50063A, Northcote's Diary, 7 May 1880.
[40] Ibid., Add. MS. 50041, 11 Sept. 1880.

our favour. When the contest becomes one of money we are in most places no match for our opponents.[41]

Gorst's comments on Northcote's letter were a good deal less amiable:

The Goat has been at it again and under colour of a friendly letter about organisation and obstruction, he has coolly proposed the dissolution of the Fourth Party and that its members should 'quietly' (fancy Randolph and Wolff doing anything quietly) take their places in the main body. What a good joke it would be to go and sit next session where Clarke does and carry on our operations with as much vigour as ever from there. In answering his letter I have praised the loyalty and determination of the Fourth Party and ignored the suggestion of dissolution altogether. But don't you think these repeated attempts upon our individual political virtue are most disreputable. I often fancy the Goat has his eye upon a possible coalition with the Whigs. In some quarters this has been spoken of as the next political combination. This would account for his hostility to us; a leader who really meant fighting would have our association at least until by experience he had proved we were incapable of being managed or led.[42]

Northcote saw eye to eye with Gorst on avoiding corrupt practices. He rightly felt that first-class men would never take part in organization as long as such practices prevailed. The General Election of 1880 had given rise to the appointment of eight Royal Commissions to report on the English boroughs where election petitions had been successful. Northcote asked Gorst to consider the bearing of this on party organization and to draw up a reform programme based on four main proposals:

(1) Prohibition of paid canvassers—(2) substitution of an organised staff of messengers, provided by local authorities, and hired from them by the Candidates—(3) regulation of Conveyance of Voters,—which I think might lead to 'voting papers'; and (4) if we got voting papers, let the names of voters be published after the Election, but *before* the time for petitioning had expired.[43]

[41] Ibid., Add. MS. 50041, 15 Sept. 1880. The Hon. Fitzroy Stewart was the new secretary at the Central Office.
[42] Balfour Papers, Add. MS. 49791, Gorst to Balfour, 15 Sept. 1880.
[43] Iddesleigh Papers, Add. MS. 50063A, Northcote's Diary, 23 Oct. 1880. For the aftermath of the 1880 Election in terms of petitions and inquiries into corrupt practices, see Cornelius O'Leary, *The Elimination of Corrupt Practices in British Elections, 1868–1911* (1962), Chapter V.

When Gorst resumed charge of the Central Office, he also started to write again to Beaconsfield on matters of organization. The most interesting of these letters is a report on the work of the Central Office in 1880:

Ordinary work of Conservative Central Office

Registration. Enquiries are made as to the residence & qualification of the outvoters of all counties in England & Wales. Forms, instructions, & advice are furnished to both Counties & Boroughs.

Elections. Local leaders are assisted in finding suitable candidates. Forms, instructions, and election literature is supplied. County outvoters are canvassed.

Organization. Formation of new Associations is promoted and assisted. Model rules &c are supplied. An annual list of clubs & associations is compiled.

Meetings. The continual holding of small local meetings is advised and encouraged. Speakers and hints for speeches are provided. Special meetings (as for example on the Irish question) are from time to time recommended and promoted.

Publications. Pamphlets & Leaflets on current political topics are issued: important speeches are reprinted and circulated.

Press. A weekly publication, called the 'Editors' Handysheet', is issued to provide materials for political articles to the Conservative Provincial Press. Political telegrams are sent from the Lobby to several provincial papers.

Parliamentary. All Bills affecting the interests of the party are circulated amongst the local leaders. Petitions are from time to time promoted.

Statistics. Facts respecting elections, Parliamentary & Municipal, are collected & tabulated. An Index of political events during the past 10 years is in course of formation.

Correspondence. Enquiries are answered upon such subjects as Finance, Foreign Affairs, Army & Navy administration, Election statistics & procedure, India, Irish affairs, Licensing, Education, Friendly Societies, &c. &c.

Interviews. People of every class call at the office on political business, and every endeavour is made to treat them with courtesy & consideration.

Visits. Constituencies are visited by emissaries from the Central Office of two sorts:

    (a) Experienced agents to advise on the registration & electoral machinery.

(b) Gentlemen to stir up dormant constituencies, & recommend local organisation & effort.

Special Work of Conservative Central Office since August 1880

The Hon. FitzRoy Stewart (our new Secy.) has read up the correspondence of the last 6 years respecting each constituency.

He has seen a great number of candidates for Parliament, & has made out a list of candidates with their qualifications.

He has also appended to each constituency the names of suitable candidates, amongst whom a selection could be made in case of a vacancy.

As the candidates for any constituency become definitely fixed, they are of course noted.

A great deal of his time has been taken up by interviews with persons who have schemes for starting every description of newspaper, and who persist in explaining them to somebody who represents the Party.

The National Union which broke out into discord with the Party managers after the general election has been brought into concord.

A new association 'The Constitutional Union' formed by barristers in the Temple, has been induced to act in harmony with the Central Office.

Constituencies have been visited by the agents of the Central Office & reports made upon their electoral prospects. Stewart has commenced visiting those in which the organisation is unsatisfactory. Arrangements are being made for several gentlemen of position to assist Stewart in this work.

A committee on County organisation has been formed by Hon. E. Stanhope, which has held many meetings & examined a large number of County members: it is to report to the Central Committee.

A Committee on Ireland has held one meeting & holds its second on Feby. 25th. It has been delayed until Col. Taylor's arrival from Ireland.

A Committee is now being formed to consider the Corrupt Practices Bill.

Mr. Dawson, an Oxford B.A., has been employed since January under the supervision of Stanhope in making an Index of Political Events of the last 10 years for reference.[44]

This report and much of the correspondence between Gorst and Smith at this period show that routine rather than startling activity was the order of the day at Conservative Central Office.

[44] Hughenden Papers, B/XXI/Gorst, to Beaconsfield, 24 Feb. 1881.

Political conditions did not favour striking initiatives at that moment. No revival of the fortunes of the Conservative party was as yet in sight and the central organization could do little but wait and hope for increased signs of local activity. Gorst wrote to Smith on the day after Lord Beaconsfield's death:

> Political activity seems to me to depend on causes too wide and deep to be controlled. A gardener might as well try to stimulate the rising of sap in the spring. We may to some extent guide political activity when it does arise into useful channels—but create it—no. We can gain thoroughly reliable information as to the state of the constituencies and we can let the local leaders know that there is a body at headquarters to communicate with. Further than this we cannot go until the local feeling awakes. Shaw's method is like putting a plant into a hothouse, which only dies the more surely when the artificial stimulus is withdrawn.[45]

During the summer recess Smith complained that Gorst had left town prematurely and without making adequate arrangements to cover the party organization. Gorst defended himself in a long letter:

> Experience has brought me to the opinion (in which I am glad to see that you concur) that the constituencies are best left alone during the next two months to work their registration with such arrangements and organization as they possess. I believe, however, that we are ready to recommence our efforts in October when the time for further operations comes. Stewart and Rowe have been through all the constituencies of England and Wales with me during the month previous to my leaving town, reporting the latest intelligence received from each place and advising as to the further treatment which each place should receive from headquarters. The arrangements for propaganda by lectures and speeches were left to be concerted by Lord Percy and myself. We have drawn up the conditions on which lecturers will be supplied in a little printed form which Stewart could show you, using as we thought desirable the name of the National Union in the matter and the scheme has been pressed in personal interviews upon the attention of persons from Bristol, Manchester, Leeds, Newcastle, Darlington and other places. It has also been considered by the Scotch Committee and pressed upon the consideration of several people of influence from Ireland. I propose in October to go myself to Yorkshire, Glasgow, Belfast, Dublin and Cork—chiefly with the view of getting a system of Con-

[45] Hambleden Papers, Series I, packet A, Gorst to Smith, 20 Apr. 1881.

servative lectures and speeches adopted—though with ulterior designs of getting the people to stir in organisation. . . . I do not credit the rumours of an autumn dissolution—they generally prevail at this time of the year—of course if there is any serious ground to believe that Gladstone contemplates any such thing I should return to London at once. . . . We are certainly not as well prepared for a dissolution now as in 1874; but then we had a long series of victories at by-elections and the Government had been unpopular for years. We have no real advantage now. Unless a dissolution is imminent there is no good in sending men to hopeless unorganised places. There are some places where the only motive to organisation is the hope of attracting a candidate. As soon as one is found the local people begin to fleece him and think of organisation no more.[46]

The complaint that Gorst was not giving enough time to the affairs of the party was also echoed by Shaw, the travelling agent, about whose encouragement of corrupt practices Gorst was so indignant. Northcote, after a visit to Sheffield, reported to Salisbury that he had had a heart-to-heart talk with Shaw, with whose work at Sheffield he was much impressed:

I shall be very glad to talk over the organisation question quietly with you. We hardly seem to have got into the right way yet: but how we are to do it, without offending some who ought not to be offended, I do not clearly see. I have had a long talk with Mr. Shaw, who has certainly done a great work here, and who is fully persuaded that he could organise the whole constituencies of the United Kingdom, but does not think himself appreciated or properly supported at head quarters. . . . He is jealous of Fitzroy Stewart and Rowe: does not like being called 'Travelling Agent' instead of 'Organising Secretary'; thinks Gorst has not time, or at all events does not give enough time, for the work; and seems even to disbelieve in Smith. As far as I can make out he would like to see some man like Charles Wortley at the head of the Executive in London, and to be the head of the Provincial Organization himself. Without adopting all his views I think he might be turned to very good account; and perhaps it might not be a bad idea to give a little work to Charles Wortley in connection with our existing Staff, and let him take the department of Provincial organisation under Edward Stanhope.[47]

[46] Ibid., Series I, packet A, Gorst to Smith, 10 Aug. 1881.
[47] Salisbury Papers, Northcote to Salisbury, 3 Sept. 1881. Charles Stuart-Wortley was member for Sheffield.

In the absence of a political revival, Gorst was active in promoting other schemes to attach the working-class voter to the Conservative party. Thus he proposed to start a building society, to be called 'The Conservative Freeholders' Company Limited'. Its object was to carry out 'upon a national scale and through the medium of funds subscribed by the people themselves the conversion of rents into sinking funds, whereby the tenants of houses, market gardens, farms and other holdings may, within a limited period, become owners'. The Radicals had floated a similar company. Smith regarded the scheme with suspicion and doubted its financial soundness.[48]

In the meantime an extraordinary correspondence had passed between Gorst and Smith which showed the former from his most 'crotchety' side. The subject was the remuneration to be paid him for his services. A thousand guineas was fixed for the period from June 1881 to June 1882. Gorst claimed that there had been an agreement that the same sum should be paid retrospectively for the year up to June 1881. This claim was apparently not accepted by Smith and the party leaders, who handed him a cheque for five hundred guineas, half the sum claimed, simply as a general recognition of services rendered and outside the agreement covering the year 1881-2. No satisfactory arrangement could be reached, though Gorst eventually waived his claim for the year 1880-1. During his first period as party agent Gorst refused to be paid, but now, after many political disappointments, he wanted his pound of flesh. When he did not get it he was, not surprisingly, unwilling to give the affairs of the Central Office precedence over a holiday in the country.[49]

In 1882 there was still little sign of a Conservative revival in the constituencies. Perhaps this, as much as personal friction and clashes of policy, accounted for the *malaise* in the Conservative party organization. There was still much debate about the methods to be used in stimulating local activity. Thus the agents sent by the Central Office came under criticism again. Two of them, Peters and Kelly by name, were, from time to time, used and subsidized to stir up an agitation amongst

---

[48] Ibid., Smith to Salisbury, 6 June 1881.
[49] Hambleden Papers, Series I, packet A, 27 May, 23 June, 15 July, 16 July, and 18 July 1881. H. E. Gorst, *The Fourth Party*, p. 32.

the working classes at borough elections. Their activities often did not gain the approval of the local leaders and Edward Stanhope and others at the centre were opposed to their continued employment.[50] In August, when parliamentary events on the Arrears Bill brought a dissolution within the realm of possibility, Gorst made the following report to Salisbury:

As in the event of a dissolution of Parliament I shall be held personally responsible for the opinion which I have submitted to the leaders of the party as to the probable result of such a step, I hope you will allow me to place on record that which I have already stated verbally. I have carefully considered the information which has been collected since the election of 1880 as to each constituency in the United Kingdom; I can on a comprehensive view see no reasonable prospect that the result of a present appeal to the country would be the return of a Conservative majority. I cannot even say that I think it likely that the Government majority would be materially diminished except by the transfer of a certain number of seats from the Home Rule supporters of the Government to the Home Rule adherents of the Land League. The condition of the Conservative party in the constituencies does not warrant the expectation of any considerable accession to our strength; and even a still further diminution is not impossible. The recent withdrawal of the Corrupt Practices bill has reduced the number of candidates prepared to contest seats and has increased the number of borough members who will retire, and has thus altered our prospects in the boroughs considerably for the worse. I abstain from expressing any opinion as to the general policy of promoting a dissolution in the present state of public affairs because I am writing officially on consideration of the statistics before me and not as an independent member of the party.[51]

Gorst's time as party agent was rapidly coming to an end. During the autumn session of 1882, called to deal with the problems of obstruction, the Fourth Party was still pursuing its independent course in the House of Commons. In November 1882 there appeared in the *Fortnightly* an unsigned article,

[50] Salisbury Papers, Stanhope to Salisbury 14 Apr. 1882. Peters and Kelly were agitators employed by the National Fair Trade League for work among labour organizations; they had an unsavoury reputation. See Benjamin H. Brown, *The Tariff Reform Movement in Great Britain, 1881–1895*, p. 31. Also below, p. 215.
[51] Salisbury Papers, Gorst to Salisbury, 8 Aug. 1882.

'Conservative Disorganisation', which was thought to have come from Gorst's pen. Here all the familiar arguments were rehearsed again. The Tory party was too much of an aristocratic clique and must become more popular. The aristocratic members of the party had taken no interest in organization or the new associations before 1874, but had then rushed in to share the spoils. Since 1874 social influence had become predominant again, the distinction between country and borough members had been revived, there had been misdirection of patronage. The Conservative government, in its legislation, had neglected borough interests in favour of its traditional supporters, as in dropping the Merchant Shipping Bill for the Agricultural Holdings Act.[52]

Gorst's resignation may have been precipated by a resolution passed by the Chelsea Conservative Association on 14 November complaining that he had, as 'the salaried agent of the Conservative Party', behaved disloyally towards the recognized leaders, and calling for his replacement by a man who was not an M.P. Lord Claud Hamilton, under whose chairmanship the resolution had been passed and who was never a friend of Gorst's, forwarded it to Northcote with a strong endorsement.[53] Northcote wrote to Gorst and by return received a letter of resignation:

> I was discussing with Lord Percy and Mr. Balfour a fortnight ago whether I had not better resign my semi-official position in the party, but the Preston election and other matters caused a postponement of the question which I greatly regret as it would have probably rendered your letter of today's date unnecessary. I will at once relieve you of all further embarrassement on my account by resigning.[54]

Gorst's path in party management had never been smooth. The difficulties were partly personal: Gorst no doubt had his 'crotchets', as Dyke put it, and also came from a different background from most of the men who concerned themselves with party management. They were a tightly knit group, some of them known as 'the Kent gang', because, like Dyke himself,

---

[52] 'Conservative Disorganization' (Part I of 'The State of the Opposition'), *Fortnightly Review*, vol. 32, Nov. 1882, p. 668.
[53] Iddesleigh Papers, Add. MS. 50041.
[54] Ibid. Add. MS. 50041, Gorst to Northcote, 17 Nov. 1882.

Colonel Talbot, Holmesdale, and Akers-Douglas, they had connections with that county. Gorst was not one of them. More important than personal disharmonies were differences of political outlook. As is evident from his correspondence, Gorst saw the Tory party as a mass party with a wide following among a large electorate; Tory Democracy was to him both a reality and a necessity; he looked at the boroughs more than the counties, because his methods had as yet little scope in the counties; organization was to him a means towards full political democracy which he did not fear. Many of the 'old identity' in party management still saw the Tory party as a parliamentary grouping predominantly based on the landed gentry, and the electoral system as a means of maintaining this position rather than as a method of representation; the large borough electorates were on the periphery of their awareness. History, however, was marching with Gorst. The need for his methods was now much greater than it had been ten years earlier, and in resigning Gorst was perhaps already planning to make organization the battleground in a major power struggle within the party. Freed from the restraints of his official engagement, he was certainly a man the party leaders had to beware of.

On Gorst's departure Smith also decided to resign from his position as Chairman of the Central Committee. Raikes, who had, like Gorst, played a part in the organization of popular Toryism, but preferred to remain in the good books of the party leaders, regarded the double resignation as 'an acute crisis in our party organisation'.[55] Stanhope took Smith's place and reported to Salisbury on 4 December that temporary arrangements had been made at the Central Office to allow the day-to-day work to continue, while a search was being made for Gorst's successor. In Stanhope's opinion the new agent should not be in Parliament, but need not necessarily be a lawyer.[56] Northcote's absence delayed matters, so that the meeting to discuss the affairs of the Central Office did not take place until 14 February 1883. Both Northcote and Salisbury were invited to it, as were Stanhope, Winn, Balfour, Percy, Dyke, Noel, and Taylor, who was probably prevented from coming by illness.[57]

[55] Salisbury Papers, Raikes to Salisbury, 9 Dec. 1882.
[56] Ibid., Stanhope to Salisbury, 4 Dec. 1882.
[57] Ibid., Stanhope to Salisbury, 8 Feb. 1883.

Abergavenny, who was making himself unpopular with the party managers by his activities in connection with a new political club, the Constitutional, was reluctantly invited and only on the insistence of Salisbury, who pointed out how much the party relied on Peers 'financially and territorially'.[58] The result of the discussions was a definite decision to seek Gorst's successor outside the ranks of Conservative M.P.s. This did not prove as easy as Stanhope had originally hoped. Northcote had an offer from Ashmead Bartlett who was prepared to become Gorst's successor without remuneration.[59] Bartlett was then, and remained, one of Northcote's most persistent supporters in his battles with Lord Randolph Churchill and the Fourth Party; but even if anyone had been inclined to consider this verbose and excitable intriguer for the post of party agent, he was automatically debarred as soon as it had been decided not to appoint an M.P. Finally Mr. G. C. T. Bartley was appointed to succeed Gorst. He had previously been Manager of the National Penny Bank and was later to become an M.P.

Bartley's tenure of office until 1885 covered two changes which were of immense importance in the field of party organization as a whole, and which closely affected the position of the Central Office and its relations with the constituencies: the Corrupt Practices Act of 1883 and the Reform Bill of 1884. The effect of the former was described by Bartley himself in a talk to party organizers on "The Condition of the Conservative Party in the Midlands". He quoted examples of the enormous reduction in expenditure on elections entailed by the new Act. Thus about £100,000 was spent in fifty-five Midland constituencies by the Conservative party in 1880. The new permitted maximum would be about £37,000. In Leicestershire North, with an electorate of 6,849, the expenditure of 1880 was £6,306 (nearly £2 for each of the 3,369 Conservative votes cast) while it would now be limited to £1,425. Bartley warned his audience that much greater reliance would in future have to be placed on voluntary help. Such voluntary work would not be forthcoming unless the individual party supporter could be made to feel that he had a place and a voice in the organi-

[58] Iddesleigh Papers, Add. MS. 50020, Salisbury to Northcote, 20 Jan. 1883.
[59] Ibid., Add. MS. 50041, Ashmead Bartlett to Northcote, 8 Jan. 1883.

zation.[60] The same point had earlier been made by Smith in a letter to Salisbury:

I do not set my judgment up against Stanhope's and Cross's—but I do not like the Corrupt Practices bill and I do not think it will work well for our friends if it becomes law. You know quite as much as I do of the habits and customs of the Tory but I have not found them to be eager volunteers in canvassing or organisation. The machinery of an election has had to be provided at somebody's cost hitherto, and much of this is to be prohibited in the future. The result will be I am afraid that we shall not poll anything approaching our strength. The Radicals have the Trade Unions, the Dissenting Chapels and every Society for the abolition of property and morality working for them. Our supporters only want to be let alone, to be allowed to enjoy what they have: and they think they are so secure that they will make no sacrifice of time or of pleasure to prepare against attack or to resist it. So, to stave off the evil day as long as possible, I should wish to retain the power of fighting elections by paid agency if necessary as in the past, but I am afraid I am in a small minority in the party in the House of Commons who only think of one thing, issuing the cheque to be drawn on their bankers.[61]

In the long run the effect of the Corrupt Practices Act was to increase the meaning of party and lessen the power of influence. Thereby the weight which the Central Office carried was also increased: it had a firm network of local organizations to deal with, and could gradually gain a bigger voice in the selection of candidates, since candidatures depended no longer so much on influence and wealth. The conception of party management which Gorst had advocated could come more into its own, as opposed to the electoral habits of the 'old identity' who still preferred to work through influence and corruption.

It was not to be expected, however, that the effects of the Corrupt Practices Act should show themselves rapidly and certainly not before the next general election. The immediate prospects, from the point of view of the party organization, showed little improvement. At the end of the year Stanhope was still complaining to Salisbury about the absence of candidates in many constituencies. He put the chief blame on the laziness of local leaders, or jealousies between them, though he

---

[60] *Minutes of the National Union Conference, 1883.*
[61] Salisbury Papers, W. H. Smith to Salisbury, 14 Aug. 1883.

admitted that the list of candidates at the Central Office was also not satisfactory. They hoped to hold meetings in various parts of the country to arouse the constituencies within that region, and they asked Salisbury and Northcote for a letter which might be sent to sluggish constituency associations.[62]

The years 1883 to 1884 witnessed the great struggle over the National Union of Conservative Associations precipitated by Lord Randolph Churchill and his supporters. The party organization was in the public eye as it had never been before. This controversy is discussed in the next chapter. In the meantime, in spite of all the sound and fury of the dispute over the National Union, the Conservative Central Office, now under Bartley, continued to carry out its appointed tasks. A real electoral recovery still eluded the Tories, in spite of the stormy passage which the Gladstone government had had ever since it came into office. Moreover, the last and perhaps greatest upheaval of the nineteenth century was about to remould the electoral system, with unpredictable consequences for the party. The organization of the Central Office itself in the spring of 1884 is set out in a document evidently prepared for Lord Salisbury, at a time when the controversy with Lord Randolph Churchill was forcing him to give thought to the relations between the Central Office and the National Union:

The Conservative Central Office and the National Union

Present distribution of work

(1) Conservative Central Committee

Executive Member	Mr. Bartley
Secretaries	{ Hon. Fitzroy Stewart { Mr. W. H. Rowe

Duties	*Department*
Negotiations with constituencies respecting candidates, interviews with candidates and others	} Mr. Bartley and Mr. Stewart
Superintendence of organising agents	Mr. Bartley
Organisation of provincial meetings to stimulate activity	} Mr. Bartley

[62] Ibid., Stanhope to Salisbury, 29 Dec. 1883. For the effect of the Corrupt Practices Bill, see O'Leary, op. cit., Chapter VI; also William B. Gwyn, *Democracy and the Cost of Politics in Britain* (1962), pp. 89 ff.

Assisting members and candidates with
political information, references,
statistics, etc.   } Mr. Bartley and
                                                  Secretaries

Editing annual List of Agents and
Associations   } Secretaries

Finance: (1) Account of Central Fund
     (2) A/c of Registration Assoc.
     (3) Subagents expenses
     (4) Lecture Fund
     (5) Office expenses

Sub-Committees

County Organisation	Mr. Akers Douglas	Chr.
Reform Bill	Sir M. Beach	Chr.
Scotch Organisation	Mr. McLeod	Secy.
Irish do.	Mr. Barton	Secy.

Preparation and supply of Election and
Registration Forms and instruction   } Mr. Rowe

General Correspondence averaging 1500
letters received per month   } Mr. Bartley and
                                                  Secs.

Occasional Conferences in London on
matters relating to Organisation   } do.

National Union

Supplying lecturers and obtaining
speakers at meetings (say 500 per annum)   } The Secretaries

Collection of information as to condition
of Associations   } The Secretaries

Publication of Pamphlets, Leaflets, etc.   do.

Promoting meetings on current political
questions   } do.

Promoting petitions to Parliament   do.

Organising Annual Conference and Banquet   do.

Finance:
Accounts of Nat. Union and of late
Metropolitan Cons. Alliance, absorbed   } do.[63]
in N.U.

Bartley impressed on the party leaders the need to give
encouragement to the secretaries and active members of Con-

[63] Salisbury Papers, filed with Lord Randolph Churchill letters, undated.

servative Associations and Working Men's Clubs, especially in London. He suggested that Conservative noblemen should throw open their country houses to visiting parties of such men, thus bringing into play long-standing Tory habits of deference.[64] Winn, then Chief Whip, frequently criticized Bartley on the ground that his experience of election management had been gained entirely in large boroughs and that he knew nothing of the counties.[65]

Winn and Bartley also clashed on the franchise and redistribution question in 1884. Winn was convinced that, in a reformed House of Commons, the Conservatives would be swamped by a vast Radical majority. He was in favour of using the Tory majority in the House of Lords to force a dissolution on the Franchise Bill. He hoped that in an election fought on the old electorate the Conservatives would improve their position sufficiently to block parliamentary reform entirely.[66] Bartley, on the other hand, was anxious that the Conservative party should take up the middle ground in politics and, by publishing a redistribution scheme of their own, show that they were in earnest in wishing to settle the parliamentary reform question on a equitable basis. Bartley's general approach to the political scene in 1884 can best be seen from a memorandum he prepared for Salisbury and Northcote:

> There is no doubt that the Government has acted wisely from their party point of view in managing to run the whole line of public thought in the direction of the franchise and diverting it from the much more serious matters of public policy in which they have so seriously failed.
>
> I am of opinion, however, that the Liberal demonstrations of the autumn have not come up either in number or enthusiasm to that which the Radical party contemplated.
>
> I am also sure that the Conservative demonstrations were much more numerous, enthusiastic and important than the Radical party anticipated. The result so far has been satisfactory to our party though I very much doubt whether, owing to this clever party move of the Government, our part at the present moment would stand so well at a General Election, as it would have done if a dissolution had taken place in July last.

[64] Ibid., Bartley to Salisbury, 7 July 1884.
[65] Ibid., Winn to Salisbury, 15 Oct. 1884.
[66] Ibid., Winn to Salisbury, 6 Oct. 1884.

The result of the demonstration has been to prove clearly that the Conservatives as well as the Liberals are prepared to give the Franchise, and to emphasize to a great extent that the difference between the two parties is one which, from a practical point of view, should be easily got over, supposing that both are in real earnest.

The Conservative party has everything to gain by getting rid of the Franchise agitation, if it can do so on a fair and proper basis, so that the attention of the public may be drawn to other matters in which the Government have so seriously jeopardised the interests of the Empire. On the other hand, the Liberal party has everything to gain by intensifying the agitation. The getting rid of the subject by an unfair compromise, or by the Lords giving way, is of course not to be thought of, but the question of putting our party, and the Lords right with the country and for the General Election is all important.

I feel, however, that if the agitation is to go on, particularly as indications have been recently seen of riot on the part of the Radicals, serious damage will be done to our case unless the steps we now take are such as to ensure the sympathy and support of that great mass of the soberminded public, who lie between the Radicals and the Conservatives, and whose oscillation from one side to the other is amply sufficient to control the result of the elections. These people do not see the fine distinctions which induce the actions of party, but they judge roughly by results and are even now hesitating on which of the two parties they shall lay the fault of the impending deadlock. Everything therefore to my mind depends on our clearly showing this large section of the public that the Conservative party is not the horse to be saddled with the deadlock. I believe that anything like the following action will seriously alienate this party from us:

1st   Any obstruction, whether direct or indirect, in the House of Commons, to delay the division on the Franchise Bill, as it stands.
2nd Mere objection to a Government scheme or redistribution unless that objection is coupled with a clear and distinct statement of the view that the Conservative party take of redistribution and a distinct statement of the line on which we should ourselves adopt a redistribution bill.[67]

It cannot have been helpful to the smooth conduct of party affairs that the Chief Whip and the Principal Party Agent took so different a view of the central political question of the day. It is also remarkable that Bartley was so persistent in putting his opinions on a matter of high policy to the party leaders. He

[67] Ibid., Bartley to Salisbury, 25 Oct. 1884.

seems to have taken a more elevated view of his functions as party agent than any of his predecessors and, like Gorst, he had strong political ambitions. During the dispute with Lord Randolph Churchill, Bartley considered it his duty to lay before the party leaders a memorandum telling them how to conduct their business. He proposed the setting up of 'Opposition Cabinet Councils' in other words a formalized Shadow Cabinet. This would decide the Opposition tactics on current parliamentary business and would also serve as a means of recruiting fresh blood to the front bench while the party was in opposition.[68] Salisbury had earlier been strongly opposed to Shadow Cabinets and attributed to them much of the trouble in the party.[69]

In August 1884, Bartley had written to Salisbury that he felt that the office of party agent could be most efficiently performed by a member of the House of Commons. If at the time of the next general election the party leaders still could not share this view he would want to reconsider his party appointment.[70] Now he was shocked by the scant regard the party leaders paid to his recommendations and, on the eve of the Conference between Government and Opposition leaders on redistribution in November 1884, he wrote a letter of resignation, curiously reminiscent of similar outpourings by his predecessors:

I regret to have to place in your hands my resignation from the office of agent of the Conservative party. The reason I am compelled to do this is that the position is altogether different from that which I anticipated and from that which I consider to be necessary if the duties are to be performed in a satisfactory manner. I feel I am not in the confidence of the leaders of the party. I have not been asked to be present on any occasion when the policy of the party has been discussed and I know nothing of what is going on or what is to be done except through the newspaper reports. My opinion is rarely if ever asked and little or no use is made of the knowledge which I presumed it was the agent's duty to obtain concerning the party outside Parliament. The agent is simply the secretary of the Conservative Central Office, a useful officer no doubt for clerical and

---

[68] Ibid., Churchill letters, Memorandum from Bartley, 5 Mar. 1884.
[69] Iddesleigh Papers, Add. MS. 50020, Salisbury to Northcote, 10 July 1883.
[70] Salisbury Papers, Bartley to Salisbury, 4 Aug. 1884.

detailed work but a position which I should never have consented to hold and am not disposed to retain.

Very much is required to place our party in its proper position. The organisation throughout the country is most inefficient. Many of the agents are apathetic and new ones of a different class are needed in many places. The Conservative press is miserable—good candidates are not forthcoming—candidates neglect their proposed constituencies. The new Franchise bill has not yet been prepared for and the policy on the great question of redistribution on which our future depends has not even been broadly determined. Such is some of the work to be accomplished but to carry this out requires in my judgment someone as agent who is not made into a clerical secretary and treated as such but one who will enjoy the full confidence of the party leaders and receive from them their constant direction support and assistance. I see no indication yet of being treated in this manner and I therefore prefer to retire.

Again the policy now being pursued with reference to the franchise question will immensely influence the party especially at the next General Election. I am convinced we are steadily losing ground by the line we are pursuing. At the same time I am keenly sensible to the fact that as the so-called agent to the party I shall after the General Election be held largely responsible for the consequences of the very neglect which I point out and which in my present position I am powerless to prevent.[71]

Bartley was induced to withdraw his resignation. Northcote managed to humour him sufficiently to make him stay on till the next general election. Stanhope was inclined to go further and hint to Bartley that the clause requiring the agent to remain out of the Commons might be withdrawn, but Northcote stopped this move.[72] Winn did no better than Bartley in gaining the ears of his leaders. After the meeting at 10 Downing Street between Salisbury and Northcote on the one side and Gladstone, Granville, Hartington, and Dilke on the other, Northcote informed his principal colleagues in the House of Commons of the general character of the redistribution scheme discussed with the Government. He did not take Winn into his confidence and wrote to Salisbury; 'I have seen Winn this evening. He is very Cassandra-like, and thinks us in evil case. I of course told him very little about the scheme.'[73]

[71] Ibid., Bartley to Salisbury, 8 Nov. 1884.
[72] Ibid., Northcote to Salisbury, 12 Dec. 1884.
[73] Ibid., Northcote to Salisbury, 20 Nov. 1884.

With the end of the 1880 Parliament both Bartley and Winn left the sphere of party management. Bartley fought and won North Islington in the General Election of 1885 and Winn was translated to the Lords as Lord St. Oswald. Bartley was succeeded by Captain Middleton, who at last proved to be the ideal party agent, and Winn by Akers-Douglas, an able Chief Whip.[74] Bartley, like Gorst before him, wrote an article in the *Fortnightly*, though unlike his predecessor he signed it and called it 'Conservative Organisation' rather than 'Disorganisation'.[75] It is less critical than Gorst's three years earlier, and deals more with the future than with the past, but the burden of Bartley's comments is very similar.

The old aristocratic predominance in the party and in organization was passing. The Conservatives were at any rate beginning to pat the working classes on the back, but the time was coming when there would be a genuine Conservative organization for the working man. Bartley saw a danger of too much power falling into the hands of wire pullers. This could only be counteracted by broadening the base and the Tories must not be afraid of this. They must trust the people to conserve what is good for the welfare of the country and throw away the rest. It is perhaps hardly surprising that those, like Bartley and Gorst, concerned with maintaining the electoral position of the Conservative party against the advance of political democracy, were acutely aware of the gulf between the masses of the working and middle classes, whose support as voters and active local leaders was required, and the leadership of the party. No one could anticipate that the Conservatives were in fact on the threshold of twenty years of virtually uninterrupted power.

[74] For Middleton's relations with Salisbury, see Lady G. Cecil, *Life of Salisbury*, vol. iii; for Akers-Douglas, see Viscount Chilston, *Chief Whip* (1961).
[75] *Fortnightly*, vol. 37 (1885), p. 611.

VII

THE NATIONAL UNION 1880-5

THROUGHOUT the 1870s the National Union was an integral part of the Conservative Central Office, and served mainly as an agency for the distribution of political literature. The aims of its founders, that it should represent all Conservative associations in the country and serve as a channel of communication between the rank and file and the leaders, had not been realized. Not all constituencies had properly constituted Conservative associations and some important associations were not affiliated to the National Union. No significant political impulses were transmitted to the leaders through the National Union. In the 1880s, however, the National Union was for a brief moment propelled into the limelight of controversy.

Apart from some minor discord, such as the separate appeal for funds reported by Gorst in September 1880, the first attempt to use the National Union for a wider political purpose was precipitated by the death of Beaconsfield in April 1881. There was doubt about Northcote's position, following the election of Salisbury to succeed Beaconsfield in the Lords. Some members of the Fourth Party tried to use the National Union Council to get Salisbury accepted as the sole leader of the party, and Northcote's son reported to his father:

Yesterday at the National Union Council a proposition was sprung on the meeting that a circular should be sent to every Conservative Association throughout the country notifying them that the Union had selected Lord Salisbury as leader of the party. Lord Percy and Bartlett, with some half-hearted support from Gorst, got the meeting adjourned till Tuesday on which day we are all going down to squash the idea summarily.

De Worms wishes you to know that he is working in your favour— in fact everybody is doing so with the exception of Churchill and Drummond Wolff—who I hear are the men who tried to spring this mine on the party. De Worms says he can vouch for this. I am

sorry to say Raikes supported them—at least so Bartlett reports. . . .
I understand that Wolff's idea was purely his own interests i.e. that
Lord Salisbury had given him the Rumelian post, and would, he
thought, be *certain* to employ him again. I fancy Churchill must have
some other brief.[1]

Northcote was annoyed by press reports casting doubt on his
position, but it is unlikely that these moves in the National
Union Council added significantly to his uneasiness, which was
in any case rapidly allayed by Salisbury's loyal support for the
dual leadership. The National Union, closely integrated with
the Central Office and without significant funds of its own,
was not a suitable instrument for fighting a battle within the
party.

Yet only two and a half years later, Lord Randolph Churchill
made the National Union the pivot of his fight for Tory Democracy and for his personal advancement in the party leadership.
There can be little doubt that his choice of battleground was at
least partly determined by the fact that his close ally in the fight
was Gorst, who had a more intimate knowledge of the party
machine than anyone. From Gorst's career as a party organizer
it emerges clearly that he had always seen the problem as a
struggle between democratic and aristocratic principles in the
structure of the Conservative party. Gorst's son suggests that
his father became Lord Randolph's ally in the assault on the
party machine somewhat unwillingly, and only because he had
burnt his boats in his relations with the party leaders.[2] This is
to some extent borne out by the manner of his resignation from
the post of party agent; while his reluctance to join with Lord
Randolph in the fight for the organization is perhaps indicated
by the fact that he spent three months in India on legal
business, when the controversy was at its height. Harold Gorst
wrote his book on the Fourth Party in the early years of this
century, when his father's career had ended in relative failure.
The old man was more than ever embittered and mulled over
his grievances against the various people who at crucial moments
in his career had failed, as he saw it, to treat him according
to his deserts. He was therefore at pains to emphasize his

[1] Iddesleigh Papers, Add. MS. 50040, H. S. Northcote to Sir S. Northcote, 30 Apr. 1881. See also above, p. 37.
[2] H. E. Gorst, *The Fourth Party*, p. 246.

differences with Lord Randolph and to depict himself as motivated by principle while his associate turned out, in the end, to be concerned mainly with self-advancement.

We may grant, however, that the approach of the two men to the National Union conflict was different. Churchill, increasingly a political heavy-weight, saw this conflict as only one aspect of a fight to remould the party in his own image. No doubt the principles of Tory Democracy and his own drive for advancement were inseparable in his mind. In so far as he used the National Union as a base for his offensive, he may have been influenced by the example of Chamberlain's progress with the aid of the National Liberal Federation. Gorst had built for himself an important parliamentary position, but he was only in the second rank as a politician and had still to find a way of effectively pushing his claims for office. He was interested in the reform of the party organization and the introduction of new electoral methods as ends in themselves. He must have known however that the National Union was not at all comparable with the National Liberal Federation, which had grown up as a powerful pressure group, independent of the parliamentary party. He must have realized that the National Union was not very suitable as a platform from which an attack against the official leadership might be launched.

By July 1884, when the controversy was resolved, Lord Randolph had become, quite independently of the fight over the party organization, so potent a figure in the party that it was in any case advisable for the leaders to reach an accommodation with him. Gorst, on the other hand, had become, if anything, more obnoxious than ever in the eyes of the leaders, and was seen at times as the evil councillor behind Churchill in the organization battles. Many in the party establishment had seen him in this guise ever since the Fourth Party drew attention to itself. 'Gorst is, I feel convinced the real motive power in this business, the clever intriguer, D. Wolff his accomplice, and R. Churchill, the monkey, who pulls their dirty chestnuts out of the fire—a pretty trio . . .' So Barrington wrote to Northcote when Churchill's letters attacking the leadership appeared in *The Times* in the spring of 1883.[3] By the summer of 1884 Gorst's

[3] Iddesleigh Papers, Add. MS. 50041, Barrington to Northcote, 4 Apr. 1883.

only chance of political promotion depended on the willingness of Lord Randolph to press his claims.

Both Gorst and Churchill knew that, by making the National Union their chosen battleground, they would be able to canalize the pressure for recognition and influence that was increasingly coming from middle-class provincial Tory leaders. Gorst had incessantly nagged the party leaders about their neglect of this stratum of the party. By his militant stance in and out of Parliament, Lord Randolph appealed to the same groups. To talk the language of Tory Democracy was, however, not free of complications. It also implied an appeal to the working masses, to the 'democracy which supports the Tory Party', as Lord Randolph later put it, and meant simultaneously gaining the support of the working classes as voters and the urban middle classes as leaders. Gorst had thought in such terms ever since the early seventies and Churchill pursued the same goal, a harmony of classes under Tory aegis, in his speeches in the eighties. It was only too easy to lose one's balance and to slip into the language of class warfare, and thus to disturb the harmony. This happened to Forwood, one of Lord Randolph's keenest supporters, when he fought and lost, in December 1882, the by-election in Liverpool caused by Sandon succeeding his father as third Earl of Harrowby. Forwood was blamed for setting 'the mob against the Upper Ten',[4] Smith considered his political faith curious[5] and the *Standard* took the opportunity to declare that it might be more appropriate if Tory Democrats formed a Fifth Party.[6] Forwood defended himself in an article in the *Contemporary Review* in which he reaffirmed his faith in the harmony of classes. He believed that the Tory party stood for established institutions and that it was possible to attach the working classes permanently and genuinely to this cause, for reasons of advantage, emotion, and deference.[7] Churchill and Gorst in their struggle for control of the party organization,

---

[4] Harrowby Papers, L/265, Lord Claud Hamilton to Lord Harrowby (Viscount Sandon), 14 Dec. 1882. See also above, p. 98.

[5] Salisbury Papers, Smith to Salisbury, 9 Dec. 1882.

[6] *Standard*, 9 Dec. 1882. For a discussion of the concept 'Tory Democracy', see William J. Wilkinson, *Tory Democracy* (Studies in History, Economics and Public Law, Columbia University, Vol. CXV, *No. 2*, 1925).

[7] A. B. Forwood, 'Democratic Toryism', *Contemporary Review*, Feb. 1883, p. 294.

were clearly fighting the battle of middle-class Conservative activists, while the Tory working-class voters watched the conflict from a distance. It could be assumed, without stretching anybody's credulity, that Churchill and Gorst, in fighting for a greater share of power in the party for middle-class leaders, were working to broaden the base of the party and were acting in the interest of the Tory masses as well.

Yet it would be an over-simplification to assume that Lord Randolph Churchill and his friends were consistently heading a movement that came up from the grass roots or responding to deep sociological changes in the nature of Toryism.[8] Among those battling for supremacy at National Union Conferences and on the National Union Council, some prominent representatives of urban Conservatism took the side of Lord Randolph: Stone and Hopkins of Birmingham, Wainwright of Blackpool, and Forwood of Liverpool, for example. Others belonged to the loyalists: Charley of Salford, Houldsworth of Manchester, Whitley of Liverpool. Whitley and Forwood, both closely connected with the Conservative party in Liverpool, had been at daggers drawn for years.[9] Edward Clarke, who had worked with Gorst and Raikes as far back as 1867 in founding the National Union, consistently supported the leaders because he considered that Lord Randolph's schemes for the reform of the party organization were unrealistic.[10] Maclean, a strong supporter of Churchill in the National Union Council, switched sides at a crucial moment, because he wanted to end the dual leadership, but preferred Lord Salisbury to Lord Randolph.[11] Similar motives inspired Howorth, a prominent Lancashire Tory: he felt the dual leadership was damaging to the party; he acknowledged Churchill's skill in opposition and appeal as a platform orator, but did not want to boost him in the leadership stakes.[12] Mitford, another Churchill supporter and member of the National Union Council elected at the

---

[8] James Cornford, 'The Transformation of Conservatism in the Late Nineteenth Century', *Victorian Studies*, Vol. VII, No. 1 (Sept. 1963), pp. 41–53, for a discussion of this issue.
[9] Harrowby Papers, particularly Vol. L on Liverpool politics.
[10] Sir Edward Clarke, *The Story of My Life* (1918), pp. 213 ff.
[11] J. M. MacLean, *Recollections of Westminster & India* (1902), p. 68.
[12] Iddesleigh Papers, Add. MS. 50042, H. H. Howorth to Northcote, 26 Feb. 1884.

Birmingham Conference in October 1883, was evidently anxious to maintain friendly relations with Northcote, but he also emphasized the serious aspirations represented by the Churchill faction:

> I must thank you many times for your kind note and the wishes for my success in my contest which you so cordially express. It is a great satisfaction to me to find that both you and Lord Salisbury accept the view expressed by me in our conversation on Sunday, that the course I had deemed it right to pursue in supporting the majority of the Council of the National Union in their endeavour to give effect to the resolution passed at the annual conference held at Birmingham in October last, in no way implies disloyalty to the leaders or a desire to create a division in the party. I trust you will, however, forgive me if I repeat the observation I made to you on Sunday, viz, that, if the masses composing the Conservative Associations throughout the country were, at any time, to realise that their representatives on the Council of the National Union had, through the action of the Central Committee, been unable to carry out the instructions of those Associations as communicated by their delegates at Birmingham the result would probably be deplorable, as an impression might not unnaturally arise that the party organisers in London were indisposed to trust the people. I venture to think that if you and Lord Salisbury can, as our leaders, see your way to smooth our present difficulties, and, by securing the co-operation of all concerned, facilitate the object which the majority of the Council have in view, viz. to meet the wishes of the Conservative Associations, great good will result therefrom.[13]

While urban Conservatism was thus not solidly ranked behind Churchill, those opposing him were by no means united either. Abergavenny, Lord Henry Thynne, and others of the 'old identity' were very critical of Stanhope as a party manager and strongly disliked the Central Committee. Ashmead Bartlett suspected Bartley of supporting the initial attempt in October 1883 of Churchill and his friends to pack the National Union Council.[14] Party organization was the kind of battlefield where personal rivalries often entirely obscured any points of substance that might have been at issue. At a crucial moment of the controversy, on May 1884, when the quarrel was nearly settled,

[13] Iddesleigh Papers, Add. MS. 50042, P. Mitford to Northcote, 29 Apr. 1884.
[14] See below, p. 174.

Salisbury expressed the view that 'the matter is now narrowed down very much to R.C.'s hatred of Stanhope'.[15]

If Churchill and his friends represented an important principle, namely the need to make the Tory party more democratic, the party leaders were by no means unaware of this need. But they could not forget that they were leading a party still very dependent on the counties and the aristocratic position in the country generally, nor that Churchill often on public platforms, used language offensive to many Tory supporters. 'I see R.C. is doing his best to set the owners of property against him', wrote Salisbury to Northcote on 2 April 1884, when the National Union battle was in full swing; 'He will hardly carry Birmingham on those terms.'[16] Moreover, the party leaders had justifiable doubts about whether the National Union was really representative of the movement of Conservative associations in the country:

I rather doubt the expediency of recognising the National Union as 'the representative of the associations on whom the work of the party really depends'. Our ambitious friends will found tremendous claims on such a basis. And I doubt whether the statement is true. There are a good many associations which are not in the Union; and of those which are, there are many which take no real interest in the elections to Council. If the National Union is to be made of greater importance its constitution ought to be carefully revised.[17]

There is no need to retell the course of events between October 1883, when Churchill and his friends started the battle for the National Union at the Birmingham conference, and July 1884, when the controversy was finally laid to rest. The fullest account is still that given by Sir Winston Churchill in the biography of his father.[18] Some sidelights may, however, illustrate how the progress of the battle was viewed by some of the participants

[15] A. J. Balfour, *Chapters of Autobiography* (1930), p. 166.
[16] Iddesleigh Papers, Add. MS. 50020.
[17] Salisbury Papers, Northcote to Salisbury, 24 Feb. 1884.
[18] W. S. Churchill, *Lord Randolph Churchill*, 2 vols. (London 1906, references are to this edition; the biography was republished in one volume in 1951). Other important accounts are to be found in A. J. Balfour, *Chapters of Autobiography;* H. E. Gorst, *The Fourth Party*; R. R. James, *Lord Randolph Churchill* (1959). The first academic discussion of the controversy is to be found in M. Ostrogorski, *Democracy and the Organisation of Political Parties* (1902), vol. i.

at various stages. Northcote received alarmist reports from his faithful but self-interested follower, Ashmead Bartlett, about the plans of the Fourth Party for the Birmingham Conference:

> I feel it my duty to let you know what has just reached me here, as it seems very important that counteracting steps should be taken at once. A confidential circular has been sent round to the various delegates (I have seen a printed copy) from Conservative Associations who will attend the forthcoming conference at Birmingham on 1st October to ask them to vote for a printed list of gentlemen as members of the new Council of the National Union. This circular is signed by Lord Randolph Churchill, Mr. Gorst and two others. The plan is as follows—to elect a Council on which the 'Fourth Party' can command a regular majority, and then use it as a representative (a good cry) body of the whole party and in a way generally favourable to their views. One of the first steps will be to choose a leader. Now all this may be and no doubt is 'ultra vires', but in my opinion the plan should be met and overthrown at once—i.e. at Birmingham on 1st October. Otherwise we shall have the greatest mischief done to the party. To countervail this carefully organised scheme there are only two methods (1) the presence at Birmingham of several prominent leaders of the party: I would suggest Mr. Stanhope and Sir R. Cross (2) an immediate effort to influence the local delegates not to support the list in question. I shall be at Birmingham but I cannot fight them singlehanded. I can do much, however, if the leaders of the party head the opposition.
>
> I think the whole scheme new and offensive, and very much like the means by which Mr. Chamberlain established his influence in the Liberal party. You have to deal with clever men, tolerably unscrupulous and acquainted with the material among whom they are working. Mr. Bartley is perhaps with them. No-one less than Mr. Stanhope will be of any avail.[19]

Northcote inquired of Smith if he knew of any of their colleagues going to Birmingham,[20] but he did not allow himself to be stampeded by Ashmead Bartlett and refused to intervene:

> I need hardly say that I am much obliged to you for your information, the importance of which I fully appreciate. I will take care to keep your name entirely secret. It is extremely difficult to see how

[19] Iddesleigh Papers, Add. MS. 50041, Bartlett to Northcote, 20 Sept. 1883.
[20] Viscount Chilston, *W. H. Smith*, p. 180.

to meet such a move as you describe without doing as much harm as good. Suppose I were to take any steps to influence the members of the National Union to vote against the proposed list, I should at once publish the existence of a split in the party and in a manner which would give it much more consequence than it ought to have. Perhaps too, if I were successful in getting a list more to my mind, I might find that I had created a Frankenstein's creature with which it would hereafter be more difficult to deal. As matters stand at present the National Union is a body which has no authority whatever and should it begin to assert any claim to the character of a representative body there would be no great difficulty in meeting it, and in disputing any authority which it might pretend to. Certainly if it were to take upon itself to 'choose a leader' it would be easy enough to expose its conduct and to bring the matter properly before the party. On the whole I am averse to any initiative move on the part of the leaders. But I will not neglect your warning and I will communicate with one or two friends, taking care not to mention you. I doubt whether Stanhope is in England.[21]

A few days later Ashmead Bartlett again pressed Northcote to act, and asked him to send Stanhope and Clarke to Birmingham.[22] As can be seen from Lord Randolph's biography, the Fourth Party move to pack the National Union Council did not fully succeed, but as twelve more members were to be co-opted subsequently, Churchill and his friends could still hope to dominate it. Cranbrook, who attended the Birmingham meeting, sent an interesting account of his experiences to Northcote:

The meeting last night was very large but the room not a very agreeable one to speak in. However I got a fair audience and the 'getters-up' appeared to be satisfied. This morning the meeting of delegates took place at Birmingham and I went in with Lord Dartmouth. On the resolution to confirm the report a rider was moved obviously at the instigation of Randolph Churchill and Gorst 'directing the Council to take steps to assert its legitimate influence in party organisation'. I am not sure of the words as I have no copy. The sense was as I write. Before this Randolph Churchill addressed the gathering being first received with quite tumultuous applause. He urged that the Council ought to hold the place of the Central

[21] Iddesleigh Papers, Add. MS. 50041, Northcote to Bartlett, 26 Sept. 1883.
[22] Ibid., Add. MS. 50041, Bartlett to Northcote, 30 Sept. 1883.

Committee which was secret, an agent of corruption not publishing accounts and that the funds which it held should be transferred to the Council! He was foolish enough to assert that in managing election business there was nothing to conceal and that full accounts ought to be given to the world or they would by the body to which he wished to assign the funds. An Executive Committee of that body would undertake electioneering management etc. etc. All was easy and so on. He insinuated rather than stated that the party was ill-led and wanted vigour imparting to it which would come from the united association. . . . I thought it best to say a few words which I did cautiously saying that while the rider in itself conveyed no very dangerous meaning that if interpreted by Lord Randolph's speech it would probably work to disunion, that the funds could not be at the disposal of the Council as they were not subscribed for it and that it was not representative of constituencies in general but only of affiliated associations which by no means covered the ground. That all wished that the just pretensions of so powerful a body should be admitted but that they ought not to claim too much. This to some extent modified the feeling which had been roused and some of the influential men among the delegates spoke in the same sense. Ashmead Bartlett did the same and very ably on many points. Gorst backed Randolph Churchill saying that all would be easy, no danger of 'splits', etc. etc. But the meeting was becoming reasonable and when Percy with much tact summed up in the sense of accepting the rider without a division but with the distinct understanding that Randolph Churchill's interpretation was not to commit anyone there was a very general if not universal assent.[23]

Ashmead Bartlett was less hopeful and thought it his duty once more to warn Northcote:

I can assure you that the party is passing through a very serious crisis. Lord Randolph Churchill and his friends are *very popular* and very bitter; and the only way in which they can be met is by fair fight inside the National Union. To suppress the Union would raise a storm among the rank and file of the party and give the Fourth Party a fine handle. Lord Cranbrook's presence was very salutary. He will no doubt tell you how extremely Lord Randolph Churchill

[23] Iddesleigh Papers, Add. MS. 50041, Cranbrook to Northcote, 2 Oct. 1883. The full text of the rider was 'that this conference of the National Union while thanking the Council for their services directs the Council for the ensuing year to take such steps as may be requisite for securing to the National Union its legitimate influence in the party organisation'. (McKenzie, *British Political Parties*, p. 169).

and Mr. Gorst spoke. Their words were an almost verbatim repetition of the article in the Fortnightly last April.[24]

After the Birmingham Conference twelve members (on the whole favourable to Churchill) were duly co-opted on to the National Union Council and this enlarged council elected an Organization Committee consisting mainly of Churchill's supporters. Neither Stanhope nor Salisbury nor Northcote were unduly alarmed by these developments. Stanhope reported to Northcote:

I have now heard all that is at present known of the recent proceedings of the National Union. It is perhaps as well that I should tell you that the first meeting of the new Organisation Committee of the Union was held on Saturday. The secretaries (Rowe and Stewart) were excluded from the room. Percy was present, but does not wish to disclose personally anything that took place. They first displaced Percy who according to practice would have taken the chair ex officio, and elected Randolph. They then agreed to present their case to Lord Salisbury as the leader of the party.

An effort is also being made to collect funds but I find that it is only proposed to collect small subscriptions, and ostensibly at any rate for the purpose of carrying on the business of lectures and distribution of political literature.

I have had a long talk with Percy and he is of the opinion that an attempt will shortly be made to carry the war into the constituencies, and that some sort of crisis in the relations between this new Committee and the Central is inevitable: and he also thinks that it will not be well to postpone it, but rather to let it take place during Gorst's absence.

My own view is that nothing has at this moment happened which should induce the Central Committee to make any move. But that the moment any step is taken which clashes with or interferes with our action, we must be prepared with a line. In my opinion the time will then have come for the course I once before suggested, a conference between the Central Committee and Lord Randolph in the presence of Lord Salisbury and yourself.

We could of course at any time precipitate a crisis by withdrawing the pecuniary assistance we gave to the Union. This would, I think, be at present unwise, for as yet nothing has been done by Lord

[24] Iddesleigh Papers, Add. MS. 50041, Bartlett to Northcote, 2 Oct. 1883. The article referred to is Lord Randolph's famous piece 'Elijah's Mantle'.

Randolph and his Committee to our knowledge, which is outwardly
inconsistent with loyalty. The resolution of the Conference at Birmingham is capable of being interpreted as meaning only to suggest
a more adequate representation of the National Union upon the
Central Committee. If the matter could be resolved, nothing would
be simpler, provided always that any new representation of the
National Union should be loyal to the existing leaders of the party.
At present, out of 7 members, 2 are members of the Council of the
Union. And it would be easy in February—when I shall in any case
suggest that the Central Committee shall lay down their office
before the body that created them last year, and ask for fresh
appointment—to add, in place of one of our existing members, the
name of someone from the Council of the Union.

The upshot of all this is that I think we should decide when we
want the crisis and then act promptly and decisively.

You also ask me about the 'Primrose League'. I cannot at present
find anything alarming about it. Percy has the papers relating to it.
But I shall gradually get more information.[25]

An interview was now arranged between the party leaders
and the Organization Committee. The request was addressed
to Lord Salisbury, since it was Lord Randolph's declared aim
to end Northcote's share in the leadership. Northcote seems
at first to have been inclined to leave Salisbury to deal with the
matter, but then changed his mind.[26] He did not want to give
Lord Randolph any chance of driving a wedge between himself
and Salisbury, or to make good his claim that Salisbury was to
be considered the sole leader of the party. Lord Randolph's
most recent biographer feels that Northcote, by his lukewarm
attitude, lost the goodwill even of men like Percy who initially
supported him and caused them to transfer their allegiance to
Salisbury.[27] He also sees the controversy being handled increasingly between Salisbury and Churchill, thus emphasizing
Northcote's decline. This decline was certainly a fact, but it
may be doubted if the course of the National Union controversy
contributed much to it. Salisbury was receiving advice from
his nephew, Arthur Balfour, who had drifted away from the

[25] Iddesleigh Papers, Add. MS. 50042, Stanhope to Northcote, 13 Dec.
1883.
[26] Salisbury Papers, Northcote to Salisbury, 15, 18 (telegram) Dec. 1883,
Christmas Day 1883. Also Iddesleigh Papers, Add. MS. 50063A, Northcote's Diary, 14 Dec. 1883.
[27] R. R. James, op. cit., p. 156.

Fourth Party by this time and had just publicly differed from Churchill over the Reform question. Balfour's advice was to keep calm in the organization battle,[28] to let Lord Randolph take the initiative and put himself in the wrong. This was exactly what Northcote was doing. Both leaders wanted to avoid a fight if they possibly could.

The battle entered a more serious phase in February 1884, with the resignation of Percy from the chairmanship of the National Union Council. Stanhope was now pressing for more decisive action. 'Unless a strong move is now made', he wrote to Salisbury, 'the Central Committee may put up its shutters very soon'.[29] On 29 February 1884, Salisbury sent his so-called 'Charter' letter to the Organization Committee. Northcote anticipated that Churchill would base large claims upon it. Salisbury's attempt to clear up the misunderstanding and the National Union Council's decision to adopt the Organization Committee's Report, which Salisbury had refused to accept, much exacerbated the quarrel. Abergavenny, who was by no means hostile to Churchill, felt that the young man had gone too far and that 'the sinews of war' must be withheld from him. Perhaps with reference to Gorst, Abergavenny told Salisbury that Churchill had 'evil councillors behind him'.[30]

Bartley's letter threatening to eject the National Union from its offices, no doubt a tactical mistake, followed on 17 March and brought the dispute to white heat.[31] Bartley's letter had, however, the immediate effect of making Churchill and Gorst put out feelers for peace:

Capt. Fellowes, Randolph's brother-in-law, has been talking with me about the great schism, and is very anxious that you and I should have a quiet talk with Churchill, Gorst and Winn, and should try to arrive at some kind of arrangement.

Can you manage this? I think we ought to prevent an open split at such a time as the present.[32]

Hicks Beach also acted as peacemaker.[33] A meeting between

[28] A. J. Balfour, op. cit., pp. 163 ff.
[29] Salisbury Papers, Stanhope to Salisbury, 7 Feb. 1884.
[30] Ibid., Churchill letters, Abergavenny to Salisbury, 16 Mar. 1884.
[31] A draft of this letter is quoted by R. R. James, op. cit., p. 144.
[32] Salisbury Papers, Northcote to Salisbury, 18 Mar. 1884.
[33] Ibid., Hicks Beach to Salisbury, 18 Mar. 1884.

Churchill, Gorst, Salisbury, Northcote, and Winn took place on 21 March. The decisive point in the controversy had been reached: was the National Union to be given real control over election expenditure, selection of candidates, and policy, or was it to remain the servant of the leaders, useful as a propaganda and publicity agency, but without a decisive function of its own? The leaders never wavered from the latter view and it was put with considerable cogency in a memorandum prepared at this moment by Northcote:

Party Organisation   Very Confidential

(1) The Parliamentary leaders must be held responsible for the direction of the political action of the party. It is of course incumbent on them to maintain free relations both with the members of the party in the two Houses of the legislature and with the great body of Conservatives out of doors. The former object is to be attained by occasional party meetings, but still more by personal intercourse with members, and by the aid of the Whips. The latter object is to be pursued by some kind of organisation calculated to bring Conservatives together, to enlighten them as to the questions of the day and as to the action which their leaders are taking with reference to these questions, and to assist them to give effect to their opinions by returning proper candidates.

(2) It is obvious that the action of the party will be stimulated and directed from two different quarters. There will be the motive power exercised from the centre, and that exercised by the various local associations. We ought to avail ourselves of both classes of influence, taking care to avoid anything which may bring about a conflict between them. The most active elements of political life are to be found in the local associations, and the future prospects of the Conservative party depend largely upon the proper working of these associations. While they undoubtedly promise the best results, if they are well managed, they are exposed to serious danger, and may conceivably be converted into centres of mischievous political agitation, if they are allowed to fall into the hands of rash, or self-seeking, or incompetent guides.

(3) The question whether it is wise and desirable to bring the various local associations into connection with the central body such as the National Union, is one which it is not necessary to discuss. The step has already been taken; and what we have now to do is this, to enquire how we may turn it to the best account. It is

observed by some that the Union although to some extent a representative body, does not really represent the great mass of the Conservatives throughout the country: and it may be added that its machinery gives but little direct power to the great mass of its members. The power really lies with the Council; which is indeed annually elected; but which, when once chosen, can act pretty much as it likes. That power will be greatly increased by the changes which it is sought to introduce into the relations between the Council and the Central Committee of the party.

(4) It becomes then a question whether steps should be taken to give the union a more truly representative character than it at present possesses; or whether on the other hand it is better to keep it in a less perfect state of organisation and to act upon it, through the agency of the Central Committee, or in some other manner so as to prevent its becoming too strong or going too wild. I myself am of opinion that the latter is the safer course, and that the leaders of the party should keep as firm a hand as they can upon the Council, treating that body as a good servant but a bad master. Only we must take care not so to weaken it as to render its influence for good nugatory.

(5) On the whole then I am disposed to recommend:

   (a) That the National Union should be allowed to remain at St. Stephen's Chambers.

   (b) To retain the services of the Secretaries.

   (c) To receive a moderate annual sum from our funds, subject to reduction in case of our contributions falling off.

   (d) That the Party Whip or Whips should be ex officio members of the Council.

   (e) That in the event of the leaders of the party desiring to confer with the Council upon any matters of party interest, they should have the right to ask for a special meeting.

   (f) That it should be understood that the Council have nothing to do with the selection of candidates for seats in Parliament.

   (g) That in the event of any question being raised upon matters of general politics it should be decided only at a special meeting, of which due notice should be given to the party leaders, who should have the right to attend such meetings.[34]

Gorst, who had returned from India only at the beginning of March, was anxious not to let matters go too far, and had a private talk with Northcote:

[34] Ibid., Churchill letters, undated.

Sir Stafford Northcote to Lord Salisbury, 28 March 1884.

Gorst came to me last night and asked for a private interview this morning. I have seen him. He is very anxious to come to some terms, and, if possible before their Council meeting next Friday. I told him frankly that the real question was whether the National Union was going to work with us or against us; and I gave him my view as to the mischief they had been doing with their secret circulars, and private inner cabinets, and so forth. He said some things had been done in his absence which he did not approve of; and he especially thought the way Percy had been treated was wrong. They were, however, most anxious for harmony and were prepared to come to almost any terms he suggested. They wished to nominate an Executive Committee at their meeting on Friday, and would submit the list to us, and add or strike out any names we wish. They were also ready to explain that by the phrase 'large principles of general policy' (or whatever the words are) they did not mean political questions properly so-called, but only principles of organisation. Further they would undertake not to interfere in the selection of candidates.[35]

This sounded accommodating enough, but when Gorst gave Northcote the names of those who were to serve on the proposed Executive Committee the latter thought them of a 'queer colour'. All but Percy were Churchill men, and Northcote doubted if Percy would be prepared to serve on such a body.[36] Salisbury and Northcote now prepared a carefully worded letter to Churchill as Chairman of the Organization Committee, which, while conditionally withdrawing the notice 'to quit', contained the suggestion made by Northcote in his memorandum that the Whips should sit *ex officio* on the National Union Council. Churchill treated this letter as an insult, summoned a meeting of the Organization Committee and sent Salisbury a lengthy and harshly worded reply.[37] Northcote's comment on it to Salisbury was; 'This is not encouraging. Perhaps, however, his Council will place the matter on a rather more reasonable footing. Probably we shall have to fight sooner or later.'[38]

Northcote's expectations proved correct: Churchill for the

[35] Ibid., Northcote to Salisbury, 28 Mar. 1884.
[36] Ibid., Northcote to Salisbury, 28 Mar. 1884.
[37] W. S. Churchill, op. cit., pp. 537–44.
[38] Salisbury Papers, Northcote to Salisbury, 4 Apr. 1884.

moment prevailed at the meeting of the National Union Council on 4 April, but at the next meeting on 2 May he was outvoted, as a result of Maclean changing sides and carrying a motion which Lord Randolph considered tantamount to a vote of no confidence. In the month between 4 April and 2 May the forces of compromise were fully at work. That this should have been so, after the harsh words that had passed, shows that Churchill and his friends were aware of the limitations of their case. The party leaders were certainly not giving way on the essentials, although they were prepared to give the National Union more financial backing. Abergavenny, who, owing to his dislike of both Stanhope and the Central Committee, could be considered a neutral third party, lent his good offices. His report to Salisbury shows that on matters of substance Churchill was prepared to recognize the authority of the leaders and of the Whips and party agent acting under them:

Keith-Falconer has at my request had an interview with Randolph Churchill as to the unfortunate state of affairs relative to the National Union. Randolph Churchill complains that the Central Committee had thought fit to give notice to the National Union to quit, that you and Northcote had sanctioned their action and that consequently he will have no further intercourse with the Committee. He states that the National Union will leave as requested, that he will appeal through its Council for funds throughout the Kingdom and will explain the cause of the breach between the Union and the leaders of the party and so far as I understand he appears to be sanguine as to the result of his appeal. As to the interference in the selection of candidates he states distinctly that it had never been contemplated and agrees that were such action to be taken by the Union it would place the leaders and Whips of the party in an impossible and intolerable position. He further states that were the Central Committee dissolved and the party management placed in the hands of the Whips and Head Agent as heretofore the leaders might count on the hearty and loyal co-operation of the National Union and that he would move at the next annual conference that the Whips whould be ex officio members of the Council. He considers that as the National Union has been cast off by the party, for the present any further co-operation with the Central Committee has become impossible. It is now some weeks since I had any conversation with Randolph Churchill but from what he then told me and from what I have since heard from others I have no doubt that he feels much hurt and is greatly annoyed at the National Union receiving notice to leave St. Stephen's Chambers. I am, however, of opinion that were that letter to be withdrawn it is possible he might be persuaded to act in a more friendly spirit. As to the Central Committee I feel certain that the sooner it is abolished the better and I may add that the National Union as at present constituted will refuse to work with them.[39]

Salisbury's draft of a reply to Abergavenny shows him prepared to dissolve the Central Committee in the long run, but not immediately in response to pressure from Lord Randolph:

We must talk over the matter when we meet with our friends, as it is one of no small difficulty. R.C. has flown, quite gratuitously, at the throats of the C.C. and to dissolve them now, after his letter to me, which being official is generally known, would be to throw them over, without cause or blame on them, at his dictation. Such a step would be a grave slight on very good men without any justification and would alienate many people in the party which are quite as important to it as R.C. Moreover it would place us in a position which neither N. or I should like to occupy. That if the C.C. is not dissolved it is quite clear that R.C. and his Union, after their anathemas, cannot possibly work together with them and they must have separate establishments.

However, it is a matter wh. can be better discussed by word of mouth. P.S. Do not understand me to be wedded to the plan of a C.C. There is a great deal to be said the other way. It is their dissolution *now* wh. seems to me to be out of the question.[40]

It is not surprising that, by the end of April 1884, Salisbury felt that there was little left in the conflict apart from Churchill's hatred of Stanhope. Stanhope himself felt uneasy about the compromise that was in the offing.[41] It is not true, as Churchill's biographers state, that Salisbury broke off negotiations with Lord Randolph as soon as he became aware of the motion put down by Maclean for the National Union Council meeting on 2 May.[42] Winn wrote to Churchill on 1 May suggesting a meeting between two or three representatives of the leaders and the National Union Council to arrive at 'a basis of arrangement'.[43] This letter was sent with the approval of Salisbury,

[39] Salisbury Papers, Abergavenny to Salisbury, 14 Apr. 1884.
[40] Ibid., Salisbury to Abergavenny, 19 Apr. 1884.
[41] Ibid., Stanhope to Salisbury, 1 May, 1884.
[42] W. S. Churchill, op. cit., i. 325, R. R. James, op. cit., p. 148.
[43] Salisbury Papers, Winn to Salisbury with enclosure Winn to Churchill 1 May 1884.

Northcote, and Stanhope. A compromise was therefore being planned right up to the day of the National Union Council meeting. Then, the largely fortuitous course of events arising from Maclean's motion threw matters once more into the melting pot. Renewed attempts at compromise followed. A deputation led by Forwood saw Salisbury on 8 May. They were prepared to accept two House of Commons Whips as members of the National Union Council, but demanded as a *quid pro quo* that the Chairman of the Council, Lord Randolph himself, if he resumed the office, should be an *ex officio* member of the Central Committee. Lord Salisbury refused an answer on this point. The deputation disclaimed any desire to interfere with the Central Committee and denied that they held 'democratic or destructive ideas'.[44] Churchill's re-election to the Chairman-ship of the National Union Council on 16 May theoretically put the clock back to where it had been at the end of April. Yet the most bitter phase of the dispute began now. This was due as much to events in the House of Commons as to the battle over organization.

The Conservatives were hopelessly split over the Reform Bill. Lord Randolph, who at Edinburgh the previous December had spoken against Reform, now gave up all opposition to it, perhaps because many of the Conservative associations in Lancashire and the Midlands were in favour of it. A split in the Conser-vative party and a realignment of parties were once more within the bounds of possibility. Northcote still did not want to get into a fight with the Fourth Party if it could be avoided, and was sceptical about efforts to influence elections to the National Union Council[45] Yet by early June he was writing to Salisbury of his fears that the party might tear itself apart:

> It seems like the opening of a new parallel by the 4th Party, and I fear it bodes a great deal of trouble. They may get up these meet-ings in some of the Northern towns, and embarrass not only the House of Lords but the whole Conservative Party. Various indica-tions lead me to think that Randolph is going in boldly, and will ride 'Tory Democracy' pretty hard. If he does, we may come to a split, and the line of cleavage may alter, and some new adjustment of party forces may take place. If it is to be by a rapprochement

[44] Ibid., Churchill letters, Minutes of Meeting of 8 May, 1884.
[45] Ibid., Northcote to Salisbury, 19 May 1884.

between the Tory Democrats and the Radical Democrats, our case must be to keep our Tory Working Men from falling into the snare. If you can say anything to strengthen their hands it will be very useful.

Of course any real co-operation between Radical and Tory Democrats may affect our relations with the Whigs. I have no faith in them: but we must not needlessly alienate them.[46]

Nevertheless neither Salisbury nor Northcote were eager to put themselves forward too prominently in the National Union battle.[47] This made Northcote reluctant to back up the so-called 'loyal party', men like Percy, Chaplin, and Ashmead Bartlett. In particular he pressed for a postponement of the National Union Conference, to be held in Sheffield at the end of July 1884.[48] He was thereby cutting the ground from under the feet of the loyalists who were anxious to confront their enemies. Ashmead Bartlett wrote him a bitter letter complaining about the lack of reward for his long record of loyalty and for the great political risks he had taken.[49] No doubt this timid conduct weakened Northcote's position in the party even further. Salisbury, on the other hand, continued to declare his firm support for Stanhope and the Central Committee only a month before the final settlement produced the resignation of the one and the dissolution of the other:

I am very much distressed to hear that a proposition has been made to you to appease Churchill by consenting to the abolition of the Central Committee: and that it has been represented as having our sanction. You may understand that I have given to it no countenance whatever. In my judgment you have done very valuable service, at a great cost of labour energy and time: and that if after your self-sacrificing efforts, a slur were cast upon you because of the animosity which one or two men have conceived against you, no man in the party could henceforth trust his neighbour.[50]

The Sheffield conference took place in spite of Northcote's misgivings. It provided a considerable but by no means unequivocal triumph for Churchill.

[46] Ibid., Northcote to Salisbury, 3 June 1884.
[47] Ibid., Northcote to Salisbury, 12 June 1884.
[48] Ibid., Northcote to Salisbury, 22 June 1884.
[49] Iddesleigh Papers, Add. MS. 50042, Bartlett to Northcote, 27 June 1884.
[50] Salisbury Papers, Salisbury to Stanhope, 22 June, 1884.

Then followed the sudden reconciliation which has never
been quite satisfactorily explained. Balfour's view was that
Lord Randolph had simply changed his mind when he saw
that 'the National Union was essentially incapable of giving
him the kind of assistance he wanted' and that he now no
longer needed it, having clearly established himself as one of
the leaders of the party.[51] Gorst, in retrospect, saw the move as
the 'Great Surrender' and felt that it marked the abandonment
by Lord Randolph of the principles of Tory Democracy.[52] Lord
Randolph's most recent biographer feels that his aim was no
more than to 'democratize' the National Union and that he in
fact achieved this.[53] The main concession made by the party
leaders was the dissolution of the Central Committee. It may
be, though it cannot be stated with certainty, that this move
was in preparation even before the Sheffield meeting. Stanhope
sent a report on the activities of the Central Committee to
Salisbury and Northcote on 17 July. The tone of the accompanying letter suggests that it was their swan song:

I send you a report of the proceeding of the Central Committee
since their reconstitution which has been drawn up by Mr. Balfour,
Mr. Whitley, Lord Percy and myself. In sending this to you, and to
Lord Salisbury we desire to thank you for the support you have
always extended to us, and we are sure that you will believe that our
main object throughout has been to support your authority, and to
provide the best interests of the party.[54]

If the party leaders, who were well aware of the criticism of
the Central Committee in quarters other than the Churchill
faction, had decided to drop it this would make Lord Randolph's
peace move less surprising.

Apart from the dissolution of the Central Committee and the
resignation of Stanhope in consequence, the changes affecting
the National Union were insubstantial. Akers-Douglas, one of
the Whips, became a Vice-Chairman and Bartley was made
Treasurer. The party leaders thus secured the official representation on the National Union which they had earlier
proposed. Hicks Beach became Chairman as 'a sort of peace

[51] A. J. Balfour, op. cit., pp. 169–71.
[52] H. E. Gorst, op. cit., p. 312.   [53] R. R. James, op. cit., p. 155.
[54] Iddesleigh Papers, Add. MS. 50042, Stanhope to Northcote, 17 July
1884.

offering'.[55] Places were found for Balfour and Gorst as Vice-Chairmen. None of these arrangements proved of great consequence in the future. Even the abolition of the Central Committee was not of decisive importance, because it was, after all, only a more formalized way of arranging for the supervision of the party organization by the Whips, the party agents, and some of the leaders, a system which in essence continued. The growing importance of local Conservative associations owed far more to the impending reform and redistribution bills, introducing household suffrage and single-member constituencies, and to the Corrupt Practices Bill passed in 1883. Everyone now recognized Churchill as one of the leaders, but this was a position he had carved for himself by his public and parliamentary performance. Gorst, as he had feared, found himself isolated and the object of much venom. In spite of public reconciliation the rise of Churchill was another stage in the decline of Northcote.

One more result of the compact between Churchill and the leaders should be mentioned: the recognition of the Primrose League.[56] According to Lady Dorothy Nevill, the idea of such an organization orginated at one of the luncheons which members of the Fourth Party used to have at her house.[57] Wolff is said to have conceived the idea when he saw many of those attending the unveiling of the Beaconsfield Memorial coming away with primroses in their button holes. He may also have thought of bodies like the Oddfellows, Buffaloes, Foresters, and Freemasons or of the Orange Loyal Institution. Both Salisbury and Northcote received the idea very coldly. Northcote wrote to Wolff; 'I am not much in favour of declarations of secrecy and obedience. They smack a little of Ribbonism! And how are men to make them without knowing to whom they are binding themselves? Your Ruling Council will certainly justify one half of your motto (Imperium) but the condition of the ordinary members will hardly be expressed by the

---

[55] Salisbury Papers, Beach to Salisbury 7 July 1885. For the part played by Hicks Beach, see Lady V. A. Hicks Beach, *Life of Sir Michael Hicks Beach* (1932), vol. i.

[56] For the Primrose League generally, see Janet Henderson Robb, *The Primrose League 1883–1906* (Columbia University Political Science Ph.D., 1942).

[57] Ralph Nevill (ed.), *The Reminiscences of Lady Dorothy Nevill*, p. 284.

other half (Libertas).'[58] Salisbury's comment was, 'I doubt the Primrose League coming to anything. There is too much unlimited obedience'.[59] For the moment the Primrose League evoked ridicule and was regarded with suspicion as a product of the Fourth Party; but in the long run it proved a useful body at a time when the party had to rely increasingly on voluntary workers.

The National Union once more came quietly to rest alongside the Central Office. As if to emphasize its essential unimportance Hicks Beach resigned in 1885 the Chairmanship into which he had been pushed the year before. The battle was over. Much of it had been shadow boxing. Churchill, Gorst, and their friends, even if they had behind them a new class of Tory activists, pushing into the citadel of party power, and even if they were pressing necessary changes in electoral methods, were always prepared to compromise and virtually give up the struggle, provided their personal position was safeguarded. The party leaders were reluctant to engage in a real fight, whatever the provocation, provided they could secure their essential control over the party.

[58] Ibid., Add. MS. 50042, Northcote to Wolff, Dec. 1883.
[59] Ibid., Add. MS. 50020, Salisbury to Northcote, 23 Dec. 1883.

VIII

ORGANIZATION AND PARTY COHESION

THE development of Conservative party organization at the centre was inseparable from what was happening in the constituencies. This emerges clearly from the National Union battle. The dissensions among the party managers in London were in large measure due to the widely differing constituencies they had to deal with, ranging from small proprietary boroughs to mass electorates in great cities. In the controversy over the National Union one of the issues at stake was the extent to which committed Conservatives might, through their organizations, share in policy making with the leaders. The outcome of the battle made it clear that this share could only be very limited. The further development and refinement of party machines since then has confirmed that parliamentary leaders must take into account the pressures from their active and committed supporters; but their response to these pressures has to be well subordinated to their awareness of the movements of public opinion at large.

So much for the transmission of pressure from below; of possibly greater significance for the rise of the modern disciplined party is pressure through organization from the centre to the periphery. As has been repeatedly shown in these pages, organization outside Parliament played little part in the cohesion of the Conservative party between the second and the third Reform bills. An examination of relations between the central and local organization, to be made in this chapter, only confirms this conclusion. On the other hand, the increasing predominance of national issues in politics exemplified by the proliferation of national pressure groups, increased the possibilities of pressure from the central party organization downwards. Pressure groups played a major role in the formation of the modern Liberal party: events in Parliament were of less importance in the process by which Whigs, moderate Liberals, and Radicals coalesced under the leadership of Gladstone than pressure from extra-parliamentary associations, such as the Liberation Society, the National Reform League or the National Education League.[1] In the making of the modern Conservative party pressure groups are much less important, and often only a pale reflection of movements on the opposite side. Nevertheless the Conservative party was increasingly caught in national political currents: these could only be satisfied by national leaders. Hence these leaders acquired increasing authority over their supporters.

Our knowledge of local party organization in the 1860s and 1870s is considerable and we owe much of it to the encyclopaedic researches of Professor Hanham. On the conservative side the campaign guide for 1874[2] listed a profusion of different types of associations: the older type of registration association often still existed in the same place alongside a Conservative Working Men's Association; regional bodies or unions in large cities further complicated the picture. The essential difference between the older and the new type of local organization was this: the registration association had as its chief object the handling of the technical side of elections, namely the contesting of claims in the registration courts and similar matters. It was concerned with attracting not so much a numerically large as a well paying membership; the membership fee was generally high. The registration association needed funds to fight claims and election contests, but it was less directed towards general political activity. The new type of organization, whatever its exact name, was mainly concerned with propaganda and the attraction of the largest possible numbers, in order to influence their ideas, get their vote and enlist voluntary workers. Yet, with both types of organization, the mainstays of the local party were still the men of influence, but the larger the electorate, the more attention they had to pay to public opinion and the greater their number became. The dividing line between bodies calling themselves Conservative Working Men's Associations and those with the simpler title 'Conservative Association' is difficult to draw. In 1867 many Working Men's Associations were founded, but Disraeli and others disliked the segregation

[1] John Vincent, *The Formation of the Liberal Party 1857–1868*, especially Chapter II.
[2] *Conservative Agents and Associations in the Boroughs and Counties of England and Wales* (1874). Published by the Central Conservative Office.

implied.[3] and after 1868 the qualification 'Working Men's' was often left out. In some cases where it remained the bodies were clubs with relatively low subscriptions, while the genuinely political functions rested with an association. There were, however, up to 1885, a large number of constituencies where organization of any kind was of little or, at most, of marginal importance. In such constituencies family interest or some other type of influence was still the decisive factor in elections.[4]

One of the oldest examples of a constituency association built up on the elective principle is the Liverpool Constitutional Association, established in 1848.[5] It had a committee of thirty, elected by the Annual General Meeting of the Association. This Committee was empowered to elect the officers of the Association, to enrol members, to regulate the affairs of the Association generally and to control the funds. Ward committees were to be set up to select their own candidates. There was a graduated scale of subscriptions from £5 to 5s; aldermen and councillors had to pay not less than £5 and only members paying more than £2 were eligible for the Committee. In his first annual report, the Secretary spoke of the work in sustaining claims of Tory voters in the Registration Courts. He also mentioned the treachery of a 'too trusted' Conservative leader, a reference to Edward Cardwell, who had followed Peel; the Secretary expressed the hope that Protectionist members would be returned. Amongst the objects of the Association, mention is made of the Empire, the Constitution, the Church, encouragement of commerce, due rewards for the artisan, the operative, the peasant, and the seaman, the promotion of national education based on religion. It was the purpose of the Association to secure the election by all legal means of M.P.s pledged to these principles.

It is clear that the Association here sketched could not be regarded as the democratic voice of Liverpool Conservatism, or representative of the great mass of Tory voters. There were special and complex reasons for the long-standing attachment

[3] *Speech of the Rt. Hon. B. Disraeli, M.P., to the Conservative Association of Glasgow, on Saturday, 22nd November, 1873.* National Union Publication No. 24, p. 4.
[4] H. J. Hanham, *Elections and Party Management*, p. 108.
[5] *Rules and Regulations of the Liverpool Constitutional Association, 1848.* Also *First Annual Report of the Liverpool Constitutional Association.*

of Liverpool to the Tory cause; one of the factors in this tradition was the strong Orange feeling aroused by the presence of a large Irish population, another, accounting perhaps for the Toryism of the business community, was the Tory defence of the slave trade. Back in the 1830s Liverpool had a strong reformist administration which was moving towards the introduction of secular education. A counter-attack, headed by the clergy and lead by Canon McNeile, whom Disraeli later appointed to the Deanery of Ripon, brought back the Tories in 1842.[6] Such local traditions were still of greater importance than party organization. On the other hand the creation and activities of the Liverpool Constitutional Association show awareness of the existence of a wider electorate and of the necessity of a reasoned appeal and constant political education and propaganda. As time went on, many Conservative organizations of various types sprang up, and after 1867 working men's clubs and associations were increasingly common here as elsewhere.

Birmingham, the birthplace of the Liberal caucus, also witnessed a Conservative attempt to pull all the existing organizations into a coherent democratic body. Up to and including the General Election of 1874, Birmingham Conservatism had been weak and badly organized and was no match for the powerful forces of Radicalism in the city. The main bodies in existence were several Conservative clubs, including the Birmingham Conservative Club, the Birmingham Junior Conservative Club and the Birmingham Association. In 1877 a Central Executive Committee was appointed, consisting of representatives from each of the sixteen wards, and thirty-six members of Conservative clubs and officers of the Association. Within this large body there was a committee of management consisting of the Secretary, the Treasurer and twelve members, which was said to stand in the same relationship to the Executive Committee as the Cabinet stands to the House of Commons.[7] The Conservative forces in Birmingham were thus unified in an organization which was at least formally democratic, though the committee of management was possibly only a way of concealing the

---

[6] A. B. Forwood, 'Democratic Toryism', *Contemporary Review*, February 1883, p. 294; also H. J. Hanham, op. cit., pp. 284–6.

[7] Asa Briggs, *History of Birmingham, Borough and City, 1865–1938* (1952), p. 176. Also *Birmingham Conservative Association. Report of the Management Committee* (1878).

activities of the men of influence behind a façade of popular sanction. After 1880, the Conservatives became increasingly strong in Birmingham and their growing hold on the masses was shown by the foundation of many working men's clubs. By 1884 they were strong enough to ask Lord Randolph Churchill and Colonel Burnaby, his close supporter, to stand as parliamentary candidates.

Manchester, another large three-member constituency, a far stronger centre of Toryism before 1874 than Birmingham, presented a confused picture. The campaign guide for 1874 listed the City of Manchester Conservative Union as the main Tory organization in the city, to which other bodies were linked. Of the linked bodies the most important was the Manchester Conservative Working Men's Association, which had an Executive Committee, and, in its turn, numerous ward branches. There was a Conservative Club in the city, John Shaw's Club, a dining club originally founded in the eighteenth century, as well as many working men's clubs. There was also a Lancashire Union of Conservative and Constitutional Associations with its seat in Manchester. The three organizations named all had W. R. Callender as President; S. C. Nicholson was Secretary of both the Working Men's Association and the Lancashire Union, and was also Secretary of the Manchester Trades Council, and all these bodies again had their offices at 4 Temple Chambers in Manchester. The registration societies in the county constituencies of Lancashire and the North of England Conservative Association, which had its seat in Manchester, were quite independent. There was also a Manchester and Salford Constitutional Association, the Secretary of which was, for financial reasons, opposed to Disraeli's visit in 1872.[8] With such a large variety of organizations in existence there could be no semblance of democratic control and the men of influence held the key to the situation.

Even in a smaller borough like Portsmouth the campaign guide listed three branches: a Conservative Club, a Working Men's Liberal Conservative Association, and a Working Men's Liberal Conservative Club. Many associations undoubtedly had little more than a paper existence, and an experienced party manager like Gorst knew this only too well:

[8] Hughenden Papers, A/IV/N; also H. J. Hanham, op. cit., p. 286.

I enclose a letter which I think ought to be brought under the notice of the party leaders. The writer is the recognised official secretary of the Conservative party in Edinburgh. Mr. Usher is the secretary of an association which exists only on paper: his specialité is inviting statesmen of distinction to Edinburgh. The difficulty thus created in Edinburgh is a type of what obtains in a great many other places.[9]

Thus, even in boroughs with larger electorates, where democratic constituency organization ought to have been most advanced, there was little sign that the forces of Conservatism were represented by single all-embracing bodies to which parliamentary candidates might have felt a sense of responsibility and by which such candidates might have been selected in a regularized manner. In smaller boroughs, so numerous still between 1867 and 1884, as well as in counties, there was as yet hardly any trace of democratic organization. When it is remembered that, out of a total of over 800 seats won by the Conservatives in the three General Elections of 1868, 1874, and 1880, less than 180 were in boroughs with more than 20,000 inhabitants the relative importance of organization can be seen more in perspective.[10] In smaller boroughs there was frequently only an agent and no organization at all. The three parliamentary boroughs in the county of Essex may be taken as a random example: in 1874 Colchester (population 26,343; 3,183 electors) had a Chairman, Secretary and agent of the Conservative Party, but no associations; Harwich (population 6,079; 712 electors) had only an agent; Maldon (population 7,151; 1,370 electors) had a Conservative Club and a Working Men's Association. In boroughs of this kind, the agent was often the local solicitor with whom the party agency in London was in the habit of working. He had, as necessity arose, built up a registration association to help him. In constituencies, borough or county, where there was strong family influence, the agent might well be the acknowledged representative of the predominant family.

It need hardly be stressed that electoral conditions up to 1885 left ample room for influence, corruption, nomination

---

[9] Salisbury Papers, Gorst to Salisbury, 26 Nov. 1881.
[10] C. Seymour, *Electoral Reform in England and Wales* (1915), p. 301. See also above, Chapter IV.

boroughs, and all the paraphernalia of an unreformed electoral system. The 1867 Reform Act and its disfranchisements of corrupt boroughs had only marginally limited these conditions; the Ballot of 1872, the next major reform, did not, in the eleven years it operated before further major reforms were undertaken, have a dramatic impact. In 1880, thirty-five boroughs still had an electorate of less than 1,000.

A few sidelights will suffice to show how much the influence of patrons was still taken for granted, and to what extent such patrons expected their views to be taken seriously by the party leaders. Lord Bath, a leading High Church Tory who became strongly opposed to Disraeli's handling of the Eastern Question,[11] wrote to Carnarvon in 1876 (the letter was sent on to the Prime Minister):

> I am in great trouble, Lopes is made a judge and there is a vacancy for Frome. I have with those who work with me the power of preventing a Conservative being returned (it will require all we can do to return one), I am most anxious for general reasons of home policy to keep our majority, on the other hand I cannot but be true to my own long held and now avowed opinions on the Eastern Question. I hope whoever stands as a Conservative will declare himself against going to war under any pretext for the maintenance of the Turkish empire. And in favour of securing the local freedom and protection of life person and property to the Christians with equality between them and the Mussulmen on borne guarantee of one or more of the Powers and on a better security than the good will and fidelity of the Turks in which we may avoid a split fatal to Government interests down here.
>
> Two points I want to mention are that if I support a Government candidate *now* my opposing the Government in public and in the House next session on the Eastern Question is not to debar me from asserting claims I might otherwise be supposed to have on them. The other that the Treasury officials should understand that any communications they have to make be made to me *direct* and not through my brother who is in no way authorised to speak for me and who does not sympathise with my views[12] [Lord Harry Thynne, the Whip, was Lord Bath's brother].

[11] For Lord Bath's views on the Eastern Question, see R. T. Shannon, *Gladstone and the Bulgarian Agitation* (1876), pp. 185–6; also above, p. 58.

[12] Carnarvon Papers, ii. 164, Bath to Carnarvon, 3 Nov. 1876. There are many such examples; the Duke of Sutherland, for instance, wrote to Beaconsfield before the Election of 1880 that he had instructed his tenants

Frome could not be regarded as a nomination borough; members of the Thynne family were frequently defeated and on this occasion the seat reverted to the Liberals. Yet great landowners like Lord Bath were still very conscious of their electoral influence and secure in this knowledge were able to treat with the Queen's ministers as equals.

Even lesser citizens had important electoral influence and did not hesitate to mention the fact when occasion demanded it. An amusing example is this letter to Beaconsfield from a disappointed applicant for the Honours list living in the Isle of Wight:

I am placed in a situation which may be styled *unique* in a Parliamentary sense: for I am absolutely 'master of the situation', and I may say without boasting that the return of a Conservative (or even Independent) candidate is,—humanly speaking—impossible without my support, that support having to be exerted with tolerable vigour. And judging by the *pathos*—one would have thought the British Empire was threatened—and *prayers* of those who made 'vows in pain', my influence was, last Election, greatly to be desired.

Mr. Cochrane was returned by a majority of nine only. I have many persons devoted to me,—not to the extent of 'giving their lives',—but their *votes* which is much more practical.[13]

In many constituencies influence was exercised by large employers, companies, and other local interests, but in such cases evidence of direct political pressure being exerted on the basis of such influence is naturally harder to come by.[14]

'to give their votes according to the principles always held by my house'. (Hughenden Papers, B/XII/K/23). See also Lord Ronald Gower, *My Reminiscences* (1895), p. 337. Lord Salisbury who as Lord Robert Cecil represented Lord Exeter's pocket borough of Stamford, was questioned by his patron about some articles in *The Saturday Review*, and told that the attacks made in them might, if persevered in, 'lead to consequences which I should deeply deplore in the event of a dissolution of Parliament'. (Lady G. Cecil, *Life of Salisbury*, i. 93–5).

[13] Hughenden Papers, C/II/B, V. Webber to A. Turnor, 5 Nov. 1878. Baillie-Cochrane, Disraeli's friend from 'Young England' days, was elected for the Isle of Wight in 1874 by 9 votes out of 3,200 cast.

[14] For influence by employers, cf. the case of the Blackburn Circular (mentioned in the notes prepared by Gorst for Disraeli, before the Lancashire visit, above, p. 119). See also *Parliamentary Papers*, 1868–9, vol. XLVIII, p. 20. For railway influence at Swindon, see P. M. Williams, 'Public Opinion and the Railway Rates Question in 1886', *English Historical Review*, vol. LXVII (1952), p. 53.

In these electoral conditions, party organization in the constituencies was patchy and democratic organization rare. The situation was remote indeed from the modern position, when the central offices of the major political parties are dealing with a comprehensive network of uniform local associations. Under modern conditions, the disciplinary pressure which the Whips can bring to bear on members is much reinforced by the existence of extra-parliamentary party organization, particularly in the constituencies. Such a situation would have been inconceivable before 1885. The reverse was still true: party leaders and Whips were liable to pressure from aristocratic and other patrons who were able to exercise political influence. Hence the very tentative and experimental method by which the Central Office had to proceed, seeking out the local leaders and attempting to persuade and guide. In some ways the Central Office had more work to do than it did later, when there was a more developed system of organization, and its task was certainly more delicate. Too much interference could prove fatal; yet in so many cases it was only encouragement and stimulation from the centre that led to any local effort at all; as Gorst put it to Smith,[15] it was only the possibility of fleecing a candidate that made many places establish organizations and attempt to obtain a candidate. The number of uncontested seats fell by nearly half over the three General Elections of 1868, 1874, and 1880, but in 1868 nearly a third of all seats had not been contested. There was a considerable rise in the number of uncontested English county seats in 1874, owing to the disarray into which the Liberal party had fallen; but this was counterbalanced by the increase in the number of contests in Ireland due to the appearance of the Home Rulers. In 1880 there were more contests everywhere, particularly in English boroughs and counties, but about a sixth of all seats still remained uncontested.[16]

The most definite and concrete move by which central party headquarters could influence the constituencies and local organizations was through the grant of money from the central party fund. The basis for this fund, when the party was in office,

[15] See above, p. 153.
[16] Trevor Lloyd, 'Uncontested Seats in British General Elections 1852–1910', *Historical Journal*, VIII, 2 (1965), pp. 260–5.

was formed by the Secret Service money at the disposal of the Chief Whip in his capacity as Patronage Secretary at the Treasury. This money amounted to £10,000 a year, but at least half of it went on the expenses of the Whips and the central party office itself. The remainder, £4,000 or £5,000 a year, could be saved, invested, and used for political purposes.[17]

Apart from this, the central fund had to be filled by collection and this was done in the main by three methods: through appeals to individuals by the Whips and others; through the National Union, the Central Conservative Registration Association and other bodies associated with the Central Office; and through the Conservative clubs in London. Fund raising quickened as soon as a general election was in the offing and it was at such times that contributions were largest and most widely given. Peers, not having election expenses, were expected to contribute handsomely. The following letter from Lord Kintore, Whip in the House of Lords, to Lord Harrowby on the eve of the 1885 Election illustrates the typical approach to a Peer:

> The receipt of a note from Lord Salisbury sending me a cheque for £2,000 towards the election fund reminds me that I have not yet written to ask you if you are disposed to contribute something. I need hardly say that we shall need all we can get. I send you a print of what was given in 1880. We propose in no case to pay more than a third of a man's expenses.[18]

Lord Harrowby apologized for not making a larger contribution (apparently he gave £200), pleading his agricultural losses, his expenses when in office (as Lord Privy Seal he drew no salary), his subscriptions to the Carlton, and the need to help with contests in his county.[19] The need to look after one's local interests was frequently given as an excuse for not subscribing more generously to the central party fund. Thus during the 1874 General Election, Richmond hesitated before replying to

---

[17] H. J. Hanham, op. cit., p. 370.

[18] Harrowby Papers, LIII/107, Kintore to Harrowby, 19 Oct. 1885. Reginald Brett reports a conversation with Harcourt and Hartington about the Liberal Election Fund on 14 Dec. 1879 (*Journals and Letters of Reginald, Viscount Esher*, i. 65), in which they mention that £500 from every Peer and M.P. would win them twenty county seats.

[19] Harrowby Papers, LIII/109, notes for Harrowby's reply to Kintore.

a request from Skelmersdale, Chief Whip in the House of Lords, until he knew how much he would have to pay in places where he had property.[20] The figure given by Kintore for Salisbury's donation compares with £10,000 raised by Disraeli from his cabinet in 1868 and with £9,000 subscribed by twelve Conservative Peers in 1856,[21] In a second letter to Harrowby in 1885 Kintore quotes £22,000 as the total subscription by all Tory Peers in 1880.[22]

If any conclusions can be drawn from these figures it is that the size of contributions, at any rate from Peers, was declining in the 1880s, mainly no doubt because of the agricultural depression. Salisbury's donation of £2,000 may be taken as exceptional, as an example set by the party leader. The Duke of Portland gave £6,000 in 1880, but normal contributions were in three figures only.[23] Between elections, subscriptions were obtained on a smaller scale from prominent men in the party:

> In June last you gave me a cheque for £100 as your subscription to our central fund. Between June and August eight other men promised a hundred pounds a year each but we decided not to ask for the money until the 1st January as most of the work in the interval would be comparatively inexpensive. We are, however, sending men out to visit and if possible organise the constituencies and we are in want of money. I have notwithstanding felt that it was not right to use your cheque and I return it to you but I hope you will send us the amount for this year.[24]

This is a guide to the scale of contributions in between elections. It is likely that the Conservative business community was also becoming an increasing source of income not only locally but at the centre. Apart from the Whips, Abergavenny was a busy collector of funds from wealthy individuals, and may have owed his influence in the party largely to his ability of extracting funds from otherwise inaccessible subscribers.

A wider body of subscribers than members of both Houses of Parliament was approached, through circulars giving them

[20] Cairns Papers, Richmond to Cairns, 3 Feb. 1874.
[21] See H. J. Hanham, 'British Party Finance', *Bulletin of the Institute of Historical Research*, vol. XXVII (1954), p. 83.
[22] Harrowby Papers, LIII/109, Kintore to Harrowby, 12 Nov. 1885.
[23] H. J. Hanham, *Elections and Party Management*, p. 374.
[24] Salisbury Papers, Smith to Salisbury, 26 Feb. 1887.

the option of subscribing either to the central fund direct or to the Central Registration Association or to the National Union. As Gorst explained to Smith, contributors were in general prepared to pay only once and a separate appeal, such as the National Union made in the summer of 1880 and again, in a more deliberately defiant manner, in 1884, could be embarrassing.[25] Most of the contributions, however, to the National Union were small and as long as they remained so and did not get in the way of the more serious fund raising no harm was done.

A circular of the National Union is going to be sent to you for your approval as President before issue. It is to beg for money to give lectures in the winter. W. H. Smith does not want it to be issued till our Central Cttee circular goes out; and that is being delayed for Winn, Ld. H. Thynne and others, to get as many large sums as possible first. I don't see much harm in the N.U. circular myself; they won't get much money, and what they do get will be well spent in propagating abuse of Gladstone, but W.H.S. is anxious on the subject and has written to me from the Levant to keep the N.U. back. As Lord Percy is Chairman and I V. Chairman of the N.U. you will wonder why we cannot keep our flock in order: but they following an illustrious example, are prolonging their patriotic labours into the end of September, when we have all at last left Town (I am writing this from the country), so that the tail of our council which still meets has everything its own way.[26]

As the balance sheet of the National Union for the year ending 1882 shows, subscription income was indeed meagre, amounting only to £926.[27] It was therefore usual for the National Union to subsidize out of the central fund rather than the other way round. It was an important part of Lord Randolph Churchill's attempt to enhance the stature of the National Union to try to obtain for it a greater share in the central party fund. The Central Registration Association fund, which, in the days when the Registration Association was an independent body, was probably of considerable importance, eventually became completely merged in the central fund; certainly this was the position by 1884.[28]

[25] See above, p. 147.
[26] Salisbury Papers, Gorst to Salisbury, no date, probably August or September 1880.   [27] *Minutes of the National Union Conference, 1882.*
[28] See above, p. 161, Memorandum on the Conservative Central Office and National Union.

The Conservative clubs in London were an important source of finance. This was by now their only remaining important function in party organization. Otherwise they were meeting places; it was still the outward and visible symbol of being an important member of the Tory party, possibly with parliamentary aspirations, to be elected to the Carlton or, if one could not rise to that eminence, to the Junior Carlton or another of the lesser clubs. The amounts which the clubs contributed to the party fund can not be exactly ascertained. In accordance with a resolution carried at the Annual Meeting of the Carlton in 1869 the Club contributed £500 to the party fund in 1870 and £900 in 1871.[29] The resolution of 1869 does not survive, but it was probably to the effect that a certain percentage of the Club's profits should go to the party fund. The Junior Carlton contributed £500 annually and made a special levy of 10s. on each of its 2,000 members at election times. In 1880 Lord Harry Thynne collected £1,000 at the Junior Carlton to help with the Oxford by-election.[30] The Junior Carlton also collected £500 for this purpose, and it was rumoured that a further £1,000 was collected outside the Club for the election. It was in connection with this episode that the Secretary of the Junior Carlton, Martin, disappeared without a trace. It was a sign of the seriousness of the internal crisis in the Tory party in the summer of 1884 that there was a threat that both the Carlton and the Junior Carlton might withdraw their contributions to the party fund.

As for the income of the clubs, Winn gave the following interesting account of the membership position at the Carlton in 1881:

1223 candidates are on the books waiting for election. It would take till 1910 before someone putting their name down now could be elected. The entrance fee at £20 is lower than for any other first-class club in London. Proposals:
(1) Increase ordinary members from 960 to 1,300 including the 91 members now in the Club in excess of establishment, leaving 249 to be elected.
(2) That of the 249 half should be selected, half taken in the ordinary course.

[29] Sir Charles Petrie, *The Carlton Club* (1955), p. 90.
[30] *Parliamentary Papers*, 1881, vol. XLIV.

(3) That the entrance fee should be raised for ordinary elections to £30, for selections to £50.

It is not believed that these additions would stretch the facilities, as most of the new members would be resident in the country, while M.P. and peer members already use the Club extensively.

Membership analysis: 1,051 ordinary members, 276 peers, 50 eldest sons of peers, 232 M.P.s, 59 abroad who do not pay. Present excess of members will take three years to remove even if no General Election intervenes; meantime there can be no more elections and only ten annual selections.[31]

Eventually an increase of the membership up to 1,100 was sanctioned. In 1883, Abergavenny was the promoter of a new club to be called the Constitutional Club. His object may have been partly to secure a new source of revenue for the party and incidentally to strengthen his own waning influence on party management. He did not consult Stanhope and the other party managers, who disliked the scheme; they, in their turn, greatly to his annoyance, refused to make him an initial grant from the party fund to get the club started.[32] Nonetheless this Club apparently achieved considerable success, not least on the financial side:

You will be glad to know our numbers still progress. The latest return being

Town life members	58	£5800
Country life members	49	£2940
	107	£8740
Town ordinary members	815	£4075
Country ordinary members	1494	£4482
	2309	£8557

making a grand total of 2416 members[33]

[31] Salisbury Papers, Winn to Salisbury, 14 Mar. 1881. The number of M.P.s who were members of the Carlton was roughly equal to the total membership of the Parliamentary Conservative Party.

[32] Salisbury Papers, Abergavenny to Salisbury, 2, 5 May 1883; Stanhope to Salisbury, 7 May 1883. See also Ralph Nevill (ed.), *The Reminiscences of Lady Dorothy Nevill*, p. 70.

[33] Salisbury Papers, Abergavenny to Salisbury, 27 May 1883.

The subscriptions of this club were therefore £100 for town life members, £60 for country life members, £5 for town ordinary members, £3 for country ordinary members. The 1870s and 1880s were a great period for clubs, and political clubs flourished in London and in the provinces.[34]

There were no clear principles governing the grant of money to candidates from the central fund. As we have seen, this was a matter which, in theory at any rate, rested ultimately with the Chief Whip; in practice any of the Whips or the principal party agent could give a promise, and little attempt was made to co-ordinate their actions. Whoever was available at the Central Office was consulted and those who were absent, when a decision was taken, might well remain in ignorance. For the general election of 1880, Colonel W. P. Talbot acted as Treasurer of the Fund and all cheques were drawn by him on an account at Drummond's which stood in Dyke's name. Colonel Talbot made no attempt to impose any system on the grant of money.[35] As to the size of the contribution to any particular contest, the maximum figure of a third of the expenses mentioned by Lord Kintore applied to the first general election after the Corrupt Practices Act of 1883. Earlier on, the sum of £500 was often spoken of as an average contri-bution from the central fund during a general election; contri-butions varied considerably, but they rarely exceeded £500. By-election contributions were almost certainly smaller, because the party fund was always at its fullest on the eve of a general election, when contributions were most easily forthcoming.

In either case, the central fund contribution did not usually amount to a large percentage of the total cost of an election, when we consider the heavy expenses of many contests even in the period between 1868 and 1883. Thus Sir Stafford Northcote contested North Devon in 1868 at a coast of £4,000, a fairly average figure for a county election.[36] Twenty-four Midland county seats cost the Conservatives £57,812 in 1880.[37] These figures, coming from private sources, are likely to be fairly

[34] See also T. H. S. Escott, *Club Makers and Club Members* (1914); H. J. Hanham, op. cit. pp. 99–105; W. F. Rae 'Political Clubs and Party Organisation', *Nineteenth Century*, vol. III (1878), p. 908.

[35] *Parliamentary Papers*, 1881, vol. XL, p. 760, vol. XLIV, p. 524.

[36] Iddesleigh Papers, Add. MS. 50037.

[37] *Minutes of the National Union Conference, 1883*, paper by Bartley.

accurate. Official statistics are also available, since the Corrupt Practices Act of 1854 had made the publication of candidates' election expenses obligatory. It was well known, however, that the published accounts often did not reveal even as much as half of the actual expenditure and never overestimated it. Official figures for the 1880 Election show heavy expenditure in the metropolitan boroughs: £6,146 for the two winning Conservative candidates at Westminster (including W. H. Smith), £3,588 for the two defeated Liberals; whereas at Chelsea the two defeated Conservatives spent £5,600 and the two winning Liberals £3,715. In boroughs outside London the situation appears to have been not much different: at Birmingham the three winning Liberals spent £6,066, the two defeated Conservatives £7,308. At Manchester the aggregate disbursement was over £20,000, at Bradford £9,500 and at Preston £6,000. James Lowther lost the family seat at York for £4,390, over £1 for each vote cast for him. Even these official figures, inadequate as they admittedly are, show that in 1880 hardly any county seat could be had for less than £3,000.[38]

In addition to election expenses, essential requirements, such as the cost of registration, bore heavily on candidates. At Liverpool in 1868, Viscount Sandon, one of the candidates, had originally contracted to pay £1,000, and the same sum was presumably also given to S. R. Graves, the other Conservative candidate. Sandon paid this sum into the Graves-Sandon election fund at the North-Western Bank in Liverpool on 18 September 1868; simultaneously he warned his agent of the necessity of extreme caution in the expenditure of this money and threw on him the responsibility of refusing any payment that might be construed as illegal.[39] Three weeks later Thomas

[38] See *Parliamentary Papers on Election Expenses*, 1868–9, vol. L; 1874, vol LIII; 1880, vol. LVII. Also W. P. Courtney 'The Cost of the General Election of 1880', *Fortnightly*, vol. XXIX, April 1881, p. 467. Lord George Hamilton spent £30,000 in his first three elections in Middlesex (Lord George Hamilton, *Parliamentary Reminiscences and Reflections, 1868–1885* [1917], p. 3); W. H. Smith spent 22s. a vote at Westminster in 1868 (Sir Herbert Maxwell, *Life and Times of W. H. Smith*, i. 150.) Middlesex, Westminster, and the other London constituencies mentioned had very large electorates. See generally C. O'Leary, *The Elimination of Corrupt Practices in British Elections 1868–1911*; William B. Gwyn, *Democracy and the Cost of Politics* (1962), especially Chapter II; H. J. Hanham, op. cit., especially Chapter XII.
[39] Harrowby Papers L/282, Sandon to Weir Anderson, 18 Sept. 1868.

(later Sir Thomas) Edwards-Moss, an influential local Conservative, made a further appeal to Sandon; he spoke of £2,000 or more having been spent in the Registration Court, yet considered the registration still not satisfactory. He asked for an additional £500 from each candidate for the contest, and mentioned that the party would have to find at least another £1,500 if there was to be any chance of carrying two candidates.[40] After reference to his father, Lord Harrowby, Sandon agreed to pay another £500, but said that £1,500 was the limit of the claims he could consider.[41]

The Oxford by-election of 1880 became notorious for heavy expenditure. It was not usual to oppose ministers seeking re-election on appointment, and in this case a deliberate effort was made to unseat Sir William Harcourt. Oxford was one of the eight boroughs for which a Royal Commission was set up after the 1880 election to enquire into corruption. In his evidence before the Commission, Dyke stated that £3,500 had been asked for from the centre and £3,000 was given. Usually any contribution given from the centre was not paid through a local bank, but made to disappear into the general fund of the candidate. The exceptional scale of the central contribution at Oxford came to light by accident.[42] The fact remains that the proportion of electoral expenses paid out of the central fund was not normally very large, but increased after the Corrupt Practices Act of 1883.

The financing of contests was not the only drain on the central fund. The Central Office and its permanent staff were a heavy expense. Even before 1870 the party agent was allowed liberal expenses and the firm of Baxter, Rose and Norton had over two hundred clerks. The National Union and other bodies connected with the Central Office had to rely on the central fund in so far as they could not meet their expenses from their own subscription income. Contributions had sometimes to be made to the legal expenses arising in Revising Barristers' Courts and towards the cost of getting up petitions. From time to time the question arose whether money from the central fund should be used for purposes other than those connected with elections,

[40] Harrowby Papers L/175, Edwards-Moss to Sandon, 7 Oct. 1868.
[41] Ibid., L/150, Harrowby to Sandon, 8 Oct. 1868.
[42] *Parliamentary Papers*, 1881, vol. XLIV; C. O'Leary, op. cit., p. 146.

petitions, and organization. Usually the Whips refused to sanction other types of expenditure. Thus Abergavenny was given no money for his Constitutional Club. Requests to help finance Conservative newspapers were frequent. In 1883 Stanhope stated categorically, in connection with an enquiry for assistance to the *Dorset County Chronicle*, that 'it was a strict rule never to spend central funds, entrusted to us primarily for organization, on newspapers'.[43] Smith does not seem to have regarded this rule as quite so strict, for in 1881 he asked Salisbury's advice about a scheme for turning the *St. James's Gazette* into a Conservative penny morning paper.[44] The purchase of the Central Press Board, mentioned earlier, and of other papers such as the *Globe* and the *Sun*, was not connected with the party fund and was arranged through wealthy supporters willing to become proprietors of such papers.[45]

Information on the central party fund, scanty and imprecise as it is, nevertheless allows the conclusion that the supply of money was the most potent weapon in the armoury of the central party managers in their negotiations with the constituencies. But before the passage of the Corrupt Practices Act of 1883 many elections were still so expensive that the central fund, however large, could not provide more than a relatively small part of the expenses of any given contest. The rest had to be found locally or by the candidate himself. From the General Election of 1885 onwards the central contributions bulked proportionately larger and hence the influence of the centre also increased. Moreover, the scale of the propaganda effort financed by party headquarters grew considerably; the size of the central office and its expenses increased and therefore the central party fund after 1885 had to be much bigger that it was before.

In the early years of this century the sale of honours became a familiar method of political fund raising. Before 1885 there is no evidence of honours being awarded in return for contributions to the party fund, though the foundations for this system were laid by Northcote's promises between 1880 and

[43] Salisbury Papers, Stanhope to Salisbury, 7 May 1883.
[44] Ibid., Smith to Salisbury, 25 Aug. 1881.
[45] Hughenden Papers, B/XXI/Keith-Falconer, to Disraeli, 3 Nov. 1873.

1885, which had later to be redeemed by Salisbury.[46] Honours and patronage, however, had their uses in the political system, apart from being a source of financial contributions to the party. They were and always had been a lubricating agent for the political machines. In this matter the Conservatives, particularly during their period in office from 1874 to 1880, were caught in a number of conflicting cross-currents. On the one hand the amount of patronage available for political purposes was decreasing, while strict criteria for the grant of honours still prevailed. On the other hand the broadening of the political base, in particular, the great organizational effort in the boroughs, increased the hunger for places and honours. The hunger was intensified by the prolonged exclusion of the Tories from office. The diminution of patronage was due to the introduction of competitive examination into the Civil Service and a general change in the climate of opinion in the direction of meritocracy. In consequence, Whips of both parties complained strongly about loss of power and influence.

Disraeli still regarded patronage as 'the outward and visible sign of an inward and spiritual grace, and this is Power' and he fought a determined rearguard action over a good many appointments.[47] A memorandum prepared for him in the course of one of these battles illustrates the narrowing of choices open to the Prime Minister:

The Patronage of the First Lord of the Treasury.

The principle of open competition with a craving for economy has within recent years considerably diminished the patronage of the Prime Minister. Nearly all minor appointments have been removed from him, and, excluding political offices which are not permanent, he is left with only those higher places which demand special knowledge, training, and great responsibility.

They may be briefly classed as follows:

Legal   The various judgeships, Queen's Proctor, numerous solicitorships.

Civil   The Heads of the great Departments of State, such as
Offices   Secretary to the Treasury, Chairman and Vice-Chairman to the Boards of Customs and Inland Revenue, also Com-

---

[46] H. J. Hanham, 'The Sale of Honours in Late Victorian England', *Victorian Studies*, vol. iii, No. 3 (Mar. 1960) p. 277.
[47] R. Blake, *Disraeli*, pp. 682 ff.

missionerships of all kinds, and various other important
staff appointments.

Art   Director, Keeper and Secretary of the National Portrait
Gallery etc.

It will be seen that the responsibility of selection imposed on the
Prime Minister is very great. He has to consider the requirements
of the particular Department, the character of the service, and the
special aptitude of the individual, and where so great an influence
for good as for evil may be exercised, he would naturally look for
proof of competency to guide his choice. The majority of applicants
are persons who having entered one branch of H.M.'s Service have
from some cause or other left it and seek somewhat late in life to
enter another branch for which they have had no training and
shown no capacity.[48]

Disraeli's Government did in fact make a larger number of
political appointments in the class of posts covered by this
memorandum than the previous Gladstone administration, but
it could not reverse the trend towards open competition.

If patronage was becoming restricted, honours were not yet
freely available. Their grant was restricted by delicate considerations of social standing and wealth. Ownership of land
was still considered a very important qualification for pro-
spective Peers and baronets. On this matter Disraeli, whose
ideas on patronage were so lax, had strong feelings. Civic
baronetcies, which had begun to sprout in the Liberal ranks,
were not for him.[49] He created fewer Peers in his six years as
Prime Minister than Gladstone had done in the five years of his
first administration and only one of his creations was from
commerce or industry.[50] The case of Mr. Barclay Walker, the
Mayor of Liverpool, exemplifies the pressures on Disraeli:

I shall be obliged to you if you would kindly bring the subject
of this letter as soon as possible before Mr. Disraeli. The present
Mayor of Liverpool, Mr. A. Barclay Walker, a very wealthy respectable and unpretending man, and a staunch Conservative, has
recently entertained with great success and with applause from both
political parties the Duke of Edinburgh for four days at Liverpool.

[48] Hughenden Papers, B/XXI/Turnor, 18 Dec. 1877.
[49] R. Blake, op. cit., p. 387.
[50] R. Blake, op. cit., p. 687; also R. E. Pumphrey, 'The Introduction of
Industrialists into the British Peerage; A Study in Adaptation of a Social
Institution', *American Historical Review*, vol. LXV, No. 1 (October 1959),
pp. 1–16.

The special objects of the visit were to lay the first stone of a stately Art Gallery, to be built opposite St. George's Hall at the sole cost of the Mayor for a sum of between £20,000 and £30,000, and presented by him to the town and to open the largest Merchant Seamen's Orphan Asylum in the country. There was also the revival of a musical festival. The royal visit was managed exceedingly well, the Duke was lodged and entertained by the Corporation all the time and altogether the town is very proud of its Mayor, who is most public spirited and munificent in every way.

I have been strongly urged by our leading friends to bring him to Mr. Disraeli's notice with a view to a baronetcy. In strict confidence, I hardly think that socially this would do, even if Mr. Disraeli, with the many other applicants he must have, was inclined to think of it, but I really think it is most desirable that the offer of knighthood should be made to him. The Radical, as well as the Conservative newspapers are all saying that he ought to have a baronetcy, the Liberal Sir William Brown who gave the Brown Library to Liverpool being made a baronet,—and our party in the town, which they say led the van in the Conservative reaction, are most anxious about it, as he is a very popular man. My colleague Mr. Torr and myself both agree that it would be a serious disappointment to our friends if knighthood was not offered—Cross I think who was at the royal visit quite agrees with us.

It is of course very important that we should do nothing as a Government to shake the Liverpool feeling (I do not mean personal; that is all safe I believe: but party). No doubt this Mayor is a great popular and Conservative favourite—only think of a net gain of over 3,000 on the last revision.[51]

Barclay Walker was knighted in 1877, but his baronetcy did not arrive until Salisbury was in office once more in 1886. Many representatives of urban Conservatism, who had played a part on one side or the other in the National Union battle, received baronetcies after 1886, a fate which was unlikely to have befallen them before 1880. Among them were men like Houldsworth, Dixon-Hartland, Forwood, R. N. Fowler, F. S. Powell, and Thomas Salt. Between 1874 and 1880 only Callender and Bates, among men of similar standing, were offered baronetcies.

We have seen the constant pressure from the party managers for liberal and judicious dispensation of patronage and honours.

[51] Hughenden Papers, B/XX/Co., Sandon to Corry, 26 Oct. 1874. Sir William Brown gave £42,000 for the library and museum which still bears his name and was made a baronet in 1863.

Gorst's persistent complaints about the neglect of prominent Conservatives in the constituencies, especially in the boroughs, furnish a striking example. These complaints cannot be attributed only to Gorst's jaundiced views; they were widely echoed. Dyke sent a report to Disraeli of a meeting of fifty agents and secretaries of Conservative associations: they were unanimous in their complaints about the Government's dispensation of patronage and alleged bias in favour of Radicals.[52] The kind of appointments these men were concerned about and which also formed the subject of many of Gorst's complaints were at a much lower level than the Civil Service Commissionerships, knighthoods, and baronetcies that took up the time of ministers: the kind of posts at issue here ranged from Church of England livings and county court judgeships down to sub-postmasterships, and messengers and cleaners in Government offices. The natural feelings of many active Tories were that the Liberals had had rich pickings in their many years of office and that the stream of benefits was not, when the Conservatives were in office, flowing sufficiently strongly in their direction.

The fact was that an increasingly wide circle of party workers and activists had to be satisfied and there was not enough to go round. When the Tories were in opposition again after 1880 they had no honours or places to give, but the pressure from the middle and lower ranks in the party was still rising. In consequence there was now a flood of letters and addresses to the party leaders asking them to speak at meetings and banquets and open bazaars and garden parties. For the small fry of the party there was some satisfaction in being able to communicate personally with the leaders and to be privileged to receive even a negative reply. Well might Salisbury say that his epitaph should be 'Died of writing inane letters to empty-headed Conservative Associations'.[53] This was the price of democracy. These developments had the effect of strengthening the hands of the central party headquarters in its dealings with local associations. Places, honours, and recognition had to come from the party leaders. The Central Office played the role of an intermediary in the process and to this extent its status was enhanced.

[52] Hughenden Papers, B/XXI/Dyke, to Disraeli, 10 Feb. (no year).
[53] Lady G. Cecil, *Life of Salisbury*, iii. 108.

Nonetheless, organization itself could only play a subordinate part in the cohesion of the Conservative party before 1885. The use of honours and patronage for political ends was, after all, in the later nineteenth century, infinitely less significant than it had been 100 years earlier. A development of more profound importance was the increasing predominance of national issues and personalities as against local ones, most clearly to be seen in the activities of pressure groups. With the enlargement of the *pays politique* in 1867, a wider public opinion could have a more direct influence on parliamentary events, and organized groups for the promotion of causes began to proliferate from the early 1860s onwards. Pressure groups were not a new phenomenon. They had been an established feature of the political scene since at least the first Reform Bill and the most famous and technically perfect example was the Anti-Corn Law League. Pressure groups sought to achieve their political objectives through local and national action. In the constituencies their most obvious line of attack was to extract pledges from candidates. Hence the great diversity of pledges and programmes to be found in election addresses. In itself this might have retarded the development of the modern party system, for most members were thus tied to a programme which might be quite independent of any national platform. But the objectives of many of the pressure groups, to which members had pledged themselves locally, could only be achieved by action at the centre and thus an M.P. would best be able to advance a cause he wanted to support by trying to further it with the leaders of his party, especially when they were in power. In this way national pressure groups enhanced the meaning of 'party' and indirectly the scope of party organization.

The great causes and their organizations were mostly on the Liberal side and the Liberal party also had in its ranks a group of wealthy Radical business men, Morley, Rathbone, Lawson, and others, who devoted much of their parliamentary careers to the promotion of a single cause.[54] The Conservatives, however, also had their pressure groups, even if these did not make an impact on the parliamentary party to anything like the same extent as on the opposition side. The Nine-Hour Movement was, in the 1860s and early 1870s, an important pressure group

[54] John Vincent, *The Formation of the Liberal Party*, p. 38.

within Labour and working-class politics. It modelled itself on the earlier Ten-Hour Movement which also acted politically mainly through the Tory party. Like its predecessor it was strong in Lancashire and Yorkshire. Callender and Fison, the Conservative candidate in the North-West Riding, were linked with the movement, and tried to plead the cause with the party leader. As their contact man they used Gorst, thus giving a classic illustration of the relationship between pressure groups, party organization and members of Parliament. Disraeli had held out hope to the leaders of the Nine-Hour Movement during his visit to Lancashire in 1872, but as long as they were in office the Liberals had a better chance of meeting their demands:

Now that the rush of the election is over and our success assured fully, I venture to avail myself of the permission which Mr. Disraeli kindly gave me and bring before you a matter of (as I think) great importance. The election in Lancashire hinged upon 2 questions— the 9 Hours bill and demands of the trade unionists. On both points every candidate for a borough constituency has had to promise compliance—my promise being only in accordance with views expressed years ago—Sir Thomas Bazley having had to explain away his votes and speeches last session.

Of the trade union question I say nothing—the 9 Hours bill is a more pressing question. At the end of last year I had some communication with Mr. Fison (who contested North-East Yorkshire) . . . and the representatives of the working men of Lancashire and Yorkshire and we had arranged through Gorst to seek an interview with Mr. Disraeli, desirous to promote the interests of the factory operatives and at the same time to do so through the chief of the Tory party.

The Masters Association had offered to compromise the question by agreeing to reduce the present 60 hours to 58 and this has been rejected, and the idea was to ask Mr. Disraeli, when the discussion came on, to propose 56 hours and enable him to say that he had the agreement of the factory workers to say that this would be accepted. Thus Mr. Mundella would have been virtually put aside and the chief of Her Majesty's Opposition would have been recognised as the channel through which our people express their wishes. It is quite clear from expressions dropped by Forster that the present Government designed to do something of the kind and it was proposed to observe the utmost secrecy. The first point to be ascertained was how far Mr. Disraeli would feel inclined to consent to our wishes—and if he had been able to do so—then the consent of the committee of the factory workers was to be obtained.

The position is now changed to our advantage and my object in troubling you is to suggest the possibility of alluding to the matter in the Queen's Speech. This would take the matter out of Mundella's hands altogether—it is in accordance with the previous vote of Mr. Disraeli, Lord John Manners and other leading members of the Cabinet—we are all so deeply pledged to it that it could not alienate our friends—and may I venture to add—it would strengthen all we have said as to the policy of the Conservative party attending to the health and comfort of the nation rather than wretched political agitation.[55]

Gorst had in fact advised Disraeli not to see Callender and Fison, because he had heard rumours that the leaders of the Nine-Hour Movement were also negotiating with the Gladstone government.[56] But this was before the announcement of the dissolution on 24 January 1874. The outcome of the elections gave the Conservatives the chance to pass the Factory Act of 1874, mainly the work of Cross.

The National Fair Trade League was a pressure group with wide ramifications in the Conservative party. Protectionist sentiments had revived in the Tory party, as far back as 1867.[57] In the 1870s a number of organizations appeared as precursors of the League and some Tory backbenchers, for example, MacIver, the member for Liverpool, were connected with them. Just before the expiry of the 1874 Parliament two Conservative borough members, Wheelhouse and Eaton, moved a Fair Trade motion but received no encouragement from their front bench. Once the Conservatives were in opposition they could afford to be less inhibited. It was at this juncture that the National Fair Trade League was founded. Its leading spirit was Farrer Ecroyd, the Conservative member for Preston, and his pamphlet *The Policy of Self-Help* was the Bible of the Fair Traders; S. S. Lloyd, of the Birmingham banking family and Conservative member for Plymouth and later South Warwickshire, was

[55] Hughenden Papers, B/XXI/Callender, to Corry, 26 Feb. 1874. For the Tories and the Ten-Hour Movement, see David Roberts, 'Tory Paternalism and Social Reform in Early Victorian England', *American Historical Review*, vol. LXIII, No. 2 (January 1958), p. 323.

[56] Hughenden Papers, B/XXI/Gorst, to Disraeli, 19 Jan. 1874.

[57] Benjamin H. Brown, *The Tariff Reform Movement in Great Britain, 1881–1895*, p. 5.

Chairman of the League.[58] Conservative Central Office had links with the League: Thomas Kelly and Samuel Peters, for instance, whose employment as agitators caused controversy at Central Office,[59] were also agents of the League. They had a dubious and chequered history in working-class politics.[60] Tory leaders were increasingly prone to take up the Fair Trade cry without committing themselves. Northcote, though privately sceptical, appeared on protectionist platforms. Raikes described his attitude on Fair Trade as 'the hands of perplexity travelling up and down the sleeves of irresolution'.[61] Salisbury evolved a cautious formulation of his attitude. Lord Randolph Churchill was bolder, but even he remained equivocal.[62]

A pressure group in the educational field, which was of great political significance in the 1870s and of permanent importance in the development of the Liberal party, was the National Education League. In many ways it became synonymous with the Radical wing of the Liberal party and grew into the National Liberal Federation. On the Conservative side the National Education Union, inaugurated in November 1869 under the chairmanship of Lord Harrowby, was the organization for promoting counter-pressure in favour of denominational education. Most of its leading members were Tories and most Conservative M.P.s were pledged to it; but there were a few prominent supporters drawn from outside the ranks of Conservative and Anglicans, among them Edward Baines, proprietor of the *Leeds Mercury*, whom Matthew Arnold had called 'the very Dissidence of Dissent, and the Protestantism of the Protestant religion', Cowper-Temple, Whig M.P. for South Hampshire, who gave his name to the famous 'non-denominational teaching' clause in the Education Act of 1870, and Thomas Hughes, the author, at this time Liberal M.P. for Frome.[63]

Pressure groups of a more purely religious nature abounded:

[58] W. Farrer Ecroyd, M.P., *The Policy of Self-Help* (1st edn. 1879); for S. S. Lloyd, see Samuel Lloyd, *The Lloyds of Birmingham* (1907).
[59] See also above, p. 155.
[60] Benjamin H. Brown, op. cit., p. 31.
[61] Sir E. Clarke, *The Story of My Life*. For Northcote's attitude, see also Cross Papers, Add. MS. 51265, Northcote to Cross, 12, 21 Sept. 1881; Iddesleigh Papers, Add. MS. 50043, folios 230–5.
[62] W. S. Churchill, *Lord Randolph Churchill*, i. 290.
[63] See F. Adams, *History of the Elementary School Contest* (1880). Also *National Education Union, Report of the Movement* (1869–70).

of particular importance for the Conservative Party were the English Church Union,[64] an organization of the High Church party, and, on the other wing of Anglicanism, the Church Association, originally formed to limit the spread of Ritualism.[65] Religious issues bulked large until the middle 1870s, when trade depression and other factors pushed economic and social problems to the fore again. We have seen how a specific problem, Ritualism, and the Public Worship Regulation Bill of 1874, caused much anxiety and division in the Tory ranks.[66] Here again, members of Parliament and party managers had to bring their misgivings privately, as well as publicly, to the notice of the parliamentary leaders, who were the only men in a position to act one way or another:

It is with great reluctance that I venture to trouble you; but I am constrained to do so by the circumstance that in my borough the clerical element predominates probably more than in any other constituency except the universities. Hence I gather the feeling of the Church not only locally but from other parts of the country. Recent divisions have manifested that the opponents of the Public Worship Regulation Bill cannot hope to stay its progress except by formal delays. They may, however, stop its passing this year by adjournments and divisions in Committee creating great irritation and full of danger to the Establishment.

The importance is great of making the question as little as possible irritating to the constituencies and embarrassing to their representatives. I venture therefore with the greatest deference to yourself and the Government to make or to support, if already made, the following suggestion, viz:

That the Government should recommend the acceptance of the Second Reading without a division, promising, after examination, to support or even to propose an amended bill next year.[67]

[64] Henry William Law and Irene Law, *The Book of the Beresford Hopes* (1925). A. J. Beresford Hope was a founder of the English Church Union in 1859.
[65] The Church Association was instituted in 1865 'to uphold the Principles and Order of the United Church of England and Ireland, and to counteract the efforts now being made to assimilate her services to those of the Church of Rome'. Among Conservatives associated with it were Abergavenny, C. N. Newdegate, M.P., Sir John Kennaway, M.P., S. S. Lloyd, and J. M. Holt, M.P. See *Annual Report 1867* (2nd edn.).
[66] See above, Chapter IV.
[67] Hughenden Papers, B/XII/F, Sir H. D. Wolff to Disraeli, 11 July 1874.

Gorst, writing as party manager to Disraeli a few months later, also drew attention to the serious damage done to the party by offending the High Anglicans:

We no doubt took on the Public Worship Regulation bill the least disadvantageous course open to us, but still the result was to alienate an important class of our supporters. The High Church party has always seemed to me to occupy on our side a position somewhat analogous to the ultra-Dissenters on the other: it has an electoral importance beyond what is due to its mere numbers, and holds opinions and principles to which party interests are subordinate. There is nothing like an open rupture yet, . . . but we must not shut our eyes to the existence of a good deal of sore feeling which future events may allay or aggravate. If the Archbishop of Canterbury pursues his career of ecclesiastical legislation, there seems to me great danger of our Government being broken up by the High Church party, as Gladstone's was by the Dissenters.[68]

Quite apart from pressure groups, members of Parliament and their leading supporters now saw public opinion swayed predominantly by national issues and by the manner in which the national leaders handled these issues. Lord Sandon, as member for Liverpool, represented one of the largest borough electorates in the country, and was also a member of the Government at a time when the public was stirred as never before by the Eastern Question. He was made aware of the conflicting views of his supporters: on the one hand patriotic fervour, particularly amongst Tory working men, is reported by Forwood, the Tory Democrat:

There are some few of our leading Conservative friends who side with Lord Derby and are a little touched with the distrust that the press propagates as to Lord Beaconsfield's policy. The bulk of our party, I mean as far as its leading men are concerned, are thoroughly at one with the 'firm policy' of the Government. Descending in the social scale the feeling is almost unanimous for firmness and determined attitude. Coming to particulars I find a strong contingent of Liberals averse to even a temporary occupation of Constantinople. Very many regret the Fleet's recall and many more are disappointed at Derby's want of courage attributing it to his idleness.[69]

Politically we are anxious and many rather 'befogged'. Derby's

[68] Hughenden Papers, B/XII/F, Gorst to Disraeli, 16 Dec. 1874.
[69] Harrowby Papers, L/84, Forwood to Sandon, 30 Jan. 1878.

resignation is not bewailed, but the Fleet's recall in January is much regretted. Let the proper authority tell the country, in as few plain English words as possible, the meaning of the respective positions assumed by England and Russia. Reserving the right to accept a discussion is Russia's roundabout phrase, let ours be very simple so that hasty readers, and they form the bulk, may comprehend.[70]

Whitley, barometer of feeling among Conservative middle-class and business circles, emphasizes more the wish for peace and a fair settlement:

You ask as to our eastern policy—as far as I can gather in Liverpool it is in favour of peace if possible. That we should not go to war unless forced by circumstances. For instance I believe the feeling would be in favour of the Dardanelles being open to all nations, not of course handed over to Russia, which would be extreme folly. That with regard to Constantinople, if taken from the Turks, that it should be a neutral city free to all nations under a protectorate. There would be a very strong feeling against Constantinople being handed over to Russia. If there is any truth in the project as to Egypt and it could be conceded to us on any fair terms I believe no stroke of foreign policy would be more popular and would tend to reconcile us very much to the opening of the Dardanelles to Russia. The Egyptian bond-holders are very numerous and these to a man irrespective of political feeling would go in favour of some such scheme.[71]

Even purely local issues were becoming increasingly dependent on central government policy, and Members of Parliament were therefore sensitive to the manner in which they were handled by the party leaders, and anxious to make their views known to them. In their arguments they tended to emphasize the question of party advantage. The grant of money to Owen's College was such an issue at Manchester, and Callender put the case to the Prime Minister:

He added an argument which he could not adduce in the presence of the deputation which waited on the Prime Minister; i.e. that the Conservative success in Lancashire can only be retained by taking advantage of every opportunity of gaining sympathy and confidence from the general public who do not take any decided party views,

---

[70] Harrowby Papers, L/90, Forwood to Sandon, 30 Mar. 1878.
[71] Ibid., L/238, Whitley to Sandon, 1 Jan. 1878. See also R. T. Shannon, *Gladstone and the Bulgarian Agitation 1876*, p. 152.

and that he considers this grant would be of great service in that way.[72]

Pressure and interest groups thus attempted to make an impact on the policies of governments by pressure on M.P.s. They in their turn had to pass the pressure on to the party leaders in order to achieve results. The party organization was increasingly used as a channel of communication. Public opinion at large was more and more focussed on the activities of national leaders—M.P.s were watching this process and report-ing it to their leaders. Hence the tendency of members to look increasingly to party interests, instead of feeling safely ensconced in their personal sources of influence. The importance of specific policies and actions was, in the light of present-day knowledge of electorates, almost overestimated: the electoral analyses of the period picture the voter as a highly rational animal who makes his decision on a careful balancing of interests and objectives. From the point of view of party organization, the result of the shift from local influence to national policy was that the party managers at the centre, acting on behalf of the party leaders, were given increased leverage in their dealings with the constituencies. Their concern with the activities of pressure groups is evident from their letters and memoranda.

Not only the policies but also the personalities of the national leaders were of growing electoral importance. In some ways over-emphasis on personality could and did retard the evolution of the party system: this was the effect of Palmerston's long predominance. The promise of general support for Gladstone or Disraeli was, no doubt, used by many a candidate to cover his personal brand of principles with a national party cry. Even so the appeal to the personalities of national leaders was part of the process by which local currents of influence were replaced in the electoral conflict by national considerations and, to that extent, the standing of the central party organizations were thereby enhanced.

The passage of the Corrupt Practices Act of 1883 and the Reform Act of 1884 together brought about a further sharp move in the direction of the modern party system. The former completed the process by which one of the main strongholds of

[72] Hughenden Papers, B/XXI/Turnor, to Disraeli, 5 Sept. 1874.

influence was finally eroded, though, perhaps even now, not completely eradicated; it was a process in which previous corrupt practices legislation, a long series of prosecutions, and the Ballot Act of 1872 formed stages.[73] Through the Reform Act of 1884 the conditions created by the existence of mass electorates, which had earlier applied to only a portion of the constituencies, became universal. The last remnant of the historic shires and boroughs disappeared almost completely, and it now became necessary for the parties to create new and uniform organizations in the new electoral districts. The central party headquarters now had a network of comprehensive constituency organizations to deal with, the absence of which between 1867 and 1884 has been noted in this chapter. Thus another era began.

The essential feature of the period between the second and third Reform Bills was that party organization, centrally and locally, became one of the characteristics of larger electorates which could not be controlled by influence; but organization was not strong enough, at any rate on the Conservative side, to weld the party together and to stamp its own laws on it. On the other hand, national policies and personalities figured increasingly in elections and a larger number of voluntary workers were needed. This meant that more regard had to be paid to the constituency organizations, while at the same time the hand of the Central Office was strengthened in dealing with them. But there was not a ready-made structure in existence even at the end of the period, of which, as at the present day, the leaders had to gain control in order to impose their policies and personalities; nor could it have been said, as it might be said today, that the very meaning of 'party' resides largely in the organizational structures outside Parliament. These formed a new part of the political system; they had their origin in the period between the first and second Reform bills, they developed mightily between the second and the third, but attained their full stature only after 1885.

[73] C. Seymour, op. cit., Chapter XIV, and O'Leary, op. cit.

APPENDIX

DISRAELI'S SECOND ADMINISTRATION
Formed in February 1874

Prime Minister and First Lord of the Treasury	B. Disraeli, cr. Earl of Beaconsfield, August 1876
Lord Chancellor	Lord Cairns, cr. Earl, 1878
Lord President	Duke of Richmond
Lord Privy Seal August 1876 January 1878	Earl of Malmesbury Earl of Beaconsfield Duke of Northumberland
Home Secretary	Richard A. Cross
Foreign Secretary March 1878	Earl of Derby Marquis of Salisbury
Colonial Secretary January 1878	Earl of Carnarvon Sir Michael Hicks Beach
War Secretary March 1878	Gathorne Hardy, cr. Viscount Cranbrook, March 1878 Col. the Hon. F. A. Stanley
Indian Secretary March 1878	Marquis of Salisbury Viscount Cranbrook
Chancellor of the Exchequer	Sir Stafford Northcote
First Lord of the Admiralty July 1877	G. Ward Hunt W. H. Smith
Postmaster-General	Lord John Manners
Chief Secretary for Ireland (entered Cabinet August 1876)	Sir Michael Hicks Beach
President of Board of Trade (entered Cabinet March 1878)	Viscount Sandon

NOT IN THE CABINET

Chief Commissioner of Works August 1876	Lord Henry Lennox Hon. Gerard J. Noel
Chancellor of the Duchy of Lancaster	Col. T. E. Taylor
Vice-President of the Committee of Council for Education March 1878	Viscount Sandon Lord George Hamilton
President of the Local Government Board	George Sclater-Booth
President of the Board of Trade March 1878	Sir Charles B. Adderley Viscount Sandon (with seat in Cabinet)
Lords of the Treasury	Viscount Mahon; Lord Crichton, 1876 Rowland Winn Sir James D. H. Elphinstone
Civil Lord of the Admiralty	Sir Massey Lopes, Bt.
Joint Secretaries of the Treasury	William Hart Dyke (Patronage Secretary) W. H. Smith (Financial Secretary)
July 1877 March 1878	Col. Hon. F. A. Stanley Sir H. Selwin-Ibbetson
Secretary of the Admiralty	The Hon. A. F. Egerton
Secretary to the Board of Trade November 1875 March 1878	G. Cavendish-Bentinck The Hon. E. Stanhope J. G. Talbot
Secretary to the Local Government Board November 1875	C. S. Read Thomas Salt
Under Secretary, Home Office March 1878	Sir H. Selwin-Ibbetson Sir M. White Ridley

Under Secretary, Colonial Office	James Lowther
January 1878	Earl Cadogan
Under Secretary, War Office	Earl of Pembroke
1875	Earl Cadogan
January 1878	Viscount Bury
Under Secretary, India Office	Lord George Hamilton
March 1878	The Hon. E. Stanhope
Paymaster-General and Judge-Advocate-General	Stephen Cave
Paymaster-General	
March 1880	The Hon. David Plunket
Judge-Advocate-General	
November 1875	G. Cavendish-Bentinck
Attorney-General	Sir J. B. Karslake
April 1874	Sir Richard Baggallay
November 1875	Sir John Holker
Solicitor-General	Sir Richard Baggallay
April 1874	Sir John Holker
November 1875	Sir Hardinge Giffard
Lord Advocate for Scotland	E. S. Gordon
1877	William Watson
Solicitor-General for Scotland	J. Millar
1877	J. H. A. Macdonald

IRELAND

Lord Lieutenant	Duke of Abercorn
1876	Duke of Marlborough
Lord Chancellor 1875	J. T. Ball
Chief Secretary	Sir Michael Hicks Beach (enters Cabinet August 1876)
January 1878	James Lowther
Attorney-General	J. T. Ball
1875	H. Ormsby
1875	G. C. A. May
1877	Edward Gibson

Solicitor-General	H. Ormsby
1875	The Hon. David Plunket
1877	G. Fitzgibbon
1878	H. Holmes

THE QUEEN'S HOUSEHOLD

Lord Steward	Earl Beauchamp
Lord Chamberlain	Marquis of Hertford
1879	Earl of Mount Edgcumbe
Master of the Horse	Earl of Bradford
Treasurer of the Household (Whip)	Earl Percy
1875	Lord Henry Thynne
Comptroller of the Household	Lord H. Somerset
Vice-Chamberlain (Whip)	Viscount Barrington
Captain of the Corps of Gentlemen at Arms	Marquis of Exeter
1878	Earl of Coventry
Captain of the Yeoman of the Guard (Whip)	Lord Skelmersdale
Master of the Buckhounds	Earl of Hardwicke
Chief Equerry and Clerk Marshall	Lord Alfred Paget
Mistress of the Robes	Duchess of Wellington

CHRONOLOGY OF THE CENTRAL
ORGANIZATION OF THE
CONSERVATIVE PARTY 1867–85

1867	April	Conference of Conservative Working Men's Associations in London.
	November	Inaugural meeting of the National Union of Conservative and Constitutional Associations.
1868	April	M. Spofforth, Principal Conservative Agent, starts Central Board, to organize religious groups for the forthcoming general election.
	September–November	Election Committee, consisting of Spofforth, Lord Abergavenny, Montagu Corry, T. E. Taylor, and the Hon. G. J. Noel, supervises conduct of general election.
1870	April	J. E. Gorst succeeds Spofforth as Principal Conservative Agent and sets up a Central Conservative Office at 53 Parliament Street, Westminster.
1871		Gorst and his assistant, Major the Hon. C. K. Keith-Falconer, become joint honorary secretaries of the National Union in succession to Leonard Sedgwick. Headquarters of the National Union moved to 53 Parliament Street.
1873	December	William Hart Dyke temporarily succeeds Noel as Chief Whip.
1874	February	Gorst's formal engagement as Party Agent ends but he continues to be available for advice. Major Keith-Falconer also leaves service of the Party. Dyke appointed Patronage Secretary. Removal of Central Office to St. Stephen's Chambers, Westminster.

1877		Gorst's connection with party management ends and he ceases to be Secretary of the National Union. W. B. Skene becomes Principal Conservative Agent.
1880	April	Skene resigns as Agent after the General Election. Committee set up under the chairmanship of W. H. Smith to enquire into the state of party organization; this becomes known as the Central Committee. The Hon. E. Stanhope is Vice-Chairman.
	July	Gorst resumes duties of Principal Agent, on the understanding that he will be given office when the Conservatives return to power. Rowland Winn succeeds Dyke as Chief Whip.
1882	November	Gorst resigns as Principal Agent. The Hon. E. Stanhope succeeds W. H. Smith as the Chairman of the Central Committee.
1883	February	G. C. T. Bartley appointed Principal Agent.
1883	October	Lord Randolph Churchill attacks party leaders at the Annual Conference of the National Union at Birmingham.
	December	Primrose League founded.
1884	March	National Union threatened with eviction from the premises of the Conservative Central Office.
	July	Quarrel between Lord Randolph Churchill and the party leaders resolved. Sir Michael Hicks Beach elected Chairman of the National Union Council. Central Committee abolished. Primrose League officially recognized.
1885		Captain Middleton succeeds Bartley as Principal Agent. A. Akers-Douglas succeeds Rowland Winn as Chief Whip.

GLOSSARY OF NAMES

(This list contains only the names of secondary personalities and Conservatives).

ABERGAVENNY (1826–1915), fifth Earl of, cr. Marquis in 1876, Viscount Nevill, K.G., J.P., Lord Lieutenant of Sussex 1892–1905. For many years one of the principal Conservative party managers.

ADDERLEY, see Norton.

ADDINGTON (1805–89), first Baron, cr. 1887, J. G. Hubbard; son of a Russia merchant, a Director of the Bank of England 1838–41; Chairman of the Public Works Loan Commission from 1853; M.P. for Buckingham 1859–68, for the City of London 1874–87. Gave much attention to taxation, coinage, ecclesiastical affairs, and education; prominent High Churchman.

AKERS-DOUGLAS, see Chilston.

AMHERST (1836–1910), third Earl, Viscount Holmesdale; Captain, Coldstream Guards, M.P. for West Kent 1859–68, for Mid-Kent 1868–80. Summoned to the House of Lords in his father's Barony in April 1880. Associated with shipping, party management and the National Union. One of the 'Kentish Gang'.

ANSON (1835–77), Hon. Augustus H. A., third son of the first Earl of Lichfield, Captain, 84th Foot 1855–8, A.D.C. to General Grant in Indian Mutiny, received V.C., M.P. for Lichfield 1859–68, for Bewdley 1869–74. One of the 'Colonels'.

ASHBOURNE (1837–1913), first Baron, cr. 1885, Edward Gibson; educ. Trinity College, Dublin, Q.C. 1872. M.P. for Dublin University 1875–85; Attorney-General for Ireland 1877–80; Lord Chancellor of Ireland with a seat in the Cabinet, 1885–6, 1886–92, 1895–1905. Regarded as the Conservative Party's expert on Irish affairs in the early 1880s.

ASHCOMBE (1828–1917), first Baron, cr. 1892, George Cubitt; M.P. for West Surrey 1860–85, for Mid-Surrey 1885–92; Second Church Estate Commissioner 1874–9. Prominent M.P. in the 1880s, active mainly on the side of the orthodox leaders.

BARRINGTON (1824–86), seventh Viscount, cr. Baron of U.K. in 1880; M.P. for Eye; Vice-Chamberlain of H.M. Household

1874–80; Captain of the Yeoman of the Guard 1885; Captain of the Corps of Gentlemen at Arms 1886. Private Secretary of the fourteenth Earl of Derby, personal friend of Disraeli, and his private secretary in the last few months of his life; a Whip in the Commons and Lords.

BARTLETT (1849–1902), Sir Ellis Ashmead, knighted 1892, of American parentage, educ. Christ Church, Oxford; President of Oxford Union 1873; M.P. for Eye 1880–5, for Sheffield (Ecclesall) 1885–1902; Civil Lord of the Admiralty 1885–6 and 1886–92. Became ardent supporter of Gladstone on Bulgarian atrocities, but later developed into a passionate imperialist, accompanying the Turkish army against the Greeks in 1897 and participating in the Boer War. Supporter of Northcote in National Union battle, became Chairman of National Union 1886–8. Much in demand as platform orator. His brother married Baroness Burdett-Coutts in 1881.

BARTLEY (1842–1910), Sir George Christopher Trant, K.C.B. 1902; educ. University College School; Assistant Director of Science Division of Science and Art Department till 1880, resigned to stand for Parliament; Principal Conservative Agent 1883–5; M.P. for N. Islington 1885–1906. Established National Penny Bank to promote thrift, 1875. Publications include 'A Square Mile in the East of London', 'Schools for the People', 'The Seven Ages of a Village Pauper'. Early advocate of old age pensions.

BARTTELOT (1820–93), Rt. Hon. Sir Walter, cr. Bt. 1875; M.P. for North-West Sussex 1860–93. Colonel, First Royal Dragoons. Prominent and respected spokesman of county Conservatism.

BASING (1826–94), first Baron, cr. 1887, George Sclater-Booth; M.P. for North Hampshire 1857–87; Parliamentary Secretary, Poor Law Board 1867–8; Financial Secretary to the Treasury, March to December 1868; President of the Local Government Board 1874–80. Responsible for the Public Health, Sale of Food and Drugs, and Rivers Pollution Acts.

BATES (1816–96), Sir Edward, cr. Bt. 1880; M.P. for Plymouth 1871–80 and 1885–92. Prominent shipping magnate. Was attacked by Plimsoll in celebrated incident in July 1875. His son married a daughter of S. R. Graves, M.P. for Liverpool.

BEAUCHAMP (1830–91), sixth Earl; M.P. for Tewkesbury 1857–63 and West Worcestershire 1863–6; Lord of the Admiralty 1859; Lord Steward of the Household 1874–80; Paymaster-General 1886–7. Prominent High Churchman, nearly resigned over the Public Worship Regulation Bill in 1874.

BENTINCK (1803–83), George W. P. A., son of Vice-Admiral William Bentinck. Contested Kendal in 1843; M.P. for West Norfolk 1852–65 and 1871–84. Pugnacious spokesman of county Conservatives, known as 'Big Ben'. Ordered his coffin to be kept open for three days after his death.

BIRLEY (1817–83), Hugh, educ. Winchester College; a partner in the firm of Macintosh & Co., indiarubber manufacturers; M.P. for Manchester 1868–83; Member of a prominent Manchester family: he and his brothers Herbert and Thomas were noted philanthropists. Chairman of the National Education Union and active on the Manchester School Board. Supporter of the United Kingdom Alliance.

BOURKE, see Connemara.

BURNABY (1842–85), Col. F. T., Correspondent of *The Times* in the Carlist camp, Spain 1874; agent of the Stafford House Committee in the Russo-Turkish war 1877–8; commanded 5th Turkish Brigade at the Battle of Taschkesin in 1877. Contested Birmingham in April 1880; was a supporter of Randolph Churchill in the National Union controversy. Made nineteen balloon ascents and crossed the Channel by balloon in 1882. Went to Egypt and was killed in the Sudan in 1885.

BUTLER-JOHNSTONE (1837–1902), Henry Alexander, M.P. for Canterbury 1826–78. His father, son of the thirteenth Lord Dunboyne, also sat for Canterbury 1852–3 and 1857–62. In 1880 Butler-Johnstone stood as an Independent candidate and later joined with Hyndman in founding the S.D.F. He consulted with Marx on the Eastern Question.

CALLENDER (1825–76), W. Romaine, cotton spinner; leading Manchester Conservative, M.P. for Manchester 1874–6. Active on National Education League in 1860s and supporter of the United Kingdom Alliance. Opponent of *laissez faire*. He died before a baronetcy conferred on him could be gazetted.

CAVE (1820–80), Rt. Hon. Sir Stephen; M.P. for New Shoreham and the Rape of Bamber 1859–80. Paymaster-General and Vice-President of the Board of Trade 1866–8; Judge-Advocate-General from Jan. 1874 to Nov. 1875. Paymaster-General 1874–80. Special envoy to Egypt 1875–6.

CAVENDISH-BENTINCK (1821–91), George, grandson of the third Duke of Portland. Contested Taunton 1859; M.P. for Taunton 1859–65 and for Whitehaven 1865–91. Parliamentary Secretary to the Board of Trade 1874–5; Judge-Advocate-General 1875–80. Well known as an art connoisseur, amateur actor, and writer of letters to

The Times on artistic matters. Published his speeches on merchant shipping legislation and contagious diseases acts.

CAWLEY (1812–77), C. E. A civil engineer and member of Institute of Civil Engineers. Alderman of Salford; M.P. for Salford 1868–death. A strong Protestant.

CHAPLIN (1840–1923), first Viscount, cr. 1916, Henry Chaplin, educ. Harrow, Christ Church, Oxford; married daughter of the third Duke of Sutherland. M.P. Mid-Lincolnshire and Sleaford division of Lincoln 1868–1906. Chancellor of the Duchy of Lancaster 1885–6; President of the Board of Agriculture 1886–93; President of the Local Government Board 1895–1900. Member of the Royal Commission on Agriculture 1881 and 1893; member of the Royal Commission on Horse Breeding 1887. Leading spokesman of agricultural Conservatives. Racehorse owner and breeder.

CHARLEY (1833–1904), Sir William Thomas, knighted 1880. Lawyer in practice in Liverpool and Salford. M.P. for Salford 1868–80, defeated in 1880, contested Ipswich in 1883 and 1885. Took prominent part in the reorganization of the Conservative Party in Lancashire and in the Metropolis after 1867. Strong Protestant. His appointment as Common Sergeant in the City in 1878 was widely criticized.

CHEYLESMORE (1816–91), first Baron, cr. 1887, H. W. Eaton; member of the firm of H. W. Eaton & Sons, silk merchants and brokers. Prominent figure in London business and club life. M.P. for Coventry 1865–80, defeated in 1880. Had considerable income and was governor of many hospitals, etc. Leading supporter of Fair Trade.

CHILSTON (1851–1926), first Viscount, cr. 1911, A. Akers-Douglas; M.P. for St. Augustine's division of Kent 1880–1911; Whip to the Conservative Party 1883, Chief Whip 1885–95; First Commissioner of Works with seat in the Cabinet 1895–1902; Home Secretary 1902–6.

COLVILLE (1818–1907), Charles J., tenth Baron and first Viscount Colville of Culross, a Representative Peer 1850–85, cr. Baron of the U.K. 1885, and Viscount 1902; Chief Equerry and Clerk Marshall to Queen Victoria, 1852–8, Master of the Buckhounds 1866–8, a Whip in the House of Lords, Lord Chamberlain to Queen Alexandra, 1873–1903.

CONNEMARA (1827–1902), first Baron, cr. 1887, Hon. Robert Bourke, third son of the fifth Earl of Mayo, Barrister, M.P. King's Lynn 1868–86, Under Secretary for Foreign Affairs, 1874–80, 1885–6, Governor of Madras 1886–90.

CORRY, see Rowton.

CRICHTON, See Erne.

CUBITT, see Ashcombe.

DALRYMPLE (1839–1916), Rt. Hon. Sir Charles, cr. Bt. 1887, son of Sir Charles Dalrymple Fergusson, fifth Bt. of Kilkerran; M.P. for Co. Bute 1868–85, for Ipswich 1886–1906; Junior Lord of the Treasury 1885–6. A Whip since 1880.

DERBY (1841–1908), sixteenth Earl of, Hon. F. A. Stanley. M.P. for Preston 1865–8, North Lancashire 1868–85, Blackpool 1885–6. Lord of the Admiralty 1868; Financial Secretary to the War Office 1874–7, to the Treasury 1877–8; Secretary of State for War 1878–80; Vice-President for Education 1885; Secretary of State for the Colonies 1885–6. Cr. Baron Stanley 1886. President of the Board of Trade 1886–8, Governor-General of Canada 1888–93. Succeeded his brother, the fifteenth Earl, in 1893.

DIXON-HARTLAND (1832–1909), Sir Frederick, cr. Bt. 1892; M.P. for Evesham 1880–5; Uxbridge division of Middlesex from 1885. A supporter of Lord Randolph Churchill on the National Union Council. Middlesex County Alderman, Director of London, City & Midland Bank.

DYKE (1837–1931), Sir William Hart, seventh Bt., educ. Harrow and Christ Church, wished to enter Navy. Started public schools racquets championships, and was one of the originators of lawn tennis. M.P. for West Kent 1865, for Mid-Kent 1865–85, for Dartford 1885–1906, when he retired. First appointed Whip in 1868, became Patronage Secretary in 1874. Chief Secretary for Ireland 1885; Vice-President for Education 1887–92.

EATON, see Cheylesmore.

EDWARDS-MOSS (1811–90), Sir Thomas, cr. Bt. 1868. Son of Liverpool banker and himself a banker. His father was connected in an oil mill business with the Forwoods. Educ. Eton; Chairman of Liverpool Constitutional Association 1866; Chairman of South Lancashire Conservative Association 1879.

EGERTON (1825–91), Hon. Algernon F., third son of the first Earl of Ellesmere; M.P. for South Lancashire 1859–68, for S.E. Lancashire 1868–80, for Wigan, 1882–5. Secretary to the Admiralty 1874–80. Was associated with the administration of the Bridgewater Canal.

EGERTON (1832–1909), cr. first Earl 1897, the Hon. Wilbraham Egerton, son of the first Lord Egerton of Tatton whom he succeeded in 1883. M.P. for North Cheshire 1858–68; for mid–Cheshire

1868–83. Chairman of Church Defence Institution; Chairman of various Royal Commissions, e.g. on the Port of London in 1900. Owned about 25,000 acres.

ELPHINSTONE (1805–86), Sir James Dalrymple-Horn-, second Bt., served in the Navy; M.P. for Portsmouth 1857–65 and 1868–80; contested Greenock in 1852, Portsmouth in 1865 and Aberdeenshire in 1866; a Junior Lord of the Treasury 1874–80.

ERNE, (1839-1914), fourth Earl of, Lord Crichton; M.P. for Enniskillen 1868–80, Fermanagh 1880–5. Lord of the Treasury 1876–80.

ESLINGTON, see Ravensworth.

FARRER (1819–99), Sir Thomas, cr. Bt 1883, cr. first Baron 1893; educ. Eton; Assistant Secretary Marine Department Board of Trade 1850, later Permanent Secretary of the Board of Trade, resigned 1886. Vice-Chairman of London County Council. Brother-in-law and close friend of Northcote.

FERGUSON (1832–1907) Rt. Hon. Sir James, sixth Bt.; educ. Rugby, married daughter of the first Lord Dalhousie. M.P. for Ayrshire 1854, 1857–65. Governor of South Australia and New Zealand Contested Frome in 1875 and Greenock in 1878. Governor of Bombay 1880–5. Under-Secretary for India 1860–7; Permanent Under-Secretary at the Home Office 1867–8. M.P. for N.E. Manchester 1885–1906; Parliamentary Under Secretary, Foreign Office, 1886–91; Postmaster-General 1891–2.

FERMOR-HESKETH (1825–72), Sir Thomas, fifth Baronet, M.P. for Preston 1862–72. Took some part in the preparations for Disraeli's Lancashire visit.

FORWOOD (1836–98), Rt. Hon. Sir Arthur Bower, cr. Bt. 1895. Merchant and ship-owner, senior partner in Leech, Harrison & Forwood, Liverpool; mayor of Liverpool 1878–9; Chairman of Liverpool Constitutional Association 1880 to death. M.P. for Ormskirk 1885. Parliamentary and Financial Secretary to Admiralty 1886–92. Prominent exponent of Tory democracy and supporter of Randolph Churchill. Published papers on housing the working classes; democratic Toryism; single-member constituencies.

FOWLER (1828–91), Sir Robert Nicholas, cr. Bt. 1885. Educ. London University; son of banker and himself senior partner in Dimsdale, Drewett, Fowler and Barnard, bankers. Became member of the Church of England having been a Quaker. Reorganized the Conservative Party in the City of London. Contested City of London 1865 and Penryn and Falmouth 1865; M.P. for Penryn 1868–74;

M.P. for City of London 1880–death. Alderman of the City from 1878.

GIBSON, see Ashbourne

GIFFARD, see Halsbury.

GILPIN (1801–82), Sir R. T., cr. Bt. 1876; M.P. for Bedfordshire 1851–80; Colonel, Bedford Militia. Spokesman on military affairs, one of 'the Colonels'.

GOLDNEY (1825–1900), Sir Gabriel, cr. Bt. 1880. M.P. for Chippenham 1865–85. Owned about 2,800 acres. Correspondent of Disraeli.

GORST (1835–1916), Sir John Eldon. Born in Preston, spent some years in New Zealand. Barrister. Contested Hastings in 1865; M.P. for Cambridge 1866–8. Conservative agent 1870. M.P. for Chatham 1875–92, for Cambridge University 1892–1906. Solicitor-General 1885–6; Under-Secretary for India 1886–91; Financial Secretary to the Treasury 1891–2; Vice-President for Education 1895–1903. Resigned from Primrose League 1906 and stood as a Liberal at Preston, 1910.

GOWER (1845–1916), Rt. Hon. Lord Ronald Sutherland-Leveson-, younger son of the second Duke of Sutherland, uncle and great-uncle of the Dukes of Argyll, Sutherland, Leinster, and Westminster. Educ. Eton and Trinity College, Cambridge; a sculptor, author of books on art and sculpture. M.P. for Sutherland, 1867–74.

GRAVES (1818–73), Samuel Robert, merchant and shipowner of Liverpool; Chairman of Liverpool Shipowner's Association 1856 and Local Marine Board 1856; Mayor of Liverpool 1860–1; M.P. for Liverpool 1865–73. In November 1868 he polled 16,755 votes, the largest number for any borough member.

GREENALL (1806–94), Sir Gilbert, cr. Bt. 1876; M.P. for Warrington 1847–68, 1874–80 and 1880–92. High Sheriff of Cheshire 1873.

GURNEY (1804–1878), Russell; M.P. for Southampton 1865–78; Recorder of the City of London 1856–78. Introduced Public Worship Regulation Bill in the Commons.

HALSBURY (1823–1921), first Earl of, cr. 1898. Sir Hardinge Giffard, cr. Baron 1885; Barrister. Solicitor-General 1875–80, M.P. for Launceston 1877–85. Lord Chancellor 1885–6, 1886–92, 1895–1905. High Steward of Oxford University from 1896. Leader of the Ditchers in 1911.

HAMILTON (1843–1925), Lord Claud, second son of the first Duke of Abercorn. M.P. for Londonderry 1865–8, for King's Lynn 1869–80, for Liverpool 1880–8, for South Kensington 1910–18; a

Lord of the Treasury 1868. Prominent on the National Union in the 1880s, as an opponent of Lord Randolph Churchill.

HAMILTON (1845–1927), Lord George Francis, third son of the first Duke of Abercorn, M.P. for Middlesex 1868–85, for the Ealing Division 1885–1906. Under-Secretary for India 1874–8; Vice-President of the Committee of Council on Education 1878–80; First Lord of the Admiralty, 1885–6 and 1886–92; Chairman of the London School Board 1894–5; Secretary of State for India 1895–1903.

HAMOND (1817–1905), Sir Charles F., knighted 1896. Barrister, Town Councillor and Alderman; shipowner and broker to 1862. Contested Newcastle-on-Tyne in 1868 and at a by-election in January 1874; M.P. for Newcastle 1874–80 and 1892–1900. Member of Newcastle School Board.

HAMPTON (1799–1880), first Baron, cr. 1874, Sir John Pakington, Bt.; M.P. for Droitwich 1837–74. Secretary of State for the Colonies 1852; First Lord of the Admiralty 1858–9 and 1866–7; Secretary of State for War 1867–8. Interested in social questions, especially education, but discredited by his indiscretion over the New Social Movement in 1871. Appointed to the newly created post of First Civil Service Commissioner in 1875.

HARROWBY (1798–1882), second Earl of, M.P. for Tiverton 1819–31, for Liverpool 1831–7; a Lord of the Admiralty 1827–8, Secretary to the India Board 1830–31. Took prominent part in the overthrow of the Melbourne Government 1841; voted for repeal of the Test Acts, for the Maynooth Grant and followed Peel as a free trader. Mediated between Derby and the free traders in 1852. Chancellor of the Duchy of Lancaster in Palmerston's first Government 1855; Lord Privy Seal 1855–7.

HARROWBY (1831–1900), third Earl of, Viscount Sandon till 1882. Made tour of the East with Carnarvon after leaving Christ Church. M.P. for Lichfield 1856–9, as a supporter of Palmerston; private secretary to Henry Labouchere, the Colonial Secretary. M.P. for Liverpool 1868–82. Member of first London School Board. Vice-President of Committee of Council on Education 1874–8; President of the Board of Trade 1878–80. Lord Privy Seal 1885–6.

HAY (1821–1912), Rt. Hon. Sir John C. D., third Bt., Admiral. Took part in Borneo and China operations. Lord of the Admiralty 1866–8; M.P. for Wakefield 1862–5; Stamford 1866–80; Wigtown Burghs 1880–5.

HEATHCOTE (1801–81), Sir William, fifth Bt., educ. Winchester and Oriel; Fellow of All Souls 1822–5; M.P. for Hampshire 1826–32; North Hampshire 1837–49; Oxford University 1854–68. His seat at Hursley Park was a centre of the Oxford Movement.

HENLEY (1793–1884), J. W., educ. Fulham and Magdalen, Oxford; M.P. for Oxfordshire 1841–78; President of the Board of Trade 1852 and 1858–9. Resigned over the 1859 Reform Bill. A High Churchman.

HERBERT (1822–76), Sir Percy E., K.C.G. 1869; second son of the second Earl of Powis; educ. Eton and Sandhurst; ensign, 43rd Foot, fought in Crimea, Deputy Quartermaster-General 1860–5 (with rank of major general); M.P. for Ludlow 1854–60; M.P. for South Shropshire 1865 to death; Treasurer of H.M. Household 1867–8. One of the 'Colonels'.

HERBERT, Hon. Sidney, see Pembroke.

HERMON (1821–81), Edward, member of the firm of Horrocks, Miller & Co., cotton spinners, M.P. for Preston 1868–81. Gave money for prizes for essays on the prevention of explosions and accidents in coal mines. Personally sworn £588,000, his pictures sold for £37,000. Typical Conservative borough member.

HILL (1825–1905), Rt. Hon. Alexander Staveley, M.P. for Coventry 1868–74; West Staffordshire 1874–85; Kingswinford division of Staffordshire 1885–1900. Recorder of Banbury 1866–1903; Counsel to Admiralty and Judge-Advocate of the Fleet 1874–80. Prominent supporter of Fair Trade.

HOLKER (1828–82), Sir John, Barrister, Q.C., M.P. for Preston 1872–82; Solicitor-General 1874; Attorney-General 1875–80. Lord Justice of Appeal 1880. His income between 1875–77 was estimated at £22,000 per annum.

HOLMESDALE, see Amherst.

HOLT (1829–1911), James Maden, educ. Christ Church, M.P. for N.E. Lancashire 1868–80. Moved rejection of Third Reading of Irish Church Disestablishment bill in 1869; introduced Ecclesiastical Offences bill in 1874. Chairman of Council of Church Association 1883–5; Treasurer of Trinitarian Bible Society.

HOPE (1820–87), Alexander James Beresford, M.P. for Maidstone 1841–52 and 1857–9. Contested Cambridge University 1859, Stoke-on-Trent 1862. M.P. for Stoke-on-Trent 1865–8 and for Cambridge University 1868 till death. Strong Churchman, opponent of Deceased Wife's Sister Bill 1859; strong opponent of 1867 Reform

Bill. Possessed great wealth and purchased St. Augustine's Abbey, Canterbury as a college for missionary clergy. Brother-in-law of Salisbury. Proprietor of *Saturday Review*.

HOPKINS (1825–98), John Satchell. Son of a Birmingham plate worker and japanner, partner in his father's business. Member of Birmingham School Board 1870; President of Birmingham Conservative Association 1880–6 and 1888–92.

HOULDSWORTH (1834–1917), Sir William Henry, cr. Bt. 1887. Landed proprietor, M.P. for N.W. Manchester 1885–1906. Member of Royal Commission on Depression of Trade and on Liquor Licensing Laws. Delegate to Monetary Conference, Brussels, 1890, and to Labour Conference, Berlin, 1892. Opponent of Lord Randolph Churchill in the National Union controversy.

HOWORTH (1842–1923), Sir Henry Hoyle, K.C.I.E. 1892, educ. Rossall, Barrister. Took an active part for many years in Lancashire politics and public life; wrote a large number of political letters to *The Times*. Archaeologist and numismatist.

HUNT (1825–77), George Ward. Educ. Eton and Christ Church; called to the Bar. Contested Northampton in 1852 and 1857. M.P. for North Northamptonshire 1857 to death. Financial Secretary to the Treasury 1866 to February 1868; Chancellor of the Exchequer February to December 1868. First Lord of the Admiralty 1874–7. Some knowledge of naval administration, but better versed in agriculture and county management. Introduced Cattle Plague Bill in 1866 and helped with Agricultural Holdings Bill in 1875.

IBBETSON, see Rookwood.

KEITH-FALCONER (1832–89), Hon. C. J. Third son of the seventh Earl of Kintore. Major, 4th Light Dragoons. After his retirement from the Army, financial difficulties forced him to seek paid employment and he was recommended to Disraeli as party organizer. Commissioner of Inland Revenue 1874–89.

KENNAWAY (1837–1919), Sir John Henry; third Bt; M.P. for East Devon 1870–1910. Father of the House of Commons 1908–10. President of the Church Missionary Society and of the London Society for the Promotion of Christianity amongst the Jews.

KINTORE (1852–1930), ninth Earl of, educ. Eton and Trinity, Cambridge; Captain of the Yeomen of the Guard 1886–9, Governor of S. Australia 1889–95; Lord-in-Waiting to Queen Victoria 1885–6 and 1895–1901, to King Edward VII 1901–5. A Whip.

KNIGHTLEY (1819–85), Sir Rainald, second Bt., cr. Baron 1892. Educ. Eton; M.P. for South Northamptonshire 1852–92. One of the best riders across country and one of the best whist players. Irreconcilable opponent of Disraeli.

KNOWLES (1824–83), Thomas. A collier boy at a pit in Ince where his father was an overman. Partner in colliery at Ince, Chairman of Pearson & Knowles Coal and Iron Company. Member of Wigan Town Council 1863–73. Mayor of Wigan 1864–6. M.P. for Wigan 1874–death On Royal Commission on Factory Acts 1875. President of Mining Association of Great Britain.

LINDSAY (1816–89), Hon. C. H., third son of the twenty-fourth Earl of Crawford; Grenadier Guards; served in Crimea. Master of the Horse to the Lord Lieutenant of Ireland 1845; Groom-in-Waiting to Queen Augusta 1866–8 and 1876 to death. M.P. for Abingdon 1865–74. C.B. 1881.

LLOYD (1820–89), Sampson Samuel. Partner in Lloyd's Bank, Birmingham, 1840–65. Managing Director of Lloyd's Bank 1865–8, Chairman of Board of Directors 1878. Manufacturer at Birmingham; founder of Birmingham Chamber of Commerce and Chairman of Associated Chambers of Commerce of the U.K. 1867–85. Contested Birmingham July 1867 and November 1868. M.P. for Plymouth 1874–80. defeated at Plymouth 1880; M.P. for South Warwickshire 1884–5, defeated in South Warwickshire December 1885. One of the leading Fair Traders in Parliament.

LOPES (1818–1908), Sir Massey, third Bt., educ. Oriel College. M.P. for Westbury 1857–68 and for South Devon 1868–85. Civil Lord of the Admiralty 1874–80. Leading county member with special interest in de-rating.

LOWTHER (1840–1904), James. Second son of the third Bt.; Barrister, M.P. for York 1865–80, for North Lincolnshire 1881–5, for Isle of Thanet 1888–1904. Parliamentary Secretary to the Poor Law Board 1868, Under-Secretary for the Colonies 1874–78, Chief Secretary for Ireland 1878–80. Right wing Tory, often regarded as the orginator of obstructive parliamentary tactics.

LOYD-LINDSAY, see Wantage.

MACLEAN (1835–1906), James Mackenzie, journalist; editor *Newcastle Chronicle*, leader-writer *Manchester Guardian*, editor and proprietor *Bombay Gazette* 1859–79, part proprietor and London contributor Western Mail, Cardiff. M.P. for Oldham 1885–92, Cardiff (Central) 1895–1900. Published books on India. Supporter of Lord Randolph Churchill.

MacIVER (1840–1907), David. M.P. for Birkenhead 1874–86 and later for Kirkdale division of Liverpool. Senior partner of David MacIver & Co., steamship owners in the River Plate trade; son of one of the founders of the Cunard Line and a partner in D. & C. MacIver, then Liverpool managers of the Cunard Steamship Co. A director of the Great Western and other Railways. Member of Liverpool City Council, Alderman. A leading supporter of the Fair Trade movement.

MARTEN (1839–1906), Hon. Sir Alfred George, knighted 1836. Educ. St. John's College, Cambridge; Q.C.; Judge of County Courts. Contested Nottingham 1865, M.P. for Cambridge 1874–80, defeated in 1880. High Churchman.

MARLBOROUGH (1822–83), seventh Duke of, Lord President of the Council 1867–8, Lord Lieutenant of Ireland 1876–80. Father of Lord Randolph Churchill, who was his secretary in Ireland.

MIDDLETON (1846–1905), Richard William Evelyn, grandson of Admiral Robert Middleton. Served in the Royal Navy 1860–77. Conservative agent for West Kent 1883–4; chief agent of the Conservative Party 1885–1903.

MITFORD (1833–84), Percy, brother of the first Lord Redesdale. Barrister and diplomat, Conservative candidate in the 1880s. Married daughter of the first Lord Egerton of Tatton.

MONTAGU (1832–1905), Lord Henry Douglas-Scott-Montagu, second son of the fifth Duke of Buccleuch, cr. first Lord Montagu of Beaulieu 1885. M.P. for Selkirk 1861–8 and for South Hampshire 1868–84. Prominent High Churchman.

MOWBRAY (1815–99), Sir John Robert, cr. Bt. 1880. M.P. for Oxford University from 1868. Father of the House of Commons from 1898. Barrister, M.P. for Durham 1853–68. Judge-Advocate-General 1858–9 and 1866–8. Church Estate Commission 1866–8 and 1871–93. Prominent High Churchman.

MUSGRAVE (1838–81), Sir Richard, eleventh Bt., contested East Cumberland 1874 and 1876. M.P. for East Cumberland 1880–death. Lord Lieutenant of Westmoreland 1876–death.

NEWDEGATE (1816–87), Charles. M.P. for North Warwickshire 1843–85. Well-known opponent of Roman Catholicism. Prominent in the fight against Bradlaugh's entry into the House of Commons.

NEVILL, see Abergavenny.

NOEL, (1823–1911), Hon. Gerard James, second son of the first Earl of Gainsborough, M.P. for Rutland 1847–83. Lord of the Treasury

1866–8, Paliamentary Secretary to the Treasury 1868. Chief Commissioner of Works 1876–80.

NORTHCOTE (1846–1911), first Baron; Sir Henry Stafford Northcote, cr. Bt. 1887, Baron 1900. Second son of Lord Iddesleigh. Educ. Eton and Merton College, Oxford. Private secretary to Lord Salisbury at Constantinople 1876–7; to his father 1877–80. M.P. for Exeter 1880–99. Financial Secretary, War Office 1885–6; Surveyor-General of Ordnance 1886–7; Charity Commissioner 1891–2. Governor of Bombay 1899–1903; Governor-General of Australia 1903–8.

NORTHUMBERLAND (1810–99), sixth Duke of, succeeded to title in 1867. Lord of the Admiralty 1858; Vice-President of Board of Trade 1859; Lord Privy Seal 1878–80.

NORTHUMBERLAND (1846–1918), seventh Duke of, Earl Percy, M.P. for Northumberland 1868–85, Treasurer of the Household 1874–5, cr. Lord Lovaine of Alnwick in 1887. Was prominent in the affairs of the National Union and opposed Lord Randolph Churchill and his friends in the 1880s.

NORTON (1814–1905), first Baron, cr. 1878, Sir Charles Boyer Adderley, M.P. for North Staffordshire 1841-78; President of the Board of Health and Vice-President of Committee of Council on Education 1858–9; Under Secretary for the Colonies 1866–8; President of the Board of Trade 1874–8.

PAKINGTON, see Hampton.

PELL, (1820–1907), Albert. Son of late Sir Albert Pell. M.P. for S. Leicestershire 1868–85. On Royal Commission for City and Parochial Charities. Assistant Commissioner in United States and Canada for Duke of Richmond's Commission 1879. Many publications in the Journal of the Royal Agricultural Society. Leading spokesman for the agricultural interest, especially the Poor Law Guardians. Opposed to outdoor relief.

PEMBROKE (1850–95), thirteenth Earl of, eldest son of Sidney Herbert whom he succeeded as second Lord Herbert of Lea in 1861; succeeded his uncle as thirteenth Earl in 1862. Under Secretary of State for War 1874–5.

PEMBROKE (1853–1913), fourteenth Earl of, Hon. Sidney Herbert, M.P. for Wilton 1877–85, for Croydon 1886–95, a Junior Lord of the Treasury 1885–6, Lord Steward of the Household 1895–1905.

PERCY, see Northumberland.

PLUNKET, see Rathmore

POWELL (1827–1911), Sir Francis Sharp, cr. Bt. 1892. Barrister, M.P. for Cambridge 1863–8, for the Northern Division of the West Riding of Yorkshire 1872–4, for Wigan 1885–1910. Contested many other seats and was a prominent figure on the National Union. Member of Royal Commission on Sanitation.

RAIKES (1838–91), Henry Cecil. Barrister; contested Derby in 1859, Chester in 1865, Devonport in 1866; M.P. for Chester 1868–80. Chairman of Executive Committee of Church Defence Institution 1867–74; Chairman of Council of National Union 1870–4. Chairman of Committees 1874–80. Defeated at Chester 1880. M.P. for Preston 1882 and for Cambridge University 1882–death. Postmaster-General 1886–death. Member of the Select Committee whose report in 1870 led to the Ballot Act.

RATHMORE (1838–1919), cr. Baron 1895. Hon. David Robert Plunket, third son of the third Baron Plunket, educ. Trinity College Dublin, Barrister, Q.C. 1868; Law Adviser to the Irish Government 1868–9; M.P. for Dublin University 1870–95; Solicitor-General for Ireland 1875–7; Paymaster-General 1880; first Commissioner of Works 1885–6, 1886–92. One of the Conservative Party's experts on Irish affairs.

RAVENSWORTH (1821–1903), second Earl, Hon. Henry George Liddell, Lord Eslington (1874). Educ. Eton, M.P. for S. Northumberland 1852–78. President of Institute of Naval Architects.

READ (1826–1905), Clare Sewell, distinguished authority on farming, M.P. for E. Norfolk 1865–8, S. Norfolk 1868–80, W. Norfolk 1884–5. Parliamentary Secretary to the Local Government Board 1874–5. Resigned as a protest against the regulations for pleuro-pneumonia not being made uniform in England and Ireland, when the farmers of England presented him with £5,500 and a service of plate.

RIDLEY (1842–1904), first Viscount, cr. 1900, Sir Matthew White Ridley, M.P. for N. Northumberland 1868–85, for Lancashire (Blackpool Division) 1886–1900. Under-Secretary, Home Office, 1878–80, Financial Secretary to the Treasury 1885–6, Secretary of State for Home Affairs 1895–1900.

RITCHIE (1838–1906), C. T., cr. first Baron Ritchie of Dundee 1905. M.P. for the Tower Hamlets 1874–85, for St. George's in the East 1885–92, and for Croydon from 1895. Secretary to the Admiralty 1885–6. President of the Local Government Board 1886–92. President of the Board of Trade 1895–1900. Home Secretary 1900–2. Chancellor of the Exchequer 1902–3.

ROOKWOOD (1826–1906), first Baron, cr. 1892, Sir Henry Selwin-Ibbetson. Moderate Churchman, contested Ipswich 1857 and 1859. M.P. for S. Essex 1865–8, N.W. Essex 1865–85, W. Essex 1885–92. Under-Secretary, Home Department 1874–8. Financial Secretary to the Treasury 1878–80. Fought for repression of rural intemperance and was an authority on the licensing laws.

ROSE (1816–83), Sir Philip, cr. Bt. 1874. Solicitor, partner in firm of Baxter, Rose, Norton & Co.; one of Disraeli's executors.

ROWTON (1838–1903), first Baron, cr. 1880, Montagu Corry, son of Henry Corry, First Lord of the Admiralty 1867, and grandson of second Earl Belmore. Barrister, private secretary to Disraeli 1866–8 and 1874–80. Secretary of the Mission for the Berlin Congress.

RUSSELL (1808–82), John Scott. Engineer and shipbuilder, joint secretary of the Royal Commission for the 1851 Exhibition and one of the nine purchasers of the Great Exhibition building; designed the great rotunda for the Vienna Exhibition 1873.

ST. OSWALD (1820–1893), first Baron, cr. 1885, Rowland Winn, M.P. for N. Lincoln 1868–85. Lord of the Treasury 1874–80; Conservative Chief Whip 1880–5.

SALT (1830–1904), Sir Thomas, cr. Bt. 1899. Educ. Rugby, private banker, director of Lloyd's Bank 1866–86 and Chairman 1886–97. M.P. for Stafford 1859–65, 1869–80, 1881–5, and 1886–92. Parliamentary Secretary to the Local Government Board 1875–6.

SANDON, see Harrowby.

SCLATER-BOOTH, see Basing.

SCOTT, Lord Henry, see Montagu.

SELWIN-IBBETSON, see Rookwood.

SIDEBOTTOM (1824–71), James, born in Stalybridge, cotton manufacturer; Mayor of Stalybridge 1864–7. M.P. for Stalybridge 1868–71. In favour of secret ballot.

SKELMERSDALE (1837–98), second Baron, cr. first Earl of Lathom 1880. Lord-in-Waiting 1866–8; Captain of the Yeoman of the Guard 1874–80; Lord Chamberlain of H.M. Household 1885–6, 1887–92, and 1895–8. Whip in the House of Lords.

SKENE (1838–1911), W. B., Treasurer of Christ Church. Educ. Harrow. Married daughter of Dean Liddell of Christ Church. Barrister, principal agent of the Conservative Party 1876–80.

SPOFFORTH (1825–1907), Markham. Educ. Barnsdale, Yorkshire. At the request of Lord Derby and Mr. Disraeli undertook the reorganization of the Conservative Party and continued principal Conservative agent for twenty years; at the time he undertook it, in consequence of Peel's defection, all the leading Tory agents had refused to act, and only about forty recognized the Carlton Club; in consequence new legal agents had to be appointed throughout the counties and boroughs of England (entry in *Who's Who*). Senior Taxing Master in Chancery 1877.

STANHOPE (1840–93), Hon. Edward, second son of the fifth Earl Stanhope. M.P. for Horncastle division of Lincoln; Parliamentary Secretary, Board of Trade, 1875–8; Under-Secretary for India 1878–80; Vice-President for Education 1885; President of the Board of Trade 1885–6; Secretary of State for the Colonies 1886–7 and for War 1887–92. Member and Chairman of Central Committee.

STEWART (1855–1914), Hon. Fitzroy, fourth son of the ninth Earl of Galloway. One of the secretaries at the Conservative Central Office in the 1880s.

STONE (1838–1914), Sir Benjamin, knighted 1892. Educ. Birmingham Grammar School, manufacturer in Birmingham; Chairman, Birmingham Conservative Association. M.P. for E. Birmingham 1895–1900.

STUART-WORTLEY (1851–1926), Charles Beilby, cr. first Baron Stuart of Wortley 1917. Barrister, Q.C., M.P. for Sheffield 1880–5 and for Hallam Division of Sheffield 1885–1916; Under-Secretary Home Office 1885–6 and 1886–92.

TALBOT (1835–1910), John Gilbert. M.P. for West Kent 1868–78; Parliamentary Secretary Board of Trade 1878–80; M.P. for Oxford University 1878. Ecclesiastical Commissioner and member of Royal Commission on Church Discipline. Associated with the work of the Conservative Central Office. Nephew of Colonel W. P. Talbot.

TALBOT (1817–1898), Sir Wellington Patrick Manvers Chetwynd, K.C.B. 1897. Educ. Eton and Sandhurst. Comptroller of the Queen's Household 1845–6. Private Secretary to Lord Derby when Prime Minister in 1852, British Resident at Cephalonia 1855–60. Lt. Col. 1st Staffordshire Militia 1833 and Honorary Colonel 1873. Sergeant-at-Arms, House of Lords 1858 to death. Treasurer of Conservative Party Fund in 1880 election.

TAYLOR (1811–83), Thomas Edward, grandson of the first Earl of Bective. Educ. Eton, Captain, 6th Dragoon Guards, Lieutenant-Colonel, Royal Meath Militia. Elected for Dublin in 1841. Acted as Opposition Whip from 1855–8, and was said to have been instrumental in bringing down Palmerston in 1858 by bringing Tories at the last moment on Lord Derby's instructions to vote against the Government. Lord of the Treasury 1858–9, Patronage Secretary 1866–8; Chancellor of the Duchy of Lancaster 1868 and 1874–80.

TENNANT (1828–1900), Robert. Educ. Leeds Grammar School. Solicitor, partner in firm of Hives and Tennant, flax spinners, Leeds. Chairman of Manston Coal Co., of Normanton Iron and Steel Co., and of West Riding Coal Owners' Association. M.P. for Leeds 1874–80, contested Peterborough in 1880. Prominent Conservative borough member.

THORNHILL (1837–1900), Sir Thomas, cr. Bt. 1885, educ. Eton and Trinity Cambridge; M.P. for West Suffolk 1875–85. Mentioned by Northcote as a Whip in 1881.

THYNNE (1832–1904) Lord Henry, second son of third Marquis of Bath, Treasurer of the Queen's Household 1875–80.

TORR (1813–80), John. A merchant in Liverpool M.P. for Liverpool 1873–death (16 Jan. 1880). Left £250,000.

WALKER (1824–93), Sir Andrew Barclay, Mayor of Liverpool 1873–74 and 1876–7. Knighted in 1877 and cr. Bt. 1886.

WANTAGE (1832–1901), first Baron, cr. 1885. Robert James Loyd-Lindsay, V.C., K.C.B. Educ. Eton, entered Scots Fusilier Guards, fought in Crimea and received V.C. for deeds of valour at Alma and Inkerman. Married a daughter of the first Lord Overstone. Great landowner in Berkshire, Northamptonshire, and other counties. M.P. for Berks 1865–85, Financial Secretary to War Office, 1877–80. Chairman of English Red Cross Society, entered Paris during siege and went to seat of war during Turco-Servian campaign, 1876. Main interests: army affairs, farming.

WHEELHOUSE (1821–86), W. St. J., knighted 1882. Barrister, Q.C. 1877, M.P. for Leeds 1868–80; contested Leeds in 1880 and W. Leeds in 1885.

WHITLEY (1825–92), Edward. Son of a Liverpool solicitor and himself a solicitor. Member of Liverpool Town Council 1866–death, Mayor 1868–9. M.P. for Liverpool 1880–5, polled 26,106 votes, the largest ever polled anywhere. M.P. for Everton division of Liverpool 1885–death. Member of the Central Committee in the 1880s.

WHITMORE (1813–76) Henry. M.P. for Bridgnorth 1852–70, Conservative Whip from 1855 till January 1869 when he resigned as a result of differences with Noel; Keeper of the Privy Seal to the Prince of Wales 1858–9 and 1866–8. Members of the Whitmore family had represented Bridgnorth for several generations.

WINMARLEIGH (1802–92), first Baron, cr. 1874, John Wilson-Patten. Educ. Eton and Magdalen, Oxford. M.P. for Lancashire 1813–31, contested Lancashire 1831; M.P. for N. Lancashire 1832–74. Chairman of Committees 1852–3. Chancellor of the Duchy of Lancaster 1867–8; Chief Secretary for Ireland September to December 1868.

WINN, see St. Oswald.

WOLFF (1830–1908), Sir Henry Drummond, son of Rev. Joseph Wolff, founder of the Irvingite Church, by Lady Georgiana, daughter of Horatio Walpole, second Earl of Oxford. Educ. Rugby. Entered Foreign Office; Private Secretary to Lord Malmesbury and Sir E. Bulwer Lytton. Contested Dorchester in 1865, M.P. for Christ Church 1874–80 and for Portsmouth 1880–5. Later active as a diplomat, appointed by Salisbury British member of the International Commission for the Organization of the Province of East Rumelia.

WORMS (1829–1912), second Baron de. Educ. University of London; head of the firm of G. & A. Worms 1856–79; M.P. for Greenwich 1880. Supporter of Northcote against Lord Randolph Churchill. Baron of Austrian Empire, of Jewish extraction.

BIBLIOGRAPHY

A. MANUSCRIPT SOURCES

(a) British Museum
Balfour Papers
Cross Papers
Iddesleigh Papers

(b) Public Record Office
Carnarvon Papers (P.R.O.)
Hambleden Papers (National Register of Archives)

(c) Private Collections
Cairns Papers (twelve typescript volumes in the possession of the Earl Cairns, Clopton Hall, nr. Woodbridge, Suffolk, made from the originals in about 1915).
Harrowby Papers (in the possession of the Earl of Harrowby, Sandon Hall, Stafford).
Hughenden Papers (in the possession of the National Trust, at Hughenden Manor, High Wycombe, Bucks.)
Richmond Papers (in the possession of the Duke of Richmond, Goodwood House, Chichester).
Salisbury Papers (in the possession of the Marquis of Salisbury, deposited at Christ Church, Oxford).
Minute Books of the National Union Conferences (in the possession of the National Union of Conservative and Unionist Associations).

B. PRINTED SOURCES

1. Newspapers:

(a) Daily:

Bolton Chronicle	*Standard*
Daily News	*Sun*
Manchester Courier	*The Times*

(b) Weekly:

The Economist	*Spectator*

2. Periodicals:

Blackwood's Magazine	*The Nineteenth Century Review*
The Contemporary Review	*The Quarterly Review*
The Edinburgh Review	*The Saturday Review*
The Fortnightly Review	*The Westminster Review*

3. Parliamentary Papers:

Interim Report of the Committee on House of Commons Personnel and Politics, 1931–2 (4130), vol. X.

Abstract of Expenses incurred by or on behalf of each Candidate at the General Election, 1868, for every County (or Division of a County), City, or Borough in the United Kingdom, 1868–9 (424), vol. L.

Return of Charges made to Candidates at Elections, 1874, by Returning Officers, number of Members returned, number of Candidates, total Expenses of each Candidate, and number of Votes polled, 1874, vol. LIII.

Return of Charges made to Candidates at Election, 1880, etc., 1880, vol. LVII.

Trial of Election Petitions at:

Beverley   Judgement, 1868–9 (120), vol. XLVIII.
            Evidence, 1868–9 (90), vol. XLVIII.
            Commission, 1870 (15 & 16), vol. XXIX.
            Other details, 1870 (310 & 344), vol. LVI.
Bridgwater   Judgement, 1868–9 (120), vol. XLVIII.
            Evidence, 1868–9 (65), vol. XLIX.
            Commission, 1870 (10, 11 & 12), vol. XXX.
            Other Papers, 1870 (79), vol. LVI.
Chester   Commission, 1881 (2824 and 2824 i.), vol. XL.
Oxford   Judgement, 1880 (337– Sess. 2), vol. LVII.
            Evidence, 1880 (349– Sess. 2), vol. LVIII.
            Commission, 1881 (2856 and 2856 i.), vol. XLIV.
Stroud   Judgement, 1874 (374), vol. LIII.
            Judgement, 1875 (342), vol. LXVII.
Totnes   Commission, 1867 (3776), vol. XXIX.

4. Works of Reference:

The Annual Register

Burke's Landed Gentry, ed. L. G. Pine, 17th edition (London, 1952).

Burke's Peerage, Baronetage and Knightage, ed. L. G. Pine, 101st edition (London, 1957).

The Complete Peerage, ed. the Hon. Vicary Gibbs and others, 13 vols. (London, 1910–53).

Conservative Agents and Associations in the Counties and Boroughs of England

and Wales, published by the Central Conservative Office (London, 1874).

The Constitutional Yearbook and Politicians' Guide, London, 1885 edition.

Dictionary of National Biography (London and Oxford, 1885–1949).

Hansard's Parliamentary Debates. Third Series.

Men of the Reign, 1885 edition, by T. H. Ward.

Modern English Biography, by Frederick Boase (Truro, 1892–1921).

The New House of Commons, published by *The Times* (London, 1880).

The New Parliament, by William Saunders (London, 1880).

Parliamentary Directory of the Professional, Commercial and Mercantile Members of the House of Commons (London, 1874).

The Parliamentary Poll Book of All Elections from the Passing of the First Reform Act in 1832, by F. H. McCalmont, 2nd edition (London, 1880).

Ross's Parliamentary Record, by C. Ross (London 1876–9).

Vacher's Parliamentary Companion, by T. B. Vacher, annual.

Walford's Shilling House of Commons, 1874 edition.

Who Was Who. 1897–1915 (London, 1920). 1916–1928 (London, 1947). 1929–1940 (London, 1947).

5. Pamphlets:

Baxter, R. D. *English Parties and Conservatism* (London, 1870). *The Results of the General Election*, 2nd edition (London, 1869).

Callender, W. R., Junr. *Trades Unions Defended* (Manchester 1870).

Carlton, a Member of the. *The Church of England, Dissent and the Disestablishment Policy* (London, 1873).

Chambers, G. F. *A Warning to Churchmen* (London, 1871). *A Record of Parliamentary Elections 1868–74* (London, 1874). *A Paper on Organisation* (Eastbourne, 1885).

Church Association. *Annual Report* (London, 1868).

Church Defence Institution. *An Accurate Analysis of the Division List on the Second Reading of the Burials Bill* (London, 1873). *Report on the Debate on Mr. Miall's Motion* (London, 1873).

Crickmay, H. J. *A Reply to Midlothian* (London, 1884).

De Ricci, J. H. *Conservatism and the People* (Leicester, 1883).

Ecroyd, W. F. *The Policy of Self-Help. Suggestions Towards the Consolidation of the Empire and the Defence of its Industries and Commerce*, 1st edition (London, 1879), 4th edition (London, 1882).

Hill, A. Staveley. *An Empire's Parliament* (London, 1880).

Hitchman, F. *The Session of 1871* (London, 1871).

Lindsay, A. W. C. (twenty-fifth Earl of Crawford). *Conservatism and its Principles, Policy and Practice* (London, 1868).

Liverpool Constitutional Association. *Rules and Regulations* (Liverpool, 1848). *First Annual Report* (Liverpool, 1850).

National Education Union. *Report on the Movement (1869–70)* (London, 1870). *Report on the Meeting of 8 April 1870* (London, 1870).
National Union of Conservative and Constitutional Associations *Publications*, First Series, Nos. I–XXVII (London 1872–5).
Rowe, W. H. *The Platform as a Conservative Agency* (London, National Union Publication, 1882).

6. Biography, Autobiography, Letters, and Speeches:

(a) Conservative:

Adderley, Sir Charles, first Lord Norton. *Life*, by William S. Childe-Pemberton (London, 1909).
Akers-Douglas, Aretas, first Viscount Chilston. *Chief Whip. The Political Life and Times of Aretas Akers-Douglas, 1st Viscount Chilston*, by Eric Alexander Viscount Chilston (London, 1961).
Balfour, A. J. *Chapters of Autobiography*, by Arthur James, first Earl of Balfour (London, 1930). *Arthur James Balfour, First Earl of Balfour*, by B. E. C. Dugdale, 2 vols. (London, 1936). *Arthur James Balfour; The Happy Life of the Politician, Prime Minister, Statesman and Philosopher, 1848–1930*, by Kenneth Young (London, 1963).
Baxter, R. D. *In Memoriam Robert Dudley Baxter*, by Mary D. Baxter (London, 1878).
Beach, Sir Michael Hicks, first Earl St. Aldwyn. *Life*, by Lady V. A. Hicks Beach, 2 vols. (London, 1932).
Bridges, John Affleck. *Reminiscences of a Country Politician* (London, 1906).
Burnaby, Col. Frederick. *The Life*, by Thomas Wright (London, 1908).
Cairns, first Earl. *Brief Memories of Hugh McCalmont 1st Earl Cairns*, by the author of 'Memoir of the Rev. W. Marsh, D.D.' (Miss C. M. Marsh) (1885).
Carnavon, fourth Earl of. *Life of Henry Howard Molyneux Herbert, Fourth Earl of Carnarvon 1831–1890*, by Sir Arthur Hardinge, 3 vols. (London, 1925).
Chaplin, Henry, first Viscount Chaplin. *Henry Chaplin: A Memoir*, by his daughter, Lady Londonderry (London, 1926).
Chilston, see Akers-Douglas.
Churchill, Lord Randolph. *Life*, by W. S. Churchill, 2 vols. (London, 1906). *Lord Randolph Churchill*, by Robert Rhodes James (London, 1959). *Randolph Spencer-Churchill, as a Portrait of his Age*, by T. H. S. Escott (London, 1895). *Speeches*, edited by L. J. Jennings, 2 vols. (London, 1889). *The Reminiscences of Lady Randolph Churchill*, by Mrs. George Cornwallis-West (London, 1908).

Clarke, Sir Edward. *The Story of My Life* (London, 1918). *Life*, by
D. Walker-Smith and Edward Clarke (London, 1939).
Cranbrook, see **Hardy.**
Cross, Sir R. A., first Viscount Cross. *A Political History, Privately
Printed for My Children* (1903).
Derby, fourteenth Earl of. *Lord Derby and Victorian Conservatism*, by
W. D. Jones (Oxford, 1956). *The Earl of Derby*, by G. E. B. Saintsbury
(London, 1892).
Derby, fifteenth Earl of. *Speeches and Addresses*, edited by T. H.
Sanderson and E. S. Roscoe, 2 vols. (1894). *Life*, by T. E. Kebbel
(London, 1890, The Statesmen Series).
Disraeli, B., Earl of Beaconsfield. *Life*, by W. F. Monypenny and
G. E. Buckle, 6 vols. (London, 1910–20); new and revised edition
in 2 vols. (London, 1929). *Disraeli*, by Robert Blake (London, 1966).
The Rt. Hon. Benjamin Disraeli, Earl of Beaconsfield, and his Times, by
A. C. Ewald, 2 vols. (London, 1883). *The Public Life of the Rt. Hon.
the Earl of Beaconsfield, K.G.*, by Francis Hitchman, 2 vols. (London,
1879). *The Earl of Beaconsfield*, by J. A. Froude (London, 1905). *The
Earl of Beaconsfield*, by H. E. Gorst (London, 1900). *Lord Beaconsfield,
A Biography*, by T. P. O'Connor (London, 1879). *Letters of Disraeli
to Lady Bradford and Lady Chesterfield*, edited by the Marquis of Zetland,
2 vols. (London, 1929). *Selected Speeches of the Late Rt. Hon. The Earl
of Beaconsfield*, edited with Introduction and Explanatory Notes by
T. E. Kebbel, 2 vols. (London, 1882).
Forwood, Sir Arthur Bower. *Recollections of a busy Life, being the
Reminiscences of a Liverpool Merchant 1840–1910*, by Sir William
Forwood (Liverpool, 1910).
Fraser, Sir William. *Disraeli and His Day*, by Sir William Fraser
(London, 1891).
Giffard, Sir Hardinge, first Earl of Halsbury. *The Earl of
Halsbury, Lord High Chancellor, 1823–1921*, by A. W. Fox (London,
1929).
Gower, Lord Ronald Sutherland-Leveson-. *My Reminiscences*, new
edition (London, 1895). *Records and Reminiscences* (London, 1903).
Halsbury, see **Giffard**
Hambleden, see **Smith.**
Hamilton, Lord George F. *Parliamentary Reminiscences and Recollec-
tions 1868–1885* (London, 1917), 2nd vol. *1885–1906* (London,
1922).
Hardy, Gathorne, first Earl of Cranbrook. *A Memoir, with
Extracts from his Diary and Correspondence*, edited by the Hon. Alfred E.
Gathorne-Hardy, 2 vols. (London, 1910).
Iddesleigh, see **Northcote.**

Kebbel, T. E. *Lord Beaconsfield and other Tory Memoirs* (London, 1907).
Knightley, Sir Rainald. *The Journals of Lady Knightley of Fawsley, 1856–1884,* edited by Julia Cartwright (London, 1915).
Loyd-Lindsay, Colonel, first Lord Wantage. *Lord Wantage, V.C., K.C.B., A Memoir,* by his Wife (H. S. L. Lindsay) (London, 1907).
Maclean, James Mackenzie. *Recollections of Westminster and India,* by J. M. Maclean (London, 1902).
Malmesbury, third Earl of. *Memoirs of an Ex-Minister,* 2 vols. (London, 1884).
Manners, Lord John. *Lord John Manners and His Friends,* by Charles Whibley, 2 vols. (Edinburgh, 1925).
Mowbray, Sir John. *Seventy Years at Westminster,* with other letters and notes, edited by his daughter (London, 1900).
Nevill, Lady Dorothy. *The Reminiscences,* edited by Ralph Nevill (London, 1906). *Leaves from the Notebooks,* edited by Ralph Nevill (London, 1907). *Under Five Reigns,* by Lady Dorothy Nevill (London, 1910).
Northcote, Sir Stafford, first Earl of Iddesleigh. *The Life, Letters and Diaries,* by Andrew Lang, 2 vols. (London, 1889).
Norton, see **Adderley.**
Pell, Albert. *The Reminiscences of Albert Pell, sometime M.P. for South Leicestershire,* edited, with an Introduction, by Thomas Mackay (London, 1908).
Powell, Sir Francis. *Sir Francis Sharp Powell, Baronet and Member of Parliament,* by H. L. P. Hubbert (Leeds, 1914).
Raikes, Henry Cecil. *The Life and Letters,* by H. St. J. Raikes (London, 1898).
St. Aldwyn, see **Beach.**
St. Helier, Lady. *Memories of Fifty Years,* by Lady St. Helier (Mary Jeune) (London, 1909).
Salisbury, third Marquis of. *The Life,* by Lady Gwendolen Cecil, 4 vols. (London, 1921–32). *Salisbury, 1830–1903,* by A. L. Kennedy (London, 1953). *The Marquis of Salisbury,* by H. D. Traill (London, 1891). *Life and Times,* by S. H. Jeyes, 4 vols. (London, 1895–6). *Speeches of the Marquis of Salisbury,* with a sketch of his life, edited by H. W. Lucy (London, 1885).
Salvidge, Sir Archibald. *Salvidge of Liverpool,* by Stanley Salvidge (London, 1934).
Shaftesbury, seventh Earl of. *Life and Work,* by E. Hodder, 3 vols. (London, 1886).
Smith, W. H. *Life and Times,* by Sir H. Maxwell, 2 vols. (Edinburgh, 1893). *W. H. Smith,* by Eric Alexander, third Viscount Chilston (London, 1965).

Wantage, see **Loyd-Lindsay.**
Wolff, Sir Henry Drummond. *Rambling Recollections,* 2 vols. (London, 1908).

(b) General:

Argyll, eighth Duke of. *Autobiography and Memoirs,* 2 vols. (London, 1906).
Bradlaugh, Charles. *Charles Bradlaugh, A Record of His Life and Work,* by H. B. Bonner, 2 vols. (London, 1895). *The Biography,* by A. S. Headingley, 2nd edition (Lucknow, 1889).
Brett, see **Esher.**
Bright, John. *Life,* by G. M. Trevelyan, new edition (London, 1925). *Public Addresses,* edited by J. E. Rogers, 2 vols. (London, 1879).
Broadhurst, Henry. *Henry Broadhurst, M.P. The Story of His Life,* Told by Himself (London, 1901).
Brodrick, George Charles. *Memoirs and Impressions, 1831–1900* (London, 1900).
Burt, Thomas. *Thomas Burt, M.P., D.C.L., Pitman and Privy Councillor* An Autobiography. With supplementary chapters by Aaron Watson (London, 1924).
Cavendish, Lady Frederick. *Diary,* ed. John Bailey, 2 vols. (London, 1927).
Chamberlain, Joseph C. *Life,* by J. L. Garvin, 3 vols. (London, 1932–3); 4th vol. by Julian Amery (London, 1951). *A Political Memoir (1880–1892),* by Joseph Chamberlain, edited by C. H. D. Howard (London, 1953). *Speeches,* edited by H. W. Lucy (London, 1885).
Childers, Hugh C. E. *Life and Correspondence, 1827–1896,* by E. S. E. Childers, 2 vols. (London, 1901).
Clarendon, fourth Earl of. *Life and Letters,* by Sir H. Maxwell, 2 vols. (London, 1913).
Coleridge, first Lord. *Forty Years of Friendship.* As recorded in the Correspondence of John Duke, Lord Coleridge, and Ellis Yarnall (London, 1911).
Dale, Robert William. *Life,* by A. W. W. Dale, 2nd edition (London, 1899).
Delane, John Thadeus. *J. T. Delane, Editor of The Times,* by A. I. Dasent, 2 vols. (London, 1908).
Dilke, Sir Charles. *Life,* by S. L. Gwynn and G. M. Tuckwell, 2 vols. (London, 1917). *Sir Charles Dilke: a Victorian Tragedy,* by Roy Jenkins (London, 1965).
Duff, Sir M. E. Grant. *Notes from a Diary, 1851–1872,* 2 vols. (London, 1897); *1873–1881,* 2 vols. (London, 1898).

Esher, first Viscount. *Journals and Letters of Reginald, Viscount Esher*, edited by M. V. Brett, 4 vols. (London, 1934–8).

Fawcett, Henry. *Life*, by Leslie Stephen (London, 1885).

Foster, W. E. *Life*, by Sir T. Wemyss Reid, 2 vols. (London, 1888).

Gladstone, W. E. *Life*, by John Morley, 3 vols. (London, 1903). *Gladstone, a Biography*, by Sir Philip Magnus (London, 1954). *The Political Correspondence of Mr. Gladstone and Lord Granville, 1868–1886*, 7 vols. (Oxford, 1952–62). *Gladstone as Financier and Economist*, by F. W. Hirst (London, 1931).

Goschen, G., first Viscount. *Life*, by the Hon. A. D. Elliot, 2 vols. (London, 1911).

Granville, second Earl. *Life*, by Lord Edmond Fitzmaurice, 2 vols. (London, 1905).

Harcourt, Sir William Vernon. *Life*, by A. G. Gardiner, 2 vols. (London, 1923).

Hartington, Marquis of, eighth Duke of Devonshire. *The Life of Spencer Compton, 8th Duke of Devonshire*, by B. Holland, 2 vols. (London, 1911).

Herbert Auberon. *Auberon Herbet, Crusader for Liberty*, by S. H. Harris (London, 1943).

Holyoake, George J. *Life and Letters*, by J. McCabe, 2 vols. (London, 1908).

Labouchere, Henry. *Life*, by A. L. Thorold (London, 1913).

Lawson, Sir Wilfred (second Bart.). *Sir Wilfred Lawson, A Memoir*, edited by G. W. E. Russell (London, 1909).

Lowe, Robert, first Viscount Sherbrooke. *Life and Letters*, by A. P. Martin, 2 vols. (London, 1893).

MacColl, Malcolm. *Malcolm MacColl, Memoirs and Correspondence*, edited by G. W. E. Russell (London, 1914).

Magee, William C., Archbishop of York. *Life and Correspondence*, by J. C. Macdonnell, 2 vols. (London, 1896).

Miall, Edward. *Life*, by A. Miall (London, 1884).

Mundella, A. J. *A. J. Mundella, 1825–1897: The Liberal Background to the Labour Movement*, by W. H. G. Armytage (London, 1951).

Osborne, Ralph Bernal. *Life*, by P. H. Bagenal (London, 1884) (for private circulation).

Palmer, Roundell, first Earl of Selbourne. *Memorials. Part II: Personal and Political, 1865–1895*, 2 vols. (London, 1896–8).

Parnell, Charles Stewart. *Parnell and his Party*, by C. Cruise O'Brien (Oxford, 1957).

Plimsoll, Samuel. *The Plimsoll Mark*, by David Masters (London, 1955).

Rathbone, William. *William Rathbone, A Memoir,* by Eleanor F. Rathbone (London, 1905).

Richard, Henry. *Henry Richard, M.P.,* by C. S. Miall (London, 1889).

Roebuck, John Arthur. *Life and Letters,* by R. E. Leader, 2 vols. (London, 1897).

Rosebery, fifth Earl of. *Rosebery: a biography of Archibald Philip, 5th Earl of Rosebery,* by Robert Rhodes James (London, 1963).

Russell, first Earl, *Recollections and Suggestions 1813–1873* (London, 1875). *The Life of Lord John Russell,* by S. H. Walpole, 2 vols. (London, 1898). *The Later Correspondence of Lord John Russell,* edited by G. P. Gooch, 2 vols. (London, 1925).

Russell, G. W. E. *Collections and Recollections* (London, 1903).

Selborne, see **Palmer.**

Sherbrooke, see **Lowe.**

Somerset, twelfth Duke of. *Letters, Remains and Memoirs* (London, 1893). *Monarchy and Democracy. Phases of Modern Politics* (London, 1880).

Stansfeld, James. *James Stansfeld: A Victorian Champion of Sex Equality,* by J. L. & B. Hammond (London, 1932).

Tait, William, Archbishop of Canterbury. *Life,* by R. T. Davidson and W. Benham, 2 vols. (London, 1891).

Torrens, William MacCullagh. *Twenty Years of Parliamentary Life* (London, 1893).

Victoria, Queen. *Letters,* Second and Third Series (1861–1901). edited by G. E. Buckle, 6 vols. (London, 1926–32).

West, Sir Algernon. *Recollections 1832–1886,* 2 vols. (London, 1899).

Wilberforce, Samuel, Bishop of Oxford and Winchester. *Life,* by R. G. Wilberforce and A. R. Ashwell, 3 vols. (London, 1880).

(c) Collected:

Atlay, J. B. *The Victorian Chancellors,* 2 vols. (London, 1908).

Escott, T. H. S. *Gentlemen of the House of Commons,* 2 vols. (1902).

Law, H. W. and Irene. *The Book of the Beresford Hopes* (London, 1929).

Lloyd, S. *The Lloyds of Birmingham* (Birmingham, 1907).

Reid, Sir T. Wemyss. *Politicians of To-day,* 2 vols. (London, 1880).

Russell, G. W. E. *Portraits of the 'Seventies'* (London, 1916). *Prime Ministers and Some Others.* A Book of Reminiscences (London, 1918).

West, Sir A. *Contemporary Portraits, Men of My Day in Public Life* (London, 1920).

7. Other Printed Works:

Adams, Francis. *History of the Elementary School Contest in England* (London, 1882).

Arnstein, Walter L. *The Bradlaugh Case, A Study in Late Victorian Opinion and Politics* (Oxford, 1965).

Beer, Samuel H. *Modern British Politics, A Study of Parties and Pressure Groups* (London, 1965).

Bateman, J. *The Great Landowners of Great Britain*, new edition (London, 1879).

Biddulph, Sir R. *Lord Cardwell at the War Office* (London, 1904).

Briggs, A. *History of Birmingham, Borough and City, 1865–1938* (Birmingham, 1952). *Victorian People: some reassessments of people, institutions, ideas and events* (London, 1954).

Brodrick, G. C. *Political Studies* (London, 1879).

Brown, Benjamin H. *The Tariff Reform Movement in Great Britain 1881–1895* (New York, 1943).

Carter, H. *The English Temperance Movement* (London, 1931).

Clapham, J. H. *An Economic History of Great Britain*, vol. ii: *Free Trade and Steel, 1850–1886* (Cambridge, 1932).

Clayden, P. W. *England under Lord Beaconsfield*, (London, 1880).

Cracroft, B. and others. *Essays in Reform* (London, 1867).

Dicey, A. V. *Lectures on the Relation between Law and Public Opinion in England during the 19th Century* (London, 1905).

Duverger, M. *Political Parties: their organisation and activity in the Modern State.* Translated from the French by Barbara and Robert North (London, 1954).

Ensor, R. C. K. *England 1870–1914* (Oxford, 1936).

Escott, T. H. S. *England: its people, policy and pursuits*, 2 vols. (London, 1881). *Club Makers and Club Members* (London, 1914).

Evans, Howard. *Radical Fights of Forty Years* (London, 1913). *Our Old Nobility* (London, 1907).

Gash, N. *Politics in the Age of Peel: a study in the technique of Parliamentary representation 1830–1850* (London, 1953).

Gorst, H. E. *The Fourth Party* (London, 1906).

Guttsman, W. L. *The British Political Elite* (London, 1963).

Gwyn, William B. *Democracy and the Cost of Politics in Britain* (London, 1962).

Hammond, J. L. *Gladstone and the Irish Nation* (London, 1938).

Hanham, H. J. *Elections and Party Management: Politics in the Time of Disraeli and Gladstone* (London, 1959).

Harris, William. *History of the Radical Party in Parliament* (London 1885).

Harrison, Royden. *Before the Socialists: Studies in Labour and Politics 1861–1881* (Toronto, 1963).

Hertz (Hurst), G. B. *The Manchester Politician 1750–1912* (London, 1912).

Hill, R. G. *Toryism and the People, 1832–1946* (London, 1929).

Jennings, Sir Ivor. *Party Politics*, 3 vols. (Cambridge, 1961).

Jephson, H. *The Platform, Its Rise and Progress*, 2 vols. (London, 1892).

Kebbel, T. E. *A History of Toryism* (London, 1886).

Kent, C. B. R. *The English Radicals* (London, 1899).

Lowell, A. L. *The Government of England*, 2 vols. (New York, 1908).

Lucy, Sir H. W. *A Diary of Two Parliaments*, 2 vols. (London, 1885–6). *Memories of Eight Parliaments* (London, 1908). *Peeps at Parliament taken from behind the Speaker's Chair* (London, 1903).

Lynd, H. M. *England in the 1880's: toward a social basis for freedom* (London, 1945).

Maccoby, S. *English Radicalism, 1832–1852* (London, 1935). *English Radicalism, 1853–1886* (London, 1938).

McDowell, R. B. *British Conservatism, 1832–1914* (London, 1959).

McKenzie, R. T. *The British Political Parties: the distribution of power within the Conservative and Labour Parties* (London, 1955).

Michaels, R. *Political Parties: a Sociological Study of the Oligarchical Tendencies of Modern Democracy*, translated from the German (London, 1915).

O'Leary, Cornelius. *The Elimination of Corrupt Practices in British Elections 1868–1911* (Oxford 1962).

O'Malley, E. L. and Hardcastle, H. *Decisions of the Judges for the Trials of Election Petitions in England and Ireland*, 2 vols. (London 1869–70).

O'Rell, Max. *John Bull and his Island* (London, 1883).

Ostrogorski, M. *Democracy and the Organisation of Political Parties*, 2 vols., translated from the French (London, 1902).

Pink, W. D., and Beavan, A. *The Parliamentary Representation of Lancashire (County & Borough) 1258–1883* (1869).

Redford, A. and Russell, I. S. *The History of Local Government in Manchester* 2 vols. (London, 1939).

Robb, J. H. *The Primrose League 1883–1906*, Columbia University Ph.D. Thesis (New York, 1942).

Rose, Richard. *Politics in England* (London 1965).

Seymour, C. *Electoral Reform in England and Wales: the development and operation of the parliamentary franchise, 1832–1885* (New Haven, 1915).

Shannon, R. T. *Gladstone and the Bulgarian Agitation 1876* (London, 1963).

Smith, F. B. *The Making of the Second Reform Bill* (Cambridge, 1966).
Smith, Goldwin. *A Trip to England* (London, 1892). *Reminiscences* (London, 1910).
Southgate, Donald. *The Passing of the Whigs 1832–1886* (London, 1962).
Stewart, J. D. *British Pressure Groups: their Role in Relation to the House of Commons* (Oxford, 1958).
Thomas, J. A. *The House of Commons 1832–1901. A Study of its Economic and Functional Character* (Cardiff, 1939).
Thompson, George C. *Public Opinion and Lord Beaconsfield, 1875–1880*, 2 vols. (London, 1886).
Vincent, John. *The Formation of the Liberal Party 1857–1868* (London, 1966).
Watson, R. S. *The National Liberal Federation* (London, 1907).
White, William. *The Inner Life of the House of Commons*, 2 vols. (London 1897).
Whitley, T. W. *The Parliamentary Representation of the City of Coventry* (1894).
Wilkinson, William J. *Tory Democracy*, Studies in History, Economic and Public Law, Columbia University, vol. CXV, no. 2 (1925).
Woodward, E. L. *The Age of Reform* (Oxford, 1938).

8. Articles:
   (a) Contemporary:
Austin, A. 'The Liberal Victory, from a Conservative Point of View', *Fortnightly*, vol. XXVII, June 1880.
Bartley, G. C. T. 'Conservative Organisation', *Fortnightly*, vol. XXXVII, May 1885.
Bear, W. E. 'The Revolt of the Counties', *Fortnightly*, vol. XXVII, Apr. 1880.
Brodrick, Hon. G. C. 'Liberals and Whigs', *Fortnightly*, vol. XXIII, May 1878.
Chamberlain, J. 'The Next Page of the Liberal Programme', *Fortnightly*, vol. XVI, Oct. 1874. 'The Caucus', *Fortnightly*, vol. XXIV Nov. 1878.
Churchill, Lord Randolph. 'Elijah's Mantle, 19th April 1883', *Fortnightly*, vol. XXXIII, May 1883.
Courtney, W. P. 'The Cost of the General Election of 1880', *Fortnightly*, vol. XXIX, Apr. 1881.
Dunckley, Henry. 'The Conservative Dilemma', *Contemporary*, vol. XLIII, Jan. 1883.
Fawcett, H. H. 'The House of Lords', *Fortnightly*, vol. X. Oct. 1871.

Forwood, Arthur B. 'Democratic Toryism', *Contemporary*, vol. XLIII, Feb. 1883.

Frisby, A. 'Voters *Not* Votes: The Relative Strength of Political Parties as shown by the last two General Elections', *Contemporary*, vol. XXXVIII, Oct. 1880. 'Has Conservatism increased in England since the last Reform Bill', *Fortnightly*, vol. XXX, Dec. 1881.

Gladstone, W. E. 'Electoral Facts', *Nineteenth Century*, vol. IV, Nov. 1878.

Harrison, Frederic. 'The Conservative Reaction', *Fortnightly*, vol. XV, Mar. 1874.

Hunter, Prof. 'Mr. Cross's Labour Bills', *Fortnightly*, vol. XVIII, Aug. 1875.

Martin, J. B. 'The Elections of 1868 and 1874', *Journal of the Statistical Society*, vol. XXXVII (1874), p. 193.

Rae, W. F. 'Political Clubs and Party Organisation', *Nineteenth Century*, vol. III, May 1878.

Raikes, H. C. 'The Functions of an Opposition', *Nineteenth Century*, vol. XIII (1883), p. 140.

Wilson, E. D. J. 'The Caucus and its Consequences', *Nineteenth Century*, vol. IV, Oct. 1878.

Unsigned. 'The Past and Future of Conservative Policy' (attributed to Salisbury), *Quarterly*, Oct. 1869. 'The Position of the Parties' (attributed to Salisbury), *Quarterly*, Oct. 1872. 'The Tory Press', by a Tory, *Contemporary*, vol. XXIII, Apr. 1874. 'Lord Beaconsfield: I. Why do we Follow Him? By a Tory. II. Why we Disbelieve in Him. By a Whig', *Fortnightly*, vol. XXXVI, Dec. 1879. 'Conservative Reorganisation', *Blackwood's Magazine*, vol. CXXVII, June 1880. 'Conservative Disorganisation' (Part I of 'The State of the Opposition'), *Fortnightly*, vol. XXXII, Nov. 1882.

(b) Learned Journals:

Armytage, W. G. H. 'A. J. Mundella as Vice-President of the Council and the Schools Question, 1880–1885', *English Historical Review*, vol. LXIII (1948), p. 52.

Aydelotte, W. O. 'A Statistical Analysis of the Parliament of 1841: Some Problems of Method', *Bulletin of the Institute of Historical Research*, vol. XXVII (1954), p. 141.

Beales, H. L. 'The "Great Depression" in Industry and Trade', *Economic History Review*, vol. V (1934–5), p. 65.

Cornford, James. 'The Transformation of Conservatism in the late Nineteenth Century', *Victorian Studies*, vol. VII, no. 1 (Sept. 1963), p. 35.

Cowling, Maurice. 'Disraeli, Derby and Fusion, October 1865 to

July 1866', *Historical Journal* VIII, 1 (1965), p. 31. 'Lytton, the Cabinet and the Russians, August to November 1878', *English Historical Review*, vol. LXXVI (1961), p. 59.

Crapster, Basil L. 'Scotland and the Conservative Party in 1876', *Journal of Modern History*, vol. XXIV (1957), p. 355.

Dunbabin, J. P. D. 'Parliamentary Elections in Great Britain, 1868–1900', *English Historical Review*, vol. LXXXI (1966), p. 82.

Dwyer, F. J. 'R. A. Cross and the Eastern Crisis of 1875–78', *Slavonic and East European Review*, vol. XXXIX (1960–61), p. 440.

Ensor, R. C. K. 'Some Political and Economic Interactions in Later Victorian England', *Transactions of the Royal Historical Society*, 4th Series, vol. XXXI (1949), p. 17.

Feuchtwanger, E. J. 'J. E. Gorst and the Central Organisation of the Conservative Party, 1870–1882', *Bulletin of the Institute of Historical Research*, vol. XXXII (1959), p. 192. 'The Conservative Party under the Impact of the Second Reform Act', *Victorian Studies*, vol. II, no. 4 (June 1959), p. 289.

Gash, N. 'Peel and the Party System', *Transactions of the Royal Historical Society*, 5th Series, vol. 1 (1951), p. 47. 'F. R. Bonham: Conservative "Political Secretary", 1832–48', *English Historical Review*, vol. LXVIII (1948), p. 502.

Goodman, Gordon L. 'Liberal Unionism: The Revolt of the Whigs', *Victorian Studies*, vol. III, no. 2 (Dec. 1959), p. 173.

Hanham, H. J. 'British Party Finance 1868–1880', *Bulletin of the Institute of Historical Research*, vol. XXVII (1954), p. 83. 'The Sale of Honours in Late Victorian England', *Victorian Studies*, vol. III, no. 3 (Mar. 1960), p. 277. 'Political Patronage at the Treasury 1870–1912', *Historical Journal*, III, 1 (1960), p. 75.

Harrison, Royden. 'The British Working Class and the General Election of 1868', *International Review of Social History*, V (Pt. 3, 1960), p. 424 and VI (Pt. 1, 1961), p. 74.

Herrick, F. H. 'The Origins of the National Liberal Federation', *Journal of Modern History*, vol. XVII (1945). 'The Reform Bill of 1867 and the British Party System', *Pacific Historical Review*, vol. III (1934). 'Lord Randolph Churchill and the Popular Organisation of the Conservative Party', *Pacific Historical Review*, vol. XV (1946).

Howard, C. H. D. 'Lord Randolph Churchill', *History*, vol. XXV (1940), p. 25. 'Joseph Chamberlain and the "Unauthorised Programme",' *English Historical Review*, vol. LXV (1950), p. 477. 'The Parnell Manifesto of 21st November 1885 and the Schools Question', *English Historical Review*, vol. LXII (1947), p. 42.

Kelley, R. 'Midlothian: A Study in Politics and Ideas', *Victorian Studies*, vol. IV, no. 2 (Dec. 1960), p. 119.

Kemp, B. 'The General Election of 1841', *History*, vol. XXXVII (1952), p. 146.

Lewis, Clyde J. 'Theory and Expediency in the Policy of Disraeli', *Victorian Studies*, vol. IV, no. 3 (Mar. 1961), p. 237.

Lloyd, Trevor. 'Uncontested Seats in British General Elections 1852–1910', *Historical Journal*, VIII, 2 (1965), p. 260.

McGill, Barry. 'Francis Schradhorst and the Liberal Party Organisation', *Journal of Modern History*, vol. XXXIV (1962), p. 19.

Pumphrey, Ralph E. 'The Introduction of Industrialists into the British Peerage: A Study in Adaptation of a Social Institution', *American Historical Review*, vol. LXV, no. 1 (Oct. 1959), p. 1.

Roberts, David. 'Tory Paternalism and Social Reform in Early Victorian England', *American Historical Review*, vol. LXIII, no. 2 (Jan. 1958), p. 323.

Salter, F. R. 'Political Nonconformity in the Eighteen-thirties', *Transactions of the Royal Historical Society*, 5th Series, vol. III (1953), p. 125.

Tholfsen, Trygve R. 'The Origins of the Birmingham Caucus', *Historical Journal*, II, 2 (1959), p. 161.

Thomas, J. A. 'The System of Registration and the Development of Party Organisation 1832–1870', *History*, vol. XXXV (1950), p. 81.

Tucker, Albert. 'Disraeli and the Natural Aristocracy', *Canadian Journal of Economics and Political Science*, vol. 28, no. 1 (Feb. 1962), p. 1.

Williams, P. M. 'Public Opinion and the Railway Rates Question in 1886', *English Historical Review*, vol. LXVII (1952), p. 37.

INDEX